The Novel of Purpose

The Novel of Purpose

Literature and Social Reform in the Anglo-American World

Amanda Claybaugh

Cornell University Press
Ithaca and London

First published 2007 by Cornell University Press

Printed in the United States of America

 Library of Congress Cataloging-in-Publication Data

Claybaugh, Amanda.
  The novel of purpose : literature and social reform in the
Anglo-American world / Amanda Claybaugh.
      p. cm.
  Includes bibliographical references and index.
  ISBN–13: 978–0–8014–4480–7 (cloth : alk. paper)
  ISBN–10: 0–8014–4480–2 (cloth : alk. paper)
  1. English fiction—19th century—History and
criticism.   2. American fiction—19th century—History
and criticism.   3. Social problems in literature.   4. Social
movements in literature.   5. Literature and society—Great
Britain—History—19th century.   6. Literature and society—
United States—History—19th century.   I. Title.
PR778.S62C57 2007
823.009'355—dc22   2006023302

Cornell University Press strives to use environmentally
responsible suppliers and materials to the fullest extent possible
in the publishing of its books. Such materials include vegetable-
based, low-VOC inks and acid-free papers that are recycled,
totally chlorine-free, or partly composed of nonwood fibers.
For further information, visit our website at www.cornellpress.
cornell.edu.

Cloth printing   10 9 8 7 6 5 4 3 2 1

For Martin Puchner

Contents

Acknowledgments

This is a book about authorial careers, and it is a great pleasure to remember the many people who have shaped mine. My first thanks go to my teachers. Lawrence Buell and Elaine Scarry, my dissertation advisors, taught me to ask my own questions and find my own language, making it possible for me to strike out on my own. Philip Fisher read my dissertation when it was finished and galvanized me with a sense of what I could yet do. Robert Ferguson was remarkably sensitive to the travails of writing and made New York a happy intellectual home. None of this would have been possible had it not been for my undergraduate teachers. Sarah Winter guided my very first efforts to think about the Victorian novel, and Elaine Hadley commented searchingly on what I had done. Kirsten Silva Gruesz taught me how to read across national boundaries, and John Rogers—quite simply—taught me how to read. Most of all, I learned from my fellow students and the dazzling example of their work. Special thanks to Kriss Basil, Nicholas Dames, Noah Heringman, Amy King, Mun-Hou Lo, Monica Miller, Patrick O'Malley, and Rebecca L. Walkowitz, my enormously encouraging readers and friends.

This book was written at Columbia University, where I received abundant support of all kinds. I am grateful for—and humbled by—the number of colleagues who set aside their own work in order to read and respond to mine: Rachel Adams, Jonathan Arac, David Damrosch, Ann Douglas, Robert Ferguson, Karl Kroeber, Monica Miller, Bruce Robbins, and especially Sharon Marcus. Edward Mendelson and James Shapiro gave me canny advice about fellowships and publishers. Other colleagues helped me less directly by sustaining the intellectual communities that make Columbia such a vibrant place, among them Nicholas Dames, Andrew Delbanco, Eileen Gillooly, Erik Gray, Ross Posnock, Maura Spiegel and Ezra Tawil, as well as the students in the Victorianist and Americanist Dissertation Colloquiums. I am grateful for the camaraderie and advice of Sarah Cole, Julie Crawford, and Jenny Davidson. And I am grateful, too, for Michael Mallick, who cheered my every day on campus and made my life easier in many ways.

In the time that I have been writing this book, many people have discussed it with me, including the members of the Victorianist Seminar at the City University of New York, the American Studies Seminar at Columbia, and the Middle Modernity Group at the University of Wisconsin–Madison. Special thanks to the denizens of the Dickens Universe, in particular Carolyn Dever, Hilary Schor and Carolyn Williams, who encouraged me when I was in the midst of this project. Special thanks as well to James Eli Adams and Shirley Samuels, who made my time in Ithaca productive and intellectually rich. And thanks, too, to Amanpal Garcha, for our many bracing conversations over the years.

Portions of chapters 1 and 3 first appeared as articles in *Novel* 37, nos. 1–2 (Fall 2003/Spring 2004) and *Victorian Studies* 48, no. 3 (2006). I am grateful to the editors of these journals for the permission to reprint.

This book is also about the often unhappy dealings of authors and publishers, which makes me all the more grateful for Cornell University Press. The manuscript was acquired by one extraordinary editor, Bernhard Kendler, and brought to press by another, Alison Kalett; it has benefited greatly from the wisdom and skill of both. Susan Tarcov was an outstanding copyeditor, missing nothing and clarifying everything. Russ Castronovo and Mary Loeffelholz were the ideal readers for this book. With a rare readiness to grant an author her *donnée*, they entered fully into my thinking, broadening, deepening and enriching it. I am indebted to their generosity, their imagination, and their rigor.

I am grateful for the people who reminded me that there was a world of ideas outside of the book: Ivan Ascher, Jon Connolly, Nikil Saval, David Lieb, Jon McKenzie, Danny Rose, Henry S. Turner, Carl Wennerlind, and especially Bernadette Meyler. And I am grateful as well for my family. My mother and father, Gloria Petit-Clair and K Wayne Claybaugh, and my stepmother, Rae Jean Claybaugh, bought me books when I was young, packed and moved my books when I was older, and in countless other ways helped the little girl who was always reading grow up to become a professor of English. My sisters, Melinda and Kelsey Claybaugh, watched all of this with patience and good humor. And Annelore, Stephan, and Elias

Puchner cheered me with their unflagging interest in the progress of my work.

A final round of thanks. Caroline Levine and Rebecca L. Walkowitz organized panels and reorganized drafts; entertained big ideas and made manageable suggestions; challenged my claims and believed in my intuitions; strategized and speculated, encouraged and commiserated, and, above all else, inspired me by their own example. James Ogilvie held this book steady in his imagination until I was able to hold it steady in mine—with him, the writing of it became first a possibility and then, astonishingly, a joy. Melinda Claybaugh has been there from the beginning, and there are no words for thanking her now.

This book is dedicated to Martin Puchner, my partner in this and all things, in gratitude for what he has created with me, a life in which love and labor are entwined.

The Novel of Purpose

Introduction

Cross Purposes

When Harriet Martineau toured the United States between 1834 and 1836, she was recognized as a social reformer who was also a woman of letters—and as a British subject who was also an Anglo-American. This latter identity was elaborated by the *Edinburgh Review* in its description of her tour. Martineau was, in the *Review*'s account, one of "that party in England" that had long maintained an unusual connection with its counterpart in the United States. The connection between them was the product of close commercial ties and even closer political and religious ones, and it manifested itself in "cousinship and similarity of manner and tone of thought."[1] With this description, the *Review* alluded to some of the many transatlantic ties that had survived the end of the War of Independence (1776–83): the religious fellowship of Unitarians in both nations; the political affiliations between British radicals and U.S. democrats; the mercantile relations linking Manchester and Liverpool to Boston and New York; and the emigration and intermarriage that sustained a literal cousinship.

Martineau embodied these residual ties, but she also highlighted, through her tour of the United States, two new modes of transatlantic interaction: the circulation of texts and the collaborations of social reform. These two modes are the subject of this book, and I begin with Martineau to throw into relief some of its central claims. More specifically, I use Martineau's career as

---

1. *Edinburgh Review*, April 1838, 181.

a reformer to sketch the workings of both nineteenth-century print culture and nineteenth-century social reform, and I use her career as a novelist to sketch the ways in which the nineteenth-century novel was shaped by reformist writings.[2]

The first central claim of this book is that *social reform depended on print.* Reform differed from earlier modes of social benevolence, such as charity, in its belief that social problems must be represented before they can be solved. As a consequence, reform gave rise to a vast number of representations. Some of these were performances, such as temperance parades and suffrage pageants, but many more were texts: governmental reports, economic treatises, medical studies, census figures, newspaper exposés, the narratives of drunkards, the narratives of slaves, sermons, poems, short stories, and novels, as well as maps, cartoons, and photographs. These texts circulated widely, ensuring that reformist ideas would move beyond the committee meeting or the lecture hall and pervade culture more generally. We can see this happen in Martineau's early reformist writings, a series of didactic short stories collectively titled *Illustrations of Political Economy* (1832–34). Written at a time when governmental elites were seeking to reform British institutions in accordance with the theories of Adam Smith, David Ricardo, and Thomas Malthus, *Illustrations* sought to explain those theories to a popular audience. "Sowers Not Reapers," for instance, shows the consequences of an agricultural tariff that has made bread more expensive than gin, while "Weal and Woe in Garveloch" shows the effects of unchecked reproduction on a limited food supply. *Illustrations* proved to be remarkably popular, with each installment selling more than ten thousand copies in Great Britain. Martineau's success at popularizing economic theories made her a figure to be reckoned with. She was invited to address Parliament, and she was petitioned by both political parties, at various times throughout her career, to popularize the results of their investigations or to write in support of their initiatives.[3]

Second, *social reform was crucially Anglo-American in scope.* Nearly all nineteenth-century reform movements involved both the United States

---

2. I use the term "nineteenth-century novel" to refer to that period in the history of the novel when realism was the predominant literary mode, which is to say, the Victorian period in the British novel and (roughly) the postbellum period in the U.S. novel. That no more satisfactory term exists to refer to these two periods together reflects both the literary-historical fact that realism came later to the U.S. novel than to the British and the disciplinary fact that the two literatures have long been studied in isolation from one another.

3. Deborah Anna Logan discusses Martineau's relation to Parliament in *The Hour and the Woman: Harriet Martineau's "Somewhat Remarkable" Life* (DeKalb: Northern Illinois Press, 2002), 19.

and Great Britain. Reformers from one nation often met with those in the other, while traveling on lecture tours or attending Anglo-American conventions against slavery or for temperance or world peace. And reformist groups in one nation offered those in the other money, moral support, and strategic advice through penny offerings, petitions, and "Friendly Addresses." But the Anglo-American scope of reform did not depend solely on direct encounters like these. More important was the transatlantic circulation of texts. In the absence of an international copyright law, texts of all kinds crossed and recrossed the Atlantic, and Martineau's *Illustrations* was part of this traffic. As popular in the United States as they were in Great Britain, *Illustrations* ensured that Martineau would be treated as an important public figure in the United States as well. She was invited not only to meet the president, Andrew Jackson, but also to settle in Texas and help the Texans write their constitution—an offer she declined.[4] The U.S. reception of *Illustrations* and of Martineau herself reminds us that the transatlantic circulation of texts created a kind of Anglo-American public sphere.[5] Through much of the nineteenth century, the people of Great Britain and the United States constituted a single reading public, and reformers in each nation shared a single imaginative horizon.

Third, *reformers in each nation allied with those in the other in order to alter both.* When Martineau arrived in the United States, she was already well known as a campaigner against slavery. One of her *Illustrations*, a story called "Demerara," had argued against slavery on economic as well as moral grounds, claiming that it not only violated the humanity of the slave but also created a lazy and inefficient workforce. Slavery was abolished in the British Empire in 1833, just a year after "Demerara" was published, and Martineau immediately redirected her antislavery efforts to the United States. As she traveled from city to city, she visited antislavery activists in each. She claimed that she had come to learn about slavery, not to teach, but the growing violence against antislavery activists in the United States eventually prompted her to take a public stand. Despite threats of violence, she began to give speeches condemning slavery. Her speeches had a special status, coming as they did from a British woman. Antislavery activists argued that Martineau, as a

---

4. Logan, *Hour and the Woman*, 20.

5. Jürgen Habermas uses this term to describe the infrastructure of newspapers and public meetings that I will describe as well (*The Structural Transformation of the Public Sphere: An Inquiry into a Category of Bourgeois Society*, trans. Thomas Burger [Cambridge: MIT Press, 1989]). But where Habermas conceives of this public sphere as separate from the private, and celebrates it as tending toward an ideal of rationality, I show that the public sphere interpenetrates the private and relies as much on affective as on rational appeals.

"representative . . . of the mother country," was a "representative of civilization" more generally.[6] The defenders of slavery, on the other hand, denied
that the "mother country" should retain any influence at all in the nation that
had rebelled against her.

But even as Martineau was seeking to influence U.S. views of slavery, her
own views of economics were being influenced in turn. In her *Illustrations*,
she had been attentive to the sufferings of industrial workers, in particular to their inadequate wages and their periodic unemployment, but she
had presented these sufferings as the inevitable consequence of unalterable
economic laws. Her economic views began to change, however, during her
time in the United States.[7] She began to recognize that the sufferings of
workers, like the sufferings of slaves, could be ameliorated by reform. In a
letter to the Massachusetts Anti-Slavery Society, she confided that industrial workers in Britain were as oppressed, and agricultural laborers as ignorant, as slaves in the United States. And she announced her new commitment to aiding workers as well.[8] This new commitment was made possible
by Martineau's encounter with alternate economic and social arrangements
during her U.S. tour. She visited New Harmony, one of the many utopian
communities that had been established in the United States. And she saw
that the social egalitarianism of the United States was not limited to its
utopian communities. In the northern states, she met a number of educated men who had once been laborers and a number of laborers who were
also educated men.[9] As a result of these experiences, Martineau no longer
believed that the conflict between workers and capitalists was inevitable
and irresoluble. On the contrary, she now sought almost socialist solutions,
arguing that a humane life was possible only where there was "community
of property."[10]

Martineau's contributions to Anglo-American reform did not end with
her return to Great Britain. She would collaborate with a U.S. activist,
Maria Weston Chapman, in writing a history of the U.S. antislavery movement, *The Martyr Age of the United States* (1839). And in the 1850s and
1860s, she would publish columns in the London *Daily News* that decried

6. Maria Weston Chapman, ed., *Harriet Martineau's Autobiography, with Memorials* (Boston:
J. R. Osgood, 1877), 127.
7. Caroline Roberts discusses the shift in Martineau's economic views in *The Woman and the
Hour: Harriet Martineau and Victorian Ideologies* (Toronto: University of Toronto Press, 2002),
35–37.
8. Quoted in Chapman, *Harriet Martineau's Autobiography*, 223.
9. Anne Hobart argues for the significance of this experience in "Harriet Martineau's Political Economy of Everyday Life," *Victorian Studies* 37, no. 2 (Winter 1934): 223–51.
10. Harriet Martineau, *Society in America*, 3 vols. (London: Saunders and Otley, 1837), 3:39.

the Fugitive Slave Law and the *Dred Scott* decision and defended the radical abolitionism of William Lloyd Garrison and, later, the Emancipation Proclamation. These columns countered the pro-southern position of the London *Times* and did much to prevent the British from supporting the Confederacy during the U.S. Civil War (1861–65).[11] But Martineau's most significant contribution to Anglo-American reform came in two books that seem, at first glance, to have little to do with reform at all. These are the books she wrote about her U.S. tour, *Society in America* (1837) and *Retrospect of Western Travel* (1838). Martineau was hardly alone in writing such travel books; more than two hundred British men and women published accounts of their travels in the United States during the first half of the nineteenth century, and an equal number of men and women from the United States published accounts of their travels in Great Britain.[12] Because each nation was central to the other's conception of reform, all of these books, whether they intended to or not, necessarily contributed to reformist debates. Martineau's descriptions of southern plantations, for instance, engaged U.S. debates about the abolition of slavery, just as her observations about U.S. manners engaged British debates about working-class enfranchisement.

Martineau's readers continued these debates. Some did so by writing texts of their own, such as the pamphlet *Slavery in America, Being a Brief Review of Miss Martineau on That Subject, by a South Carolinian* (1838), while others did so in their reviews of her books. These reviews offered an occasion for the reviewers to articulate their own positions on slavery and suffrage, positions that seldom conformed entirely to those taken by either government. The *Edinburgh Review* followed the British government in supporting the abolition of slavery and urging caution in expanding the franchise, but all other reviewers took the occasion to dissent in some way from the policies of their own governments. The conservative *Southern Literary Messenger* defended slavery and argued that enfranchisement had gone too far, while the radical *Westminster Review* took precisely the opposite position on both questions. In the responses to Martineau's travel books as in the travel books themselves, we can see the Anglo-American public sphere at work. More specifically, we can see how Anglo-American reform movements created a context in which persons within either nation could reimagine both.

11. Logan discusses the effects of Martineau's *Daily News* columns in "Harriet Martineau and the Martyr Age of the United States," *Symbiosis* 5, no. 1 (April 2001): 33–49.

12. Christopher Mulvey discusses this genre in *Transatlantic Manners: Social Patterns in Nineteenth-Century Anglo-American Travel Literature* (Cambridge: Cambridge University Press, 1990).

Just as Martineau's career as a reformer highlights the existence of an Anglo-American public sphere, so her career as a woman of letters throws into relief the structure of the Anglo-American literary field.[13] The author of reformist short stories, newspaper columns, and travel books, Martineau also wrote a treatise on protosociological methodology, defenses of atheism and mesmerism, and two novels. In the novels we can see that *there were important continuities between reformist writings and literary realism. The Hour and the Man* (1841), is openly reformist, even revolutionary. Written at a time when the pro- and antislavery factions in the United States were debating whether the freeing of the slaves would lead to insurrection, it offers an idealized portrait of Toussaint L'Ouverture, the black leader of the Haitian Revolution. But Martineau's other novel, *Deerbrook* (1839), seems to have nothing at all to do with reform, at least not at first. Focusing on a handful of families in a small country village and the courtships that take place among them, *Deerbrook* resembles a novel by Jane Austen. As it moves toward its final volume, however, it suddenly attempts a more comprehensive verisimilitude than anything Austen attempted. It shifts its attention to the many laborers who live alongside the novel's middle-class protagonists. These laborers are suffering from an unspecified economic distress, which has prompted some of them to turn to highway robbery and housebreaking and leaves all of them vulnerable to the epidemic that soon breaks out. In this way, an Austen-like courtship plot gives way to something much like one of Martineau's own *Illustrations*. This is not to suggest that *Deerbrook* becomes a reformist novel. It offers no account of what might have caused the economic distress or of how the laborers' sufferings might be alleviated. What *Deerbrook* does share with the *Illustrations*, and what the nineteenth-century novel more generally shares with the writings of reform, is a commitment to expanding the domain of representation, to depicting persons and experiences that have hitherto been ignored or treated unseriously, such as poverty, drunkenness, and disease; prisons, factories, slums, and madhouses; prostitutes, laborers, servants, and slaves.

Nineteenth-century novelists and reformist writers not only shared a representational project but also borrowed one another's formal techniques. The novel's plots and, even more, its methods of characterization were powerful tools for evoking sympathy. "There is something much more

13. I take this term from Pierre Bourdieu, who uses it to describe the overlapping contexts—sociological and economic, as well as literary—that determine the value of a given work of literature (*The Rules of Art: Genesis and Structure of the Literary Field*, trans. Susan Emanuel [Palo Alto: Stanford University Press, 1996]). Included within the literary field but not exhausted by it is the literary marketplace, which is constituted by the economic relations among authors, editors, publishers, reviewers, and readers.

human about a housebreaker than I had fancied," says one of the middle-class characters in *Deerbrook* after the robbery of her house has enabled her to speak with a laborer for the first time.[14] Reformist writings, including Martineau's own, learned from the novel how to create sympathetic characters. At the same time, the novel was learning other techniques from reformist writings. *Deerbrook*'s impulse to widen its verisimilitude is satisfied by one of the most common scenes in reformist writing: the investigative visit. This scene is used in one of the *Illustrations*, "Cousin Marshall," when a middle-class woman, a clergyman's sister, visits a workhouse to inspect its conditions. In much the same way, the epidemic in *Deerbrook* affords the middle-class characters access to the cottages on the outskirts of the villages. Entering these cottages to nurse the sick, they see—and we see through their eyes—the facts of poverty: the lack of food, the lack of fuel, the heap of rags that make up a bed.

Martineau's novels were only moderately successful, and by the end of her life even her *Illustrations* had been largely forgotten. Her most lasting legacy was to be found in the novelists she had influenced: Charlotte Elizabeth Tonna, Charles Kingsley, Harriet Beecher Stowe, Rebecca Harding Davis, Elizabeth Gaskell, Charlotte Brontë, and George Eliot. Although these novelists differ from one another—and from Martineau—in many ways, they nonetheless shared a specific conception of the novel. This conception is best captured by a term commonly used in the literary criticism of the time: the novel of purpose. The novel of purpose comprised both reformist and nonreformist novels, but it took its conception of purposefulness from reform. As a consequence, nineteenth-century novels were written, published, read, and reviewed according to expectations learned from social reform. Like reformist writings, the novel of purpose was understood to act on its readers—and, through its readers, the world. This conception of the novel did much to elevate its status. Where the novel had earlier been at best dismissed as frivolous, at worst condemned as sinful, it was now understood to be actively working for the social good.

In this way, Martineau established a model of a novelistic career that emerges out of, while remaining importantly grounded in, reformist writings. So powerful was this model that many other novelists would follow it, even those who were skeptical of or indifferent to reform. They would take up reformist subject matter without feeling any reformist commitment or without intending any reformist effect. And it is these reluctant reformist writers who are the main subject of this book. In focusing on them, I show

14. Harriet Martineau, *Deerbrook*, ed. Valerie Sanders (1839; London: Penguin Books, 2004), 520.

that the relations between social reform and literary realism, between reformist writings and the novel of purpose, are more complicated and more varied than they might at first seem. Some of these novelists oppose the reforms that they are depicting. Henry James's *The Bostonians* (1885–86) and George Eliot's *Felix Holt* (1866) take as their subject the campaigns to expand the suffrage to women and working-class men, campaigns that Eliot took to be premature and James misguided. And Charles Dickens, despite his subsequent fame as the great reformist novelist, would begin his career by mocking reform, specifically temperance reform, in his *Sketches by Boz* (1836) and *The Pickwick Papers* (1836–37). Other novelists depict reforms that they do support, but they depict them only after these reforms have been achieved: Mark Twain's *The Adventures of Huckleberry Finn* (1885) was written twenty years after the abolition of slavery; Thomas Hardy's *Jude the Obscure* (1895) was written forty years after the enactment of the right to divorce. In all of these cases, the absence of reformist intention and reformist effect prompts us to ask what other uses might be served by reform.

It is revealing, in this context, that many of the novelists I focus on take up the subject of reform at a crucial moment of transition in their careers: Dickens, when he was in the process of inventing the first serial novel; Eliot, when she turned from her early autobiographical novels to the social novels of her mature period; James, when he sought to recapture the popular audience that had once been his; Twain, when he tried to transform himself from humor writer to novelist; Hardy, when he said his last, bitter farewell to the novel and took up poetry instead. What this suggests is that these novelists found in reform a set of strategies for managing the relations among their novels, their readers, and the world. More specifically, some of these novelists, such as Dickens, Eliot, and James as well as Elizabeth Stoddard and Anne Brontë, would find in reformist writings an array of formal resources. Other novelists, such as James, Twain, and Hardy, found in reformist subject matter the occasion to present themselves and their works as purposeful.

Purposes can cross in two senses of the word. Martineau's travels and writings remind us that reformist purposes crossed and recrossed the Atlantic throughout the nineteenth century. Here, crossing names the collaborations, negotiations, and appropriations out of which both the United States and Great Britain would take shape. I discuss these crossings more fully in the next chapter, and I return to many of them throughout this book, from Dickens's tour of the United States and Stowe's and Twain's tours of Great Britain through a range of Anglo-American reform movements to the Anglo-American campaign against imperialism at the end of the century. But purposes also cross when they are at odds with one another. Here, the phrase "cross purposes" refers to the novelists I focus on most extensively, the ones who sought to make literary use of social reform. Some of these novelists borrowed from reformist writings, while others parodied them, and still others saw in these writings an effort to solve the representational problems that troubled the realist novel as well. But all of them recognized certain ideological and formal limitations in these writings, and all of them developed new representational practices in order to go beyond those limitations. In the process, these novelists, reluctant reformers all, contributed to the development of the novel of purpose and ensured that it would be the predominant nineteenth-century genre in both Great Britain and the United States.

Chapter 1

Social Reform and the New Transatlanticism

The Anglo-American world reached its zenith with the defeat of France in the Seven Years War (1756–63). From England, Scotland, and Wales, it extended west through Ireland and Labrador; south through Newfoundland and Nova Scotia and through the New England, mid-Atlantic, and southern colonies; and even farther south and east through Jamaica, Bermuda, the Bahamas, and Barbados, with outposts on the Central American and African coasts. While the Anglo-American world was weakly centered in what would be called Great Britain, it was structured less by center and periphery than by affiliations that were partial, mutable, and overlapping. Constituted and reconstituted by explorers, travelers, traders, settlers, and migrants of all kinds, the Anglo-American world was both crisscrossed and bound together by the exchange of commodities, ideas, and cultural practices. It was what the historian Bernard Bailyn has described as a "congeries of entities."[1] Over time, the Anglo-American world would be divided into discrete nation-states. A little more than a decade after the Seven Years War, the thirteen North American colonies would declare their independence. Other regions would gradually follow. But the process of nation formation did not nullify the legacy of Anglo-American interdependence, nor did it sever the many affiliations that made up the Anglo-American world.

1. Bernard Bailyn, preface to *The British Atlantic World, 1500–1800*, ed. David Armitage and Michael J. Braddick (London: Palgrave, 2002), xv.

Among the most fundamental of these legacies was the English language. The Anglo-American world was largely Anglophone, and as a consequence the literatures of the nations that would emerge within it have never been entirely distinct. Even after national boundaries had been drawn, literary works continued to move across them with ease. Works written and published in one nation were very often republished, read, and reviewed in another. This transnational literary world was, to be sure, overlaid by national prejudice and national self-assertion. National prejudice can be found in the common presumption of British preeminence. Voiced explicitly in Sidney Smith's notorious question, "In the four quarters of the globe, who reads an American book?" the presumption was more commonly expressed through silence, in literary reviews that devoted little or no space to works by U.S. or Canadian authors.[2] As for national self-assertion, it can be found in the efforts made by U.S. authors to create a distinctively American literature. In the antebellum period, the authors associated with what would come to be called the American Renaissance sought to create such a literature by renouncing their cultural inheritance from Europe. "Our day of dependence, our long apprenticeship to the learning of other lands, draws to a close," announces Ralph Waldo Emerson's "American Scholar" (1837), while the preface to Walt Whitman's *Leaves of Grass* (1855) opens with an image of European literature being carried, like a corpse, out the door.[3] In the postbellum period, by contrast, a number of U.S. authors sought to align themselves with continental literary movements to distinguish themselves from their nearer British rivals. The chief architect of this strategy was William Dean Howells, the period's most influential man of letters. Unusually cosmopolitan for a literary nationalist, Howells famously claimed, in an 1882 review of Henry James, that the United States had superseded Britain in novel writing and that this new U.S. preeminence was made possible in large part by the recent influence of the French.[4] But these statements of U.S. self-assertion, like the statements of British prejudice, were powerless to stop the transatlantic circulation of texts, which would not be regulated in any way until the 1891 ratification of an international copyright law.

As a consequence, the nineteenth-century literary field took for granted the existence of what I will call "literature in English." This category is never fully articulated or defended, but it underwrites most contemporary reviews. From time to time, reviewers would remark on national differ-

2. *Edinburgh Review* 33 (January 1820): 79.
3. Ralph Waldo Emerson, "The American Scholar," reprinted in *Ralph Waldo Emerson: Essays and Lectures*, ed. Joel Porte (New York: Library of America, 1983), 53.
4. William Dean Howells, "Henry James, Jr.," *Century Magazine* 25, no. 1 (November 1882): 28.

ences, but their more usual practice was to discuss at least some U.S. works interchangeably with British ones. This is true, for instance, of the reviews that George Eliot would write in the 1850s. In one, she notes in passing that U.S. literature is characterized by "certain defects of taste" and "a sort of vague spiritualism and grandiloquence," but in many others she reads British and U.S. authors alongside one another without alluding to national difference at all.[5] She pairs Henry Wadsworth Longfellow with Robert Browning, for instance, and Walt Whitman with Alfred Lord Tennyson. Thirty years later, critics would still be doing much the same. Indeed, the category of literature in English is the one point on which critics as different as Walter Besant and Henry James can agree. In their famous debate over the "art of fiction," Besant does not address nationality at all, simply referring as a matter of course to Oliver Wendell Holmes as well as Charles Reade, to Nathaniel Hawthorne as well as Eliot. And James, for his part, alludes to the category in a magisterial parenthesis that seeks neither to justify nor to defend. "In the English novel," he begins and then goes on to add, "(by which of course I mean the American novel as well)."[6]

In the twentieth century, by contrast, discussions of literature in English would largely give way to the study of literature nationally defined. U.S. self-assertion would ultimately lead to the establishment of American literature as a separate field and American studies as a separate discipline, which would in turn reinforce the British indifference to all but the most distinguished of U.S. writers. To be sure, a few critics continued to read across national borders. For F. R. Leavis, the "great tradition" of what he calls the "English novel" includes James and Joseph Conrad, as well as Eliot and Jane Austen.[7] And F. O. Matthiessen, in his field-defining study of the American Renaissance, emphasizes the connections between Herman Melville and William Shakespeare, Hawthorne and John Milton, Whitman and Gerard Manley Hopkins.[8] But such approaches would become increasingly rare. For a host of reasons, institutional as well as intellectual, the study of British literature and the study of U.S. literature would proceed along separate tracks for much of the twentieth century.

5. George Eliot, "Margaret Fuller and Mary Wollstonecraft," *Leader* 6 (13 October 1855): 988–989, reprinted in *Essays of George Eliot*, ed. Thomas Pinney (New York: Columbia University Press, 1963).

6. Henry James, "The *Art of Fiction*," *Longman's Magazine*, September 1884, reprinted in *Henry James: The Critical Muse: Selected Literary Criticism*, ed. Roger Gard (New York: Penguin, 1987), 204.

7. F. R. Leavis, *The Great Tradition: George Eliot, Henry James, Joseph Conrad* (New York: George W. Stewart, 1950), 1.

8. F. O. Matthiessen, *The American Renaissance* (Oxford: Oxford University Press, 1941), xiii.

In the past two decades, however, literary scholars have begun to rediscover what nineteenth-century critics took for granted: that English language works should not be read in isolation from one another. They do so at a moment when historians have also been rediscovering the significance of transatlantic ties. Indeed, the transatlantic has come to be a predominant paradigm. The historian David Armitage begins his already seminal essay "Three Concepts of Atlantic History" (2002) by announcing that "we are all Atlanticists now."[9] And Lawrence Buell, one of the founders of transatlantic literary studies, surveyed the present state of the field in a 2003 review essay and determined that "these days . . . look like boom times for transatlantic studies."[10] One sign of these "boom times" is a renewed interest in the old category of literature in English. The critical scene is newly hospitable to those scholars who follow Matthiessen and Leavis—as well as Eliot, James, and Besant—in taking the English language as their frontier.[11] Focusing on a transatlantic array of texts, these scholars are not primarily interested in accounting for or speculating about the transatlantic relation. On the contrary, the crossing of national boundaries is largely incidental to whatever argument they are seeking to make, whether it be an argument about literary movements (Richard Gravil and Leon Chai), literary genre (George P. Landow), philosophical traditions (Susan Manning), or the interrelations of literary and social phenomena (Jonathan Arac).[12]

Other scholars have taken the transatlantic relation itself as their object of study. Some focus on the whole Anglo-American world, which includes Caribbean islands and ports in Africa and Latin America as well as Great Britain, Ireland, Canada, and the United States. Others focus on the relations between two nations within that world, most commonly the United States and Great Britain.[13] This difference in focus has tended to entail a

9. David Armitage, "Three Concepts of Atlantic History," in Armitage and Braddick, *British Atlantic World*, 11.

10. Lawrence Buell, "Rethinking Anglo-American Literary History," *Clio* 33, no. 1 (Fall 2003): 66.

11. I borrow this phrase from Richard Gravil's *Romantic Dialogues: Anglo-American Continuities, 1776–1862* (London: Macmillan, 2000), xx.

12. Gravil, *Romantic Dialogues;* Leon Chai, *The Romantic Foundations of the American Renaissance* (Ithaca: Cornell University Press, 1987); George P. Landow, *Elegant Jeremiahs: The Sage from Carlyle to Mailer* (Ithaca: Cornell University Press, 1986); Susan Manning, *Fragments of Union: Making Connections in Scottish and American Writing* (London: Palgrave, 2002); and Jonathan Arac, *Commissioned Spirits: The Shaping of Social Motion in Dickens, Carlyle, Melville, and Hawthorne* (New York: Columbia University Press, 1989).

13. I am not the first to respond to the flourishing of transatlanticism by creating a taxonomy of its variants. Armitage's "Three Concepts" created an anatomy, as well as reconstructing a genealogy, of Atlantic history, and Laura M. Stevens has since applied Armitage's anatomy to literary studies ("Transatlanticism Now," *American Literary History* 16, no. 1 [Spring 2004]: (93–102).

difference in method, which has given rise to certain lacunae in the field. Those scholars who focus on the Anglo-American world have tended to excavate the material networks that constituted it, such as the slave trade (Paul Gilroy and Joseph Roach) and black newspapers in the United States, Europe, and Africa (Brent Edwards).[14] Those scholars who focus on the relations between Great Britain and the United States have tended, by contrast, to focus on relations that are imagined, not material. For Robert Weisbuch, the relevant paradigm is Freudian, by way of Harold Bloom. He finds in nineteenth-century U.S. literature a tendency to imitate and revise British writings that bears witness, he argues, to the literature's felt belatedness.[15] For Buell, the relevant paradigms come from postcolonial theory. He finds in the condescension of British reviewers and the rebelliousness of U.S. writers the first iteration of what would become a familiar relation between former colonizer and former colony.[16] More recently, Paul Giles has taken a different approach. He has proposed that what he calls "the transatlantic imaginary," far from being structured in any stable way, is instead a space of projection and free play that any author, British or U.S., can enter at will and make use of.[17]

The imagined relations between Great Britain and the United States were importantly shaped by the material networks that connected them; this, in my view, is what studies of U.S.-British relations can learn from studies of the Atlantic world. In what follows, I will focus on two of these networks, print culture and social reform. In doing so, I will throw into relief the many subnational connections between persons and groups on both sides of the Atlantic—and the complexities of the power relations between the two na-

---

Armitage's anatomy divides the field into three groups according to geographical focus; mine divides it instead into two, but more importantly pairs geographical focus with theoretical method.

14. Paul Gilroy, *The Black Atlantic: Modernity and Double Consciousness* (Cambridge: Harvard University Press, 1993); Joseph Roach, *Cities of the Dead: Circum-Atlantic Performance* (New York: Columbia University Press, 1996); Brent Hayes Edwards, *The Practice of Diaspora: Literature, Translation, and the Rise of Black Internationalism* (Cambridge: Harvard University Press, 2003). Scholars whose focus is intercontinental rather than transatlantic have done the same, excavating, for instance, the Spanish language press in North and South America (Kirsten Silva Gruesz) and patterns of immigration and migration (John Carlos Rowe). Kirsten Silva Gruesz, *Ambassadors of Culture: The Transamerican Origins of Latino Writing* (Princeton: Princeton University Press, 2002); John Carlos Rowe, "Nineteenth-Century United States Literary Culture and Transnationality," *PMLA* 118, no. 1 (January 2003): 78–89.

15. Robert Weisbuch, *Atlantic Double-Cross: American Literature and British Influence in the Age of Emerson* (Chicago: University of Chicago Press, 1986).

16. Lawrence Buell, "American Literary Emergence as a Postcolonial Phenomenon," *American Literary History* 4, no. 3 (Autumn 1992): 411–42.

17. Paul Giles, *Virtual Americas: Transnational Fictions and the Transatlantic Imaginary* (Durham: Duke University Press, 2002), 1.

tions. Critics who speculate about the transatlantic imaginary without attending to these material networks tend to emphasize British cultural authority (Weisbuch, Buell) or minimize the importance of cultural authority at all (Giles). But a range of other possibilities exists: that power exists but is dispersed; that influence flows in many directions at once. These possibilities come into view when we turn our attention to print culture and social reform. In the literary marketplace, British authors were more celebrated and British reviewers more influential, but U.S. readers were more numerous and U.S. publishing houses were increasingly more powerful. Something similar is true of social reform. Some reforms, such as temperance, began in the United States and then traveled to Britain, while others, such as antislavery activism, traveled in the opposite direction; still others, such as suffrage reform and women's rights activism, developed in tandem between the two nations.

In focusing on the Anglo-American dimensions of both print culture and social reform, I do not mean to ignore the crucial role that each played in nation formation. More specifically, nations require us to think and feel that we are more strongly connected to persons within the abstract boundary of the nation than to persons beyond it. In the nineteenth century, as a number of theorists have argued, this training in thinking and feeling took place in large part through print culture and social reform. That both were importantly Anglo-American in scope meant that the United States and Great Britain formed as nations in a transnational context. Each, that is to say, came to conceive of itself as a nation with, through, and against the other.

Anglo-American Print Culture

When critics argue that nations were formed through novels and newspapers, they are referring most obviously to the content of these texts. Newspapers inform their readers of actual events happening to actual persons elsewhere in the nations, and novels entertain their readers with the same events in a fictional mode. But these critics are also referring to the mental habits that the reading of newspapers and novels inculcates. Newspapers, as Michael Warner has argued, address us as—and in addressing us as, transform us into—persons likely to care about, even to debate, the events they describe.[18] Moreover, as Benedict Anderson has observed, the newspaper's juxtaposed events, like the novel's multiple plots, train us to keep track of

---

18. Michael Warner, *The Letters of the Republic: Publication and the Public Sphere in Eighteenth-Century America* (Cambridge: Harvard University Press, 1990).

simultaneous events. In this way, we learn to acknowledge a connection between our own lives and those unfolding elsewhere in the nation.[19] And novels can provide affective training as well. The so-called national romance, as described by Doris Sommer and Nina Silber, emplots national union or reunion through the courtship of a woman from one national group by a man from another.[20]

But while newspapers and novels contributed to nation formation, they did so in a literary marketplace that was specifically Anglo-American. As a result of the U.S. refusal to recognize international copyright law, publishers in one nation, most commonly the United States, were able to reprint works by authors from the other nation, most commonly Great Britain, without paying any compensation. This practice harmed British authors, who had easy access to, but little profit from, the growing U.S. market. It also harmed U.S. authors, who found it difficult to enter either the British market or their own: readers in both nations were reluctant to read books by U.S. authors, which not only had less cultural authority than British books, but were also more expensive. For these reasons, both British and U.S. authors campaigned, throughout the nineteenth century, for the United States to recognize international copyright law. In the 1840s, Charles Dickens and Washington Irving separately sought to rally the support of other authors to the cause; by the 1880s, authors had organized themselves into advocacy groups, specifically the Author's Society (founded by Walter Besant and chaired by Tennyson, George Meredith, and Thomas Hardy) and the American Copyright League (led by James Russell Lowell and Mark Twain).

But the harms done to British and U.S. authors and to British publishers by reprinting were balanced by the benefits reprinting conferred elsewhere. The most obvious beneficiaries were U.S. publishers, although the unchecked competitiveness of the reprinting market drove many out of business in the 1840s and nearly destroyed the young U.S. publishing industry in the process.[21] A less obvious beneficiary was the U.S. reading public, which received a steady supply of cheap and excellent books. To be sure, some U.S. authors, particularly those active in the American Renaissance, were troubled by the fact that these books were British and argued that reprinting was impeding the development of a genuinely national literature. "Every book we read, every biography, play, romance, in whatever

19. Benedict Anderson, *Imagined Communities* (1983; London: Verso, 1991).

20. Doris Sommer, *Foundational Fictions: The National Romances of Latin America* (Berkeley: University of California Press, 1991); Nina Silber, *The Romance of Reunion: Northerners and the South, 1865–1900* (Chapel Hill: University of North Carolina Press, 1993).

21. William Charvat describes this in *Literary Publishing in America, 1790–1850* (Amherst: University of Massachusetts Press, 1959), 18.

form, is still English history and manners," Emerson observed in his *English Traits* (1856). "So that a sensible Englishman once said to me, 'as long as you do not grant us copyright, we shall have the teaching of you.'"[22] But U.S. publishers replied that a democracy depends less on its authors than on its readers, and the U.S. government was persuaded, as Siva Vaidhyanathan has shown, to sacrifice national literature to national literacy.[23] Similar arguments would be made in Britain after the decisive expansion of male suffrage in 1867. In 1876, the Royal Copyright Commission was convened, and over the next two years it heard arguments both from those who wanted to expand copyright protections and those who wanted to narrow them. In the latter group, Paul Saint-Amour has shown, were reformers who argued that workers would be capable of voting responsibly only when national education was sustained by good and readily available books.[24]

Because of reprinting, the U.S. literary marketplace developed in an asymmetrical, if intimate, relation to the British. Where the British literary marketplace was centered in London and oriented toward the writing and printing of texts, the U.S. literary marketplace was, at least during the antebellum period, scattered among a number of coastal cities and oriented toward reprinting. It was thus, as Meredith McGill has argued, both "internally divided" and "transatlantic," less a national marketplace than one that was "regional in articulation and transnational in scope."[25] Indeed, McGill observes, the market's transnational scope helped to mediate the increasing regional tensions of the antebellum period. Magazines that aspired to a national circulation needed to avoid commenting on issues with the potential to be regionally divisive, such as the annexation of Texas, and they managed to do so by reprinting British commentary on those issues instead.[26] Over time, U.S. publishing began to centralize. The development of trans-Allegheny railroads in the 1850s made it possible, William Charvat has shown, for publishing firms in coastal cities to serve the interior regions, and this new infrastructure of national distribution in turn

22. Ralph Waldo Emerson, *English Traits* (1856; Cambridge: Harvard University Press, 1929), 36.

23. Siva Vaidhyanathan, *Copyrights and Copywrongs: The Rise of Intellectual Property and How It Threatens Creativity* (New York: New York University Press, 2001), 51.

24. Paul K. Saint-Amour, *The Copywrights: Intellectual Property and the Literary Imagination* (Ithaca: Cornell University Press, 2003), 59–63. Those reformers involved in colonial administration also argued that cheap books were necessary for transforming native populations into docile British subjects (64–65).

25. Meredith McGill, *American Literature and the Culture of Reprinting, 1834–1853* (Philadelphia: University of Pennsylvania Press, 2003), 7, 1.

26. McGill, *American Literature and the Culture of Reprinting*, 24.

made it possible for a national literature to emerge.[27] At the same time, the phenomenal success of such 1850s authors as Fanny Fern, Harriet Beecher Stowe, and Susan Warner demonstrated that a national literature was not only possible but even profitable. The success of Stowe's *Uncle Tom's Cabin* (1851–52) was particularly striking in this regard, since the novel proved to be so popular in Britain that it became subject to unauthorized reprint- ing by British publishers, just as British books had been reprinted by U.S. publishers.[28] In this way, *Uncle Tom's Cabin* heralded the beginning of a new era in which the literary marketplaces of the United States and Britain were more or less symmetrical, with publishers on both sides of the Atlan- tic printing works by authors from their own nation and reprinting works by authors from the other.

But while the markets were more or less symmetrical, they nonethe- less differed in one crucial way. The U.S. market had stabilized at a lower price than the British; U.S. publishers sold many copies of relatively inex- pensive editions, whereas British publishers would sell relatively few copies of expensive ones. "Copy for copy American publishers vastly outproduced English," J. A. Sutherland observes; "title for title English novelists vastly outproduced American."[29] Viewed from the perspective of writing, then, the Anglo-American literary marketplace was clearly centered in London. Viewed from the perspective of publishing, however, it was increasingly cen- tered in Boston and New York. The complexities of this doubly centered literary field are thrown into relief by such firms as Harper Brothers. On the one hand, by 1850 Harper Brothers had dwarfed its British rivals, publishing two million volumes a year.[30] As a consequence, British authors submitted to the taste of Harpers and its rivals as surely as they submitted to the taste of those circulating libraries, Mudie's and W. H. Smith most prominently, that purchased the expensive British editions of their works. On the other hand, the vast majority of what Harpers published was written by British authors; of the 234 titles in its first catalogue, 90 percent were British reprints. To consider publishing alongside writing is, then, to see that neither nation clearly dominated the literary marketplace.

27. For a fuller discussion of the effects of railroads on U.S. literature, see Charvat, *Literary Publishing*, and Ronald Zboray, *A Fictive People: Antebellum Economic Development and the Ameri- can Reading Public* (Oxford: Oxford University Press, 1993).

28. McGill discusses the consequences of this in *American Literature and the Culture of Re- printing*, 274.

29. J. A. Sutherland, *Victorian Novelists and Publishers* (Chicago: University of Chicago Press, 1976), 17.

30. Sutherland, *Victorian Novelists and Publishers*, 71.

Over time, certain accommodations were made to compensate for the lack of an international copyright law. The most respectable publishers in both nations made voluntary payments to the authors they were reprinting. They also made and honored what they called "courtesy of the trade" agreements not to poach these authors from one another once the payments had been made. Authors became savvier as well, arranging for simultaneous publication on both sides of the Atlantic so that copyright could be secured in both nations at once and selling the same work twice, once to a British and once to a U.S. magazine. Still, these accommodations were fragile, and established publishers were continually threatened by upstart rivals. Increasingly, these rivals were Canadian. Canadian reprinters did not have to respect U.S. copyright, of course, but after the Canadian Copyright Act of 1875, they did not have to respect British copyright either. They were permitted to reprint British books so long as they did not then export these reprints back to Britain. In this way, Canadian reprinting challenged the dominance of British publishers across the British Empire and also raised the specter of similar challenges in Britain itself one day.[31] Canadian reprinting thus united British and U.S. publishers and prompted them to join the authors in campaigning for an international copyright law.

In 1891, the U.S. Congress responded to this campaign by passing the Chace Act, which recognized British copyright under certain conditions. But international copyright law ended up making less of a difference than its supporters had hoped, at least in the first few decades after it was passed. U.S. printers and compositors, who belonged to one of the most powerful trade unions, had ensured that U.S. copyright protections would be extended only to those British texts that had been printed in the United States from type set by U.S. typesetters. This required British publishers to commit to two separate typesettings and printings, which they were willing to do only for authors certain to sell well in the United States.[32] As a consequence, only about 5 percent of British books were copyrighted in the United States, at least according to contemporary observers.[33] The rest remained as vulnerable to reprinting as they always had been. And the Anglo-American literary field, although beginning to divide in two, remained importantly connected.

31. Saint-Amour, *Copywrights*, 61.

32. For a fuller discussion of this, see James L.W. West, "The Chace Act and Anglo-American Literary Relations," *Studies in Bibliography* 45 (1992): 305.

33. See, for instance, Stanley Unwin, *The Truth about Publishing* (1926; Boston: Houghton Mifflin, 1927), 69.

Anglo-American Social Reform

The chapters that follow focus on a number of reform movements, includ-ing temperance and the abolition of slavery, the campaigns for women's and working-class suffrage, and also efforts to equalize marriage laws, to restruc-ture poorhouses, and to establish utopian communities and schools. This list is long and heterogeneous, to be sure, but it does not begin to exhaust the array of nineteenth-century reforms, which also included Magdalene houses for fallen women and settlement houses for immigrants and the poor, the campaign against naval flogging, the campaign for animal welfare, reform of asylums and prisons, sanitation reform, rational dress reform, vegetarianism, mesmerism, phrenology, and water cures. Surprisingly, this heterogeneous array was seen by contemporary reformers as coherent. There were some conflicts among these reforms, as well as within them, but for the most part they were understood to be part of a single project. Reformers active in one movement were nearly always active in others, new movements emerged out of existing ones, and the arguments made by one group of reformers were often borrowed by others. What united all of these reforms was an effort to improve society, specifically by changing some of its aspects while leaving others intact. This is, to be sure, an imprecise definition, but its very impre-cision usefully registers the fact that reform occupies a middle position, both historically and ideologically, and is therefore best defined in terms of what it is not. In historical terms, reform superseded charity and would, in turn, lay the foundations of the welfare state. In ideological terms, reform stands between the stasis of an ancien régime and the thoroughgoing changes of a revolution.

Reform emerged at the end of the eighteenth century as an alternative to charity, which had existed in an organized form since the early medieval period and had been coordinated by monasteries, churches, guilds, and even some local governments.[34] Charity seeks to assuage a suffering that is un-derstood to be inevitable, the result of either accident or God's will, and it does so most commonly through concrete acts of material aid. Charity thus takes the form of alms to the poor, food to the hungry, shelter and succor to the old and sick. Reform emerged as an alternative to charity once charity's fundamental presupposition, the inevitability of suffering, was doubly chal-lenged, first by the Enlightenment and then by the evangelical revivals that began in the late eighteenth century and continued through much of the

---

34. The standard histories of this are W. K. Jordan, *Philanthropy in England, 1480–1660* (London: G. Allen and Unwin, 1959), and David Owen, *English Philanthropy, 1660–1960* (Cambridge: Harvard University Press, 1964).

nineteenth. From the Enlightenment came the idea that social and political arrangements might be improved or even perfected and, with it, the idea that suffering could be lessened or even eliminated altogether. Animated by this possibility, a number of Enlightenment thinkers sought to identify the causes of phenomena that had hitherto been taken for granted, such as poverty and sickness; in the process, they developed new modes of analysis that would lead to the development of the social sciences. But while the possibility of improving society originated in the Enlightenment, it was popularized by a very different social movement, the evangelical revival that swept both the established and dissenting churches in Great Britain as well as the United States. Replacing the idea of predestination with an idea of salvation open to all, evangelicalism made it possible to imagine reclaiming persons from their sufferings on earth as they would be redeemed from their sins in heaven.[35] Indeed, a millennial strain of evangelicalism, most prevalent in the United States, made it possible to imagine a heaven achieved on earth by Christ's imminent return.[36] Moreover, the evangelical emphasis on conversion and active faith inspired adherents to transform first themselves and then their world. In this way, evangelicalism took a possibility envisioned by Enlightenment elites and made it into an imperative duty shared by all.

What emerged out of the confluence of evangelicalism and the Enlightenment was social reform. Where charity had been practiced by individuals and already existing groups, such as parishes and guilds, reform entailed new forms of association. Evangelicalism was significant here as well. Coinciding with the disestablishment of churches in the United States and the flourishing of alternatives to the established church in Great Britain, the evangelical revival offered a model of social organization distinct from the state and thus made it possible for persons to imagine more secular forms of social organization as well.[37] In this way, evangelicalism contributed to the growth of civil society, in particular to the rise of voluntary associations. Voluntary associations were most famously described by Alexis de Tocqueville, who also asserted that they were unique to the United States. "Americans of all ages, all conditions, and all dispositions constantly form associations," he observes. ". . . The Americans make associations to give entertainments, to found seminaries, to build inns, to construct churches, to diffuse books, to send missionaries to the antipodes; in this manner they found hospitals,

---

35. For a full account of the culture of evangelicalism in England, see Leonore Davidoff and Catherine Hall, *Family Fortunes: Men and Women of the English Middle Class, 1780–1850* (Chicago: University of Chicago Press, 1987), 93.

36. Robert H. Abzug makes this argument in *Cosmos Crumbling: American Reform and the Religious Imagination* (Oxford: Oxford University Press, 1994).

37. For a full account of the culture of evangelicalism in the United States, see Ann Douglas, *The Feminization of American Culture* (New York: Knopf, 1977).

prisons, and schools."[38] Historians of reform have followed Tocqueville in arguing that voluntary associations were more common in the United States than in Great Britain because the United States had no longstanding tradition of church and state institutions.[39] But voluntary associations were, in fact, quite important in Great Britain as well. In Britain they offered, as Leonore Davidoff and Catherine Hall have argued, an alternative mode of civic involvement to precisely those groups who were denied access to full democratic participation, such as middle-class men early in the nineteenth century and women and workers after that.[40]

In both nations, voluntary associations worked to supplement the state. Lauren Goodlad has recently emphasized that the British state, unlike the French, was remarkably small, and she has argued that much of what we take to be statist intervention in nineteenth-century Britain was actually in the hands of individual volunteers.[41] The New Poor Law of 1834, for instance, depended on volunteer inspectors for its enforcement, as did animal cruelty laws later in the century. And while the Blue Books were written under Parliamentary direction, other monumental texts of British reform, such as Henry Mayhew's *London Labour and the London Poor* (1861–62), were written by journalists and other independent individuals. What was true of Great Britain was even more true of the United States, where the state was even smaller. In supplementing the state, voluntary associations, particularly reformist ones, solved two problems at once. By enabling the United States and Great Britain to respond to social unrest without having to develop an elaborate state apparatus, reform managed to stave off the double threat of continental revolution and continental despotism.[42] Over the course of the century, these voluntary associations were gradually enfolded into an enlarging state, and in this way reform laid the groundwork for the welfare state of the twentieth century.

Even though many people joined reformist associations of various kinds, reform nonetheless conceived of the individual as both the agent and the site of social transformation. It is in this way that reform differs from other

---

38. Alexis de Tocqueville, *Democracy in America* (1835; New York: Modern Library, 1981), 403.

39. William B. Cohen summarizes this view in "Epilogue: The European Comparison," in *Charity, Philanthropy, and Civility in American History*, ed. Lawrence J. Friedman and Mark D. McGarvie (Cambridge: Cambridge University Press, 2003), 385.

40. Davidoff and Hall, *Family Fortunes*, 136.

41. Lauren M. E. Goodlad, *Victorian Literature and the Victorian State: Character and Governance in a Liberal Society* (Baltimore: Johns Hopkins University Press, 2003), 6.

42. For an account of fears of revolution, see Brian Harrison, *The Peaceable Kingdom: Stability and Change in Modern Britain* (Oxford: Oxford University Press, 1982), 22. For an account of fears of despotism, see Goodlad, *Victorian Literature and the Victorian State*, 6.

modes of social action. This focus on the individual is most obvious in the case of those reforms that required individuals to transform their own lives—by eating only vegetables or taking water cures, by wearing bloomers or joining utopian communities, or, most commonly, by renouncing drink. But it is equally true of reforms that entailed the transformation of lives other than the reformers' own, such as the campaigns against poverty or slavery. Reformers were only secondarily interested in providing charitable aid to the poor or the enslaved; they were primarily interested in changing the structures that made poverty or slavery possible. But structural change took place, for nineteenth-century reformers, one individual at a time. This was true not only of the persons reformers were seeking to aid but also of the reformers themselves. Not only did each fallen woman or each drunkard have to be individually reclaimed, but each reformer had to recognize, individually, that slavery was wrong and factory work cruel. Reform sought structural change, but, as Jane Tompkins has argued, it imagined structures to be the aggregate of individual beliefs.[43]

The canonical account of how such reform was understood to work can be found in Stowe's *Uncle Tom's Cabin*. In the novel's final pages, Stowe conjures up a reader who asks what any individual can do in response to the horrors the novel has described. To this question, Stowe gives a confident answer: "There is one thing that every individual can do,—they can see to it that *they feel right.*"[44] Feeling right is powerful, she goes on to claim, because our feelings diffuse from us in a circle of sympathy, altering those around us in turn. Elizabeth Gaskell makes much the same claim in the preface to her industrial novel *Mary Barton* (1848), which concludes with the hope that readerly sympathy will somehow reconcile workers with their masters and thus prevent the revolutions then taking place on the continent from breaking out in Britain as well. What must be reformed, in both novels, is not so much the slave or factory system but rather the individuals who profit from those systems, however remotely. Once these individuals come to feel sympathy, the systems themselves will wither away. And this is because sympathy is not only affective but also cognitive. To feel sympathy with a slave or a worker is to recognize that he or she is a person in some way like oneself, and this makes his or her sufferings unacceptable.

43. Josephine Guy argues that industrial novels sought to solve the problem of poverty one individual at a time by expecting individuals to make different choices (*The Victorian Social-Problem Novel: The Market, the Individual, and Communal Life* [London: Macmillan, 1996], 100). In her reading of U.S. sentimental fiction, Jane Tompkins, by contrast, emphasizes that individual choices together alter the contexts in which they are made (*Sensational Designs: The Cultural Work of American Fiction, 1790–1860* [Oxford: Oxford University Press, 1985]).

44. Harriet Beecher Stowe, *Uncle Tom's Cabin; or, Life among the Lowly* (1851; New York: Norton, 1994), 385.

While charity takes place between donor and recipient, reform takes place within an individual's own heart and mind. For this reason, its central locus is the scene of reading. And so while the defining act of charity is the giving of material aid, the defining act of reform is the production and circulation of texts.[45] So many and varied were these reformist texts that reform played an important role in the development of nineteenth-century print culture. In the United States, reformist groups such as the American Tract Society not only established new presses but introduced new printing techniques and new modes of distribution, all of which were ultimately taken over by nonreformist publishers.[46] And the printing and distribution of reformist texts, along with expansion of the lecture tours, made it possible in turn for reformers to support themselves while doing the work of reform.[47]

Reform was not only materially central to the development of nineteenth-century print culture; it was also formally intertwined with the development of the nineteenth-century novel. Of the various reformist genres, reformist novels proved the most influential and the most enduring, in large part because the novel was uniquely adapted to soliciting the kind of identifications that were central to reform. The industrial novelist Charlotte Elizabeth Tonna makes this point in the preface to her *Wrongs of Woman* (1843). "The abstract idea of a suffering family does not strongly affect the mind," she acknowledges, "but let the parties be known to us, let their names call up some familiar images to our view, and certain facts connected with their past lives be vividly brought to our recollection when they are spoken of, we are enabled much more feelingly to enter into their trial."[48] Tonna is here explaining the significance of character, its capacity to make an "abstract idea" concrete, but she is also explaining the significance of plot. If characters are most affecting when we can "recollect" events from "their past lives," when they have become "familiar" to us through long acquaintance, then they are most affecting not in brief episodes but in sustained narratives.

The identifications prompted by reformist writings were crucially nation forming. Recognizing that nations depend on imagined connections, Mary Poovey has argued that reform was one of the discourses that established

45. Indeed, Oz Frankel has shown that the British government had trouble persuading anyone to read the voluminous reports it put out ("Blue Books and the Victorian Reader," *Victorian Studies* 46, no. 2 [Winter 2004]: 308–18).

46. Steven Mintz discusses this in *Moralists and Modernizers: America's Pre–Civil War Reformers* (Baltimore: Johns Hopkins University Press, 1995), 54.

47. Ronald Walters demonstrates this in *American Reformers, 1815–1860* (New York: Hill and Wang, 1978), 16.

48. Charlotte Elizabeth Tonna, *The Wrongs of Woman*, quoted in Joseph Kestner, *Protest and Reform: The British Social Narrative by Women, 1827–1867* (Madison: University of Wisconsin Press, 1985), 97.

such connections in Great Britain: by identifying certain persons and problems as worthy of the nation's concern, reform called the nation itself into being.[49] Moreover, the agendas of some reform movements were directly connected to nation formation. Some, such as the Benthamite reform of the poor laws, altered existing state institutions and established new ones. Others sought to establish new terms for national belonging: the campaigns against slavery and for worker's or women's rights helped to determine who would count as citizens or subjects and on what terms. Even those reforms that would seem to have little to do with nation formation, such as temperance reform, ended up contributing to it as well. The temperance pledge, for instance, was often seen as a new kind of social contract. First signed by elite men in the United States who sought to reconstitute what they took to be a fragmenting social order, the pledge was subsequently taken up by the working-class Chartist movement in Britain and later by Irish nationalists, who believed that it was connected in some way to home rule.[50] And in the United States, teetotal societies held their most festive occasions on the Fourth of July, inviting attendees to sign the pledge as a way of declaring a "SECOND INDEPENDENCE" from Prince Alcohol.[51]

Finally, the very phenomenon of reform was understood to be characteristic of particular nations, namely, Great Britain and the United States. Edward Bulwer famously declared, in his *England and the English* (1833), that "the question of reform came on . . . [and] was hailed at once by the national heart."[52] Bulwer is referring specifically to the Reform Bill of 1832, which extended suffrage to middle-class men, but he is also alluding implicitly to France, whose recent revolution tried to achieve similar effects through violence. A few years later, Ralph Waldo Emerson would make a similar claim in his essay "Man the Reformer" (1841): "[T]he doctrine of reform had never such scope as at the present hour," he proclaimed, aligning the "hour" with a particular place, namely, the United States.[53] This national focus persists into the present day. The most important historian of British

49. Mary Poovey, *Making a Social Body: British Cultural Formation, 1830–1864* (Chicago: University of Chicago Press, 1995).

50. On U.S. elites, see Abzug, *Cosmos Crumbling*, 97. On Chartist temperance reform, see Brian Harrison, *Drink and the Victorians: The Temperance Question in England, 1815–1872* (Pittsburgh: University of Pittsburgh Press, 1971), 115. On Irish nationalists, see Christine Alfano, "Under the Influence: Drink, Discourse, and Narrative in Victorian Britain" (Ph.D. diss., Stanford University, 1996), 173.

51. Quoted in W. J. Rorabaugh, *The Alcoholic Republic: An American Tradition* (Oxford: Oxford University Press, 1979), 194.

52. Edward Bulwer, *England and the English*, ed. Standish Meacham (1833; Chicago: University of Chicago Press, 1970), 288.

53. Ralph Waldo Emerson, "Man the Reformer," in *Nature: Addresses and Lectures* (Boston: James Monroe, 1849).

reform, Brian Harrison, has recently argued that it is Britain's commitment to reform that distinguishes it from other nations.[54] And U.S. historians of reform make similar claims. What is striking about this historiographical tradition is that it attributes either the British or the U.S. culture of reform to an array of factors that were clearly shared by both nations: laissez-faire liberalism, a gradual expansion of suffrage, Protestantism, and a free press.

But while reform is connected to nationhood in many ways, it was itself a transnational phenomenon. The historian Frank Thistlethwaite was among the first to note that there was an Atlantic exchange in religious and political ideas as well as in goods, that there were Atlantic networks of friendship and alliance as well as of trade.[55] Reform, I argue, was a central conduit for these exchanges. Indeed, reform enabled and sustained an array of transatlantic affiliations through which both nations were imagined and strategically re-made. At times, one nation would set an example that reformers in the other nation would follow. More often, reformers in one nation would ally with those in the other in order to alter both.

We can see both of these processes at work in the Anglo-American campaign against slavery. The campaign against slavery emerged in response to the transatlantic phenomenon par excellence, the slave trade. The exchanges of goods and persons that the slave trade entailed laid down the routes of subsequent transatlantic interactions, some of which were reformist. The antislavery campaign began in the 1760s when a group of Quakers from Philadelphia appealed to the British government to abolish slavery in the colonies, and it remained importantly Anglo-American until its end. Antislavery activists in one nation were routinely invited to be corresponding members of antislavery societies in the other, and in this way activists on each side of the Atlantic were able to learn from the very different experiences of slavery on the other. In the 1780s and 1790s, for instance, the lives of freed slaves in the United States, as described by members of the New York and Massachusetts antislavery societies, were held up by British activists to argue for the thoroughgoing emancipation of slaves in the British colonies.[56] In the 1830s, antislavery groups became even more tightly intertwined. The American Anti-Slavery League was founded one year after the British league of the same name, and in 1833 William Lloyd Garrison traveled to London to meet the president of the British league, who in turn traveled to Boston the next year—with galvanizing effects on both nations. The abolition of

---

54. Harrison, *Peaceable Kingdom*, 2.

55. Frank Thistlethwaite, *The Anglo-American Connection in the Early Nineteenth Century* (Philadelphia: University of Pennsylvania Press, 1959).

56. David Turley describes this in *Culture of English Antislavery, 1780–1860* (London: Routledge, 1991), 200.

slavery in the British Empire did not put an end to these collaborations, as Harriet Martineau's U.S. tour reminds us. Martineau was only one of many British reformers who continued to serve as a source of moral example, practical advice, and financial support for groups in the United States.

In the campaign for suffrage, the transatlantic connections were less institutional but no less significant. The United States had long served as an inspiration for British radicals, most famously William Cobbett, and it continued to do so for the Chartists. "[T]he Chartist movement was reared," the historian George Lillibridge has argued, "on the American destiny."[57] Indeed, Chartist newspapers frequently invoked the United States as proof that universal manhood suffrage could be achieved. And for the more radical Chartists, the United States also exemplified the separation of church and state. In 1839, the first People's Charter was rejected by Parliament. As a consequence, a number of leading Chartists emigrated to the United States, which became a real refuge, as well as an imagined alternative.[58]

These reformist campaigns made possible a number of different relations between Great Britain and the United States. At times, the two nations used reform to articulate the differences between them. Democracy has long been crucial to U.S. self-understanding, while the antislavery campaign enabled Britain to conceive of itself, Christopher Brown has argued, as the moral alternative to its former colony.[59] We can see these processes at work in the writings of British travelers describing U.S. slaves—and U.S. travelers describing British servants. When he attends a slave auction, Thomas Grattan expects the bidding to stop when he, an Englishman, arrives.[60] Fanny Kemble expresses a similar presumption more forcefully, announcing before she travels to the southern states that "assuredly, I *am* going [south] prejudiced against slavery, for I am an Englishwoman, in whom the absence of such prejudice would be disgraceful."[61] In much the same way, U.S. travelers expressed shock when in Britain at the existence of a permanent serving class, as Christopher Mulvey has shown.[62]

57. George Donald Lillibridge, *Beacon of Freedom: The Impact of American Democracy upon Great Britain, 1830–1870* (Philadelphia: University of Pennsylvania Press, 1955), 41.

58. For a thorough account of the Chartists in the United States, see Ray Boston, *British Chartists in America, 1839–1900* (Manchester: Manchester University Press, 1971).

59. Christopher Leslie Brown, *Moral Capital: Foundations of British Abolitionism* (Chapel Hill: University of North Carolina Press, 2006).

60. Thomas Colley Grattan, *Civilized America* (London: Bradbury and Evans, 1859), 413, 417.

61. Frances Anne Kemble, *Journal of a Residence on a Georgian Plantation in 1838–1839*, ed. John A. Scott (1863; New York: Knopf, 1961), 11.

62. Christopher Mulvey, *Transatlantic Manners: Social Patterns in Nineteenth-Century Anglo-American Travel Literature* (Cambridge: Cambridge University Press, 1990), 162–71.

At other times, however, the Anglo-American scope of these two reform movements enabled groups within one nation to appeal to the other for help. Some fugitive slaves found refuge in Britain, and some of the more radical Chartists considered petitioning the president of the United States to intervene on behalf of the British working class.[63] And the antislavery movement allowed factions within each nation to imagine both nations being transformed. Black antislavery activists would, as Elisa Tamarkin has shown, align their own past with that of Britain, conjuring up an imaginary archaic England, which they claimed, astonishingly enough, as their true mother country.[64] And working-class British men would see their own future in the Republican party of the United States, which was providing working men with land even as it was also seeking to free the slaves.

The antislavery and suffrage campaigns were intertwined with one another for much of the century. The first activists for women's rights came out of the antislavery campaign, and the women's rights movement in the United States would divide, after the freeing of the slaves, over the question of whether the freedmen should be enfranchised first. The emancipation of the slaves also lent force to the contemporary campaign in Great Britain to enfranchise working-class men. Thomas Carlyle acknowledges as much in his notorious "Shooting Niagara" (1867), which argues that what he refers to as the "Settlement of the Nigger Question" will lamentably lead to the enfranchisement of all workers, which he refers to as "the Niagara leap."[65] The two causes were also linked by those who supported both. William Gladstone, for instance, argued in favor of the Reform Act of 1884, which completed the work of extending suffrage to all men, by adducing the Union victory in the U.S. Civil War. This victory showed, he argued, that nations were strongest when they were most democratic.

What the history of the antislavery campaign suggests, and the history of other nineteenth-century reform movements confirms, is that the most fundamental questions of national identity were asked and answered in the context of the Anglo-American world. These questions come up again and again in the chapters that follow. The antislavery campaign, to which Charles Dickens and Mark Twain contributed, asked who deserved to be treated as a person. The suffrage campaign, which George Eliot and Henry James de-

63. Boston discusses this in *British Chartists in America*, 16.
64. Elisa Tamarkin, "Black Anglophilia; or, The Sociability of Antislavery," *American Literary History* 14, no. 3 (2002): 44–77.
65. Thomas Carlyle, "Shooting Niagara—And After?" *Macmillan's Magazine* 16 (April 1867): 64–87.

picted, asked which citizens or subjects should be permitted to vote. And the campaigns for women's rights, which Elizabeth Stoddard and Thomas Hardy commented on, asked where rights came from and what they were useful for. In all of these instances, we see the legacy of Anglo-America at work in the nations that formed out of it.

Chapter 2

The Novel of Purpose and Anglo-American Realism

The first book-length study of the novel in English, David Masson's *British Novelists and Their Styles* (1859), was also the first to remark on the connection between literary realism and social reform. In his discussion of the nineteenth century, Masson claims that the novel was revivified, following the death of Sir Walter Scott, by two literary phenomena prompted by the revolutions of 1848: the "increase and extension of a persevering spirit of realism" and "a great development in the Novel of Purpose."[1] The "novel of purpose," as Masson goes on to describe it, is a genre grounded in the writings of social reform. Crucially defined by explicitly reformist novels (here, socialist novels, temperance novels, and novels about women's rights), it extends through sectarian novels (Catholic and anti-Catholic novels, high church and low church novels) to novels that make no reference at all to particular causes but that are nonetheless characterized by "doctrinal or didactic earnestness,"[2] which is to say, almost any nineteenth-century novel at all. The line that Masson sketches from reformism to earnestness reminds us that the reformist novel was the genre that defined the nineteenth-century novel more generally. This is a point that generations of critics have continued to make, most famously Patrick Brantlinger. In his classic study of

1. David Masson, *British Novelists and Their Styles, Being a Critical Sketch of the History of British Prose Fiction* (1859; Philadelphia: Folson Press, 1969), 257.
2. Masson, *British Novelists and Their Styles,* 291.

reform in British literature, Brantlinger observes that "Victorian fiction as-
pires to the condition of bluebooks" and "bluebooks were very often treated
like novels."[3] The same can be said of U.S. literature as well. There is no
study of U.S. literature to complement Brantlinger's, but F. O. Matthiessen
long ago said that there should be one. The history of nineteenth-century
U.S. literature could be written, he said, in two volumes: *The Age of Sweden-
borg*, about literature and religion; and *The Age of Fourier*, about literature
and reform.[4]

But if Masson predicted subsequent generations of critics in his attention to the relation between the realist novel and social reform, he and his
contemporaries conceived of this relation with more subtlety than present-
day critics tend to do. Specifically, they understood that some novelists
take up reformist subject matter without having reformist commitments
or intending reformist effects. Masson, for instance, recognizes the obvious difference between novels that support a given reform and novels
that condemn it. But he also recognizes a more fundamental difference
between novels that seek to argue for—or against—a given reform and
novels for whom a given reform is nothing but subject matter. Masson
draws a distinction, that is to say, between novels about reform that seek
to be performative, to "inculcate" reform's "doctrines," and novels about
reform that seek only to be descriptive, that treat reform as an "interesting phenomenon of the time" (264).

If we follow Masson's distinctions, we can develop a four-square taxonomy of novels that take up the subject of reform. In one corner are those
novels that seek to effect a reform that their author supports, novels such as
Harriet Beecher Stowe's *Uncle Tom's Cabin* (1851–52) or Elizabeth Gaskell's
Mary Barton (1848) or others that we readily call reformist. In the corner
below are those novels that seek to prevent a reform that their author op-
poses, antireformist novels such as John W. Page's *Uncle Robin in His Cabin
in Virginia, and Tom without One in Boston* (1853) or Fred Folio's *Lucy Boston;
or, Women's Rights and Spiritualism, Illustrating the Follies and Delusions of the
Nineteenth Century* (1855). Reformist or antireformist, these novels share a
conviction that novels can "inculcate" their "doctrines" and so intervene in
the contemporary world. In the other column, however, are those novels for
whom reform is mere subject matter, drained of any reformist effect. One
square is filled by novels whose authors happen to approve of the reforms

3. Patrick Brantlinger, *The Spirit of Reform: British Literature and Politics, 1832–1867* (Cambridge: Harvard University Press, 1977), 28.

4. F. O. Matthiessen, *The American Renaissance: Art and Expression in the Age of Emerson and
Whitman* (Oxford: Oxford University Press, 1941), viii.

they describe, such as Anne Brontë's *The Tenant of Wildfell Hall* (1848) or Mark Twain's *The Adventures of Huckleberry Finn* (1885), while the other is filled by novels whose authors happen to disapprove, such as Henry James's *The Bostonians* (1885–86) or George Eliot's *Felix Holt* (1866). Approve or disapprove, however, these novels in the second column do not primarily intend either to advocate or to condemn reform.

Why would novelists who have no reformist or antireformist intentions choose to write about reform? Nineteenth-century critics often attempted to answer this question. Masson himself, in identifying reform as an "interesting phenomenon of the time," raises one possibility: that these novelists were motivated by the desire to be topical. And William Dean Howells suggests that they may be motivated by a desire to be sensational as well. The cynical newspaper reporter who is the protagonist of Howells's *A Modern Instance* (1882) invents an abuse to be reformed because he knows that there is "nothing the public enjoys so much as an exposé."[5] Where Howells suggests that reformist subject matter is profitable because it is sensational, Eliot argues that it is profitable because it seems to be improving. The "moralising" of many authors, she argues, is prompted less by "profound conviction" than by a desire to secure a large audience by presenting their works as "eligible" for "family reading."[6] An anonymous reviewer for the *Saturday Review* makes a similar point. Some novelists may write out of a genuine sense of purpose, he acknowledges; others, however, are like "tradesmen whose chief object is to sell their goods" and who draw in customers by placing "in their shop windows placards about charity sermons."[7]

Only a few present-day critics have recognized instances in which reformist subject matter is being put to nonreformist uses. David S. Reynolds has identified a set of antebellum writers who took up reformist subject matter, as Howells's newspaper reporter would later do, because it was sensational and lurid.[8] And Wai Chee Dimock has argued that Herman Melville's attack on naval flogging, which he made after the practice had been abolished, shows how popular reformist subject matter could be.[9] But where Reynolds and Dimock focus on specific instances in which reformist subject matter

5. William Dean Howells, *A Modern Instance* (1882; New York: Penguin, 1984), 382.

6. George Eliot, "The Morality of Wilhelm Meister," *Leader* 6 (21 July 1855): 703, reprinted in *Essays of George Eliot*, 145.

7. Quoted in David Skilton, *The Early and Mid-Victorian Novel* (London: Routledge, 1993), 39.

8. David S. Reynolds, *Beneath the American Renaissance: The Subversive Imagination in the Age of Emerson and Melville* (Cambridge: Harvard University Press, 1988), 54–91.

9. Wai Chee Dimock, *Empire for Liberty: Melville and the Poetics of Individualism* (Princeton: Princeton University Press, 1989), 99–100.

was used for nonreformist ends, I discuss the phenomenon more generally. In focusing on novels whose relation to reform is strategic rather than committed, I hope to throw into relief the more ordinary workings of reformist novels and their more typical place within the nineteenth-century literary field.

The Novel of Purpose

The term "novel of purpose" was not new to the nineteenth century. It was first used in the eighteenth century to describe the works of Maria Edgeworth and William Godwin. When the term reappeared in the nineteenth century, however, it would refer to something different. The eighteenth-century novel of purpose had been didactic in its efforts to improve its readers, but the nineteenth-century version was reformist in its faith that transforming readers was a necessary step in transforming the world.[10] At first, the two terms, purpose and reform, were used interchangeably in discussions of novels. A review of Dickens, for instance, calls him both a novelist of "solemn purpose" and a "social reformer."[11] The 1849 *Southern Literary Messenger* heralded the emergence of a new genre, novels that "aim at great political reform," while the 1854 *Graham's Magazine* noted, in the course of reviewing an industrial novel, that it was the "tendency of the age" to write with a sense of "purpose."[12]

Over the course of the 1850s, however, references to "reform" became less common as the concept of the reformist novel was enfolded into a more capacious conception of the purposeful one. This shift in terminology thus reflected an expansion of the genre. Grounded in the reformist novel proper, the novel of purpose came to encompass all novels that sought to intervene in the contemporary world. And nearly all novels sought to do so. Indeed, the novel had become, in the words of the 1844 *North American*, "an essay on morals, on political economy, on the condition of women, on the vices and defects of social life."[13] An article in the 1853 *Westminster Review* adds that there is "hardly a theory, an opinion or a crotchet" that has not been made the subject of a novel; the result, the reviewer observed, was a market

---

10. In this way, nineteenth-century novelists differed from Immanuel Kant's conception of art as a "purposeful purposelessness."

11. Review of *The Chimes*, by Charles Dickens, *Economist*, 18 January 1845, 53–54.

12. *Southern Literary Messenger*, November 1849; *Graham's Magazine*, April 1854. Quoted in Nina Baym, *Novels, Readers, and Reviewers: Responses to Fiction in Antebellum America* (Ithaca: Cornell University Press, 1984), 214, 215.

13. *North American*, April 1844.

flooded with novels about atheism or factory boys, industrial novels, political manifestos, and confessions of faith.[14] In the expansion of the genre, we can see the process that would lead Masson, in 1859, to define the novel of purpose as almost any contemporary novel at all.

To be sure, a number of reviewers did criticize certain novels for putting purpose ahead of art, but these criticisms tended to mask substantive objections to the particular purpose itself.[15] Until the end of the century, only a handful of figures took a principled position against the novel of purpose as a genre. One was Edgar Allan Poe, who argued that novels should be judged according to a purely aesthetic standard: "without reference to any supposed moral or immoral tendencies (things with which the critic has nothing to do)."[16] Two others, James Fitzjames Stephen and William Makepeace Thackeray, argued that novels should instead be judged according to the standards of entertainment. Stephen was a reformer himself, deeply involved in the reform of the Indian legal code. But he nonetheless believed that reform had no place in the novel, which was capable of little more than providing amusement, and he deplored the fact that novels were nonetheless being "used for a greater number of purposes than any other species of literature."[17] Like Stephen, Thackeray acknowledged the predominance of the novel of purpose even as he railed against it: "How many Puseyite novels, Evangelical novels, and Roman Catholic novels have we had," he asked, "and how absurd and unsatisfactory are they?"[18] But Poe, Stephen, and Thackeray aside, the "novel of purpose" would be the dominant genre until the end of the century.

14. "The Progress of Fiction as an Art," *Westminster Review* 60 (October 1853): 342–74, reprinted in *A Victorian Art of Fiction: Essays on the Novel in British Periodicals, 1851–1869*, ed. John Charles Olmstead (New York: Garland, 1979), 2:92.

15. Several literary historians have argued that these criticisms show that the reformist novel was valued less highly than the didactic (Nina Baym) or the realist (Edwin M. Eigner and George J. Worth). But these criticisms were made so inconsistently as to reveal that something other than disinterested classification was at work. And so Richard Stang argues, and I agree, that reviewers condemned as unartfully purposeful only those novels whose purposes they did not accept. Baym, *Novels, Readers, and Reviewers*, 216; Edwin M. Eigner and George J. Worth, *Victorian Criticism of the Novel* (Cambridge: Cambridge University Press, 1985), 8; Richard Stang, *The Theory of the Novel in England, 1850–1870* (New York: Columbia University Press, 1959), 71.

16. Quoted in Baym, *Novels, Readers, and Reviewers*, 173. Baym notes that this review is the only one of the two thousand she has surveyed to make such a claim.

17. Eigner and Worth, *Victorian Criticism of the Novel*, 97. It seems likely that his objections to reformist novels were more personal than programmatic: he had been deeply offended by Dickens's attacks on the legal system in *Little Dorrit*. In this way, Stephen's response confirms Stang's claim that it was the specific object of reform rather than reformism itself that troubled many critics of the novel of purpose.

18. Eigner and Worth, *Victorian Criticism of the Novel*, 9.

I have revived the "novel of purpose" as a critical category because it re-covers something crucial about the self-understanding of nineteenth-century novelists.[19] Nineteenth-century novelists were united in their conviction that purposes were what novels did and should have, even if they sometimes disagreed about what these purposes should be. As a consequence, they thought of novels not as self-contained aesthetic objects but rather as active interventions into social and political life. They thought of novels as per-formative, and they took their conception of performativity from the writ-ings of social reform. The novel of purpose, emerging as it does out of the reformist novel, reminds us that what is now seen—and often dismissed—as the "earnestness" of the nineteenth-century novel was not simply moral but social, indeed political. It was actively seeking to remake the world that it was also seeking to represent.

This conception of the novel did much to elevate the novel's status. Through the eighteenth century, novels had been seen as entertaining, and the success of Sir Walter Scott, at the turn of the nineteenth century, had persuaded readers that novels could be artful as well. At the same time, how-ever, an increasingly influential evangelical movement was condemning the novel, along with card playing and theater, as immoral. Redefining the novel in terms of purpose implicitly argued that it was not entertainment at all but rather a serious engagement with the most pressing problems of social and political life. This tactic was so successful that novelists of purpose were able to turn the tables on their evangelical critics and identify themselves, rather than their rivals, as the true clergymen of the nineteenth century. Anthony Trollope compared the novelist to a minister, claiming that both were motivated by the same sense of purpose, and he was far from the only literary figure to make such a comparison.[20] Dinah Mulock Craik noted that novelists reached more people than ministers: "[T]he essayist may write for his hundreds, the preacher preach for his thousands; but the novelist counts his audience by millions."[21]

---

19. Mary Loeffelholz has recently made a complementary argument about poetry. Where I describe a literary field organized around purposeful novels, she describes a literary field orga-nized around didactic poetry. In both of our accounts, the literary field is profoundly altered at century's end—by what I call antipurposeful aestheticism and protomodernism and what Loef-felholz calls antididactic aestheticism. It is my hope that the parallels between our arguments will prompt a rethinking of the divisions too easily drawn between novels and poetry. *From School to Salon: Reading Nineteenth-Century American Women's Poetry* (Princeton: Princeton Uni-versity Press, 2004).

20. Skilton, *Early and Mid-Victorian Novel*, 38. Stang describes this as a commonplace of contemporary reviews (*Theory of the Novel in England*, 68).

21. Dinah Mulock, "To Novelists—and a Novelist," *Macmillan's Magazine*, April 1861, 442, quoted in Pauline Nestor, *George Eliot* (London: Palgrave, 2002), 2.

Anglo-American Realism

The consolidation of the novel of purpose intersected, at mid-century, with an emergent conception of realism. The term "realism" tends to be used in two different ways. Used loosely, it refers to a longstanding aspiration to represent the world as faithfully as possible, what Erich Auerbach calls "mimesis" and I call "verisimilitude." The verisimilar tradition, which begins with Homer and extends into the present day, is best described by Boris Tomashevsky's theory of literary convention. All representation is conventional, Tomashevsky argues, but only those conventions that are imperceptible achieve verisimilitude. This imperceptibility is a function not of the conventions themselves but of their placement in time: when a convention first appears, it draws attention to itself through its newness; over time, it gradually becomes more familiar and in the process imperceptible, until its very familiarity makes it perceptible once more, as tired and outworn. As a consequence, new conventions often argue for their own verisimilitude by exposing the artifice of the conventions that have come before.[22] Miguel de Cervantes's *Don Quixote* (1605; 1615) is thus the classic text of verisimilitude.

Realism has another meaning as well. If the term loosely refers to verisimilitude in general, it more strictly refers to that nineteenth-century version of verisimilitude that named itself "realist." There had been a few scattered uses of the term "realism" in British reviews of the early 1850s, as Pam Morris has observed, but at this point the term still did not refer to anything very consistent or precise.[23] It did so only after it emerged independently in France, in the mid-1850s, where it was used to distinguish a new mode of representation from neoclassicism and idealism. French artists were the first to use the term, in the debates over Gustave Courbet and the subsequent founding of the journal *Le réalisme*, and it was subsequently taken up by French novelists to describe the work of Gustave Flaubert and Ivan Turgenev, among others. The term then returned to Britain, now laden with a history of aesthetic controversy. It was first used in this new sense by John Ruskin, in the 1856 installment of his *Modern Painters* (1843–60). And it was then made available to literary criticism by Eliot, in her review of Ruskin's book.

The British novels to which the term "realist" was applied were not the product of realist theorizing, as the French realist novels had been. On the

22. Boris Tomashevsky, "Thematics," in *Russian Formalist Criticism: Four Essays*, trans. and intro. Lee T. Lemon and Marion J. Rees (1925; Lincoln: University of Nebraska Press, 1965), 92–94.

23. Pam Morris, *Realism* (London: Routledge, 2003).

contrary, they were part of a homegrown tradition of verisimilitude. This tradition begins with Daniel Defoe and extends through Samuel Richardson and Jane Austen, all of whom found verisimilitude in what middle-class readers took to be ordinary—ordinary persons, such as servant girls and merchants' sons, and ordinary events, such as those that take place in a small country village. But this tradition also includes other novelists, such as Charles Brockden Brown and Charles Dickens, who instead found verisimilitude in the low—in slums, crime, drunkenness, dirt, and disease. These latter subjects were also taken up by contemporary reformist writings. Because of this shared subject matter, there was considerable exchange between the reformist writings of the 1830s and 1840s and at least one strain of the verisimilar novel. By the 1850s, however, this exchange was coming to an end. The history of reform in canonical British literature is, as Brantlinger has argued, a "history of its disappearance."[24] In part, this was because there were simply fewer reformist writings; the 1850s were a more quiescent time than the two previous decades, at least in Great Britain. But in part this was because the verisimilar novel had nothing more to learn from the writings of reform. It had already absorbed, as Hilary Schor has shown, the formal techniques of reformist writings, along with their subject matter.[25] It had also absorbed, I would add, their purposefulness.

When the term "realism" was reimported from France, then, it was applied to precisely this mix of verisimilitude and purposefulness. And the same mix would constitute realism in the United States. Here, too, the earliest novels now identified as realist came out of a tradition of reformist writing. Rebecca Harding Davis's *Life in the Iron Mills* (1861), which is often said to be the first realist U.S. novel, is an industrial novel like those written in Great Britain in the 1840s. And there is a strain of realism lying side by side with the sentimentalism of Harriet Beecher Stowe's *Uncle Tom's Cabin* as well. These precursor novels aside, realism would not flourish in the United States until the 1880s, when it was taken up and championed by Howells. He championed it in part by attacking the conventions that had come before him, in particular, those of sentimental fiction and the romance. In his novels, most famously in *The Rise of Silas Lapham* (1884–85), he parodied sentimental fiction, and in his critical writings he delighted in, as he put it, "banging the babes of Romance about."[26] But Howells also sought to champion realism on its own terms, and so he collected his reviews into what he

24. Brantlinger, *Spirit of Reform*, 7.
25. Hilary Schor, "Fiction," in *A Companion to Victorian Literature and Culture*, ed. Herbert F. Tucker (London: Blackwell, 1999), 330.
26. Howells to Edmund Gosse, 24 January 1886, quoted in Susan Goodman and Carl Dawson, *William Dean Howells: A Writer's Life* (Berkeley: University of California Press, 2005), 276.

presented as a serious defense of realism, *Criticism and Fiction* (1891). The impulse to make such a defense was typically continental, but its content threw into relief the fact that a distinctively Anglo-American variant of realism had emerged.

Nineteenth-century readers and reviewers recognized a difference between continental and Anglo-American realist novels, and they tended to describe this difference in terms of subject matter. British and U.S. readers and reviewers delighted in distinguishing the novel in English from the novel in French on the grounds that the French novel alone took up the subject of sex. But this was not quite true. Anglo-American novelists were also free to write about sex, so long as they did so in the name of a moral or reformist purpose. James makes this point in an anecdote he borrows from the French critic Hippolyte Taine. Taine describes a dinner party at which a racy young Frenchman recounts the plot of a recent novel to "an English spinster of didactic habits." The Frenchman traces the heroine's descent from one act of wickedness to another, followed by her inevitable and painful death. Favorably impressed, the English spinster asks for the title of this book so that she might read it for herself. Its title, the Frenchman slyly replies, is "*Madame Bovary; or, The Consequences of Misconduct.*"[27] What Taine's anecdote suggests is that morality is less an attribute of the text than a phenomenon of its reception. It is the effects that a novel is imagined to have and the intentions that are imagined to have gone into its writing—what I have been calling the novel's "purpose"—that determine whether the novel is taken to be moral or immoral, purposeful or not. The only difference between *Madame Bovary* and an Anglo-American novel of adultery, such as Ellen Wood's *East Lynne* (1860–61), is that the latter seeks to teach "the consequences of misconduct."

What was true of sexual subject matter was true of realism as well: it was justified by an apparatus of purposefulness. All realists, whether Anglo-American or continental, share the same representational project. They are committed to representing the world as it is. Fernand Desnoyer begins his manifesto "On Realism" by stating this baldly: "Realism is the true depiction of objects."[28] In much the same way, Howells's *Criticism and Fiction* calls for novels to "cease to lie about life" and instead "portray men and women as they are."[29] Some novelists, Howells among them, believed that it is possible to represent objective reality, while others believed that objective real-

---

27. Henry James, "Charles de Bernard and Gustave Flaubert: The Minor French Novelists," *Galaxy*, February 1876, 219–34.

28. Fernand Desnoyers, "On Realism," reprinted in *Documents of Modern Literary Realism*, ed. George J. Becker (Princeton: Princeton University Press, 1963), 80.

29. William Dean Howells, *Criticism and Fiction* (1891; New York: New York University Press, 1959), 51.

ity can only be subjectively perceived. For instance, Eliot emphasizes, in the metafictional portion of *Adam Bede* (1859), that she portrays "men and things" not as they are but rather as "they have mirrored themselves in my mind."[30] And Courbet, in the manifesto that would give realism its name, describes his project as necessarily subjective, as "depicting the manners, ideas, and appearances of my time as I see it."[31] The differences between the objective and subjective versions of realism seem quite stark to us, particularly after a number of poststructuralist critics have attacked what they take to be realism's epistemological naïveté. But the realists themselves did not distinguish too rigorously between the two versions. Even Desnoyer's manifesto, which begins by calling realism the "true depiction of objects," ends by slipping from objective reality to subjective perception: "Let us write and paint only what is, or at least what we see, what we know, what we have experienced."[32] For the nineteenth-century realists, it seems, the objective and the subjective view were two parts of the same project.

Where the realist novelists more importantly differ is that nearly all continental realists take realism to be an end in itself, while the Anglo-American realists embed this mode within a complex of authorial intentions and readerly effects.[33] They represent the world as it is in order to bring about the world as it should be. We can see this most clearly in *Adam Bede*. Responding to an imagined reader who asks why she has not idealized the characters that her novel depicts, Eliot defends her decision in terms of its possible effects. Idealist depictions make readers impatient with human flaws, she says, while realist depictions teach us sympathy. Eliot is even more clear about her intentions in a letter: enabling her readers "to *imagine* and to *feel* the pains and joys of those who differ from themselves" is, she confides, "the only effect I ardently long to produce."[34] Howells defends realism along much the same lines in *Criticism and Fiction*, when he argues that representing common people as they are will strengthen democracy, while showing all readers

30. George Eliot, *Adam Bede* (1859; New York: Signet, 1981), 174.

31. Gustave Courbet, "Realism," in Becker, *Documents of Modern Literary Realism*, 88.

32. Desnoyers, "On Realism," in Becker, *Documents of Modern Literary Realism*, 87.

33. Edmond and Jules de Goncourt are the exceptions that prove this rule. In a preface entitled "On True Novels" (1865), they define realism in what I am arguing are characteristically Anglo-American terms. They identify realism as the literary counterpart to "universal suffrage, democracy, and liberalism." Moreover, they align the reading and writing of realist novels, if not with reform, at least with charity: "Let it show to the happy people of Paris misery which should not be forgotten; let it show to people of fashion what Sisters of Charity do not shrink from, what the Queens of olden days let their children see in the hospitals—human suffering, immediate and alive, which teaches charity." Reprinted in Becker, *Documents of Modern Literary Realism*, 118–19.

34. Quoted in Stang, *Theory of the Novel in England*, 41.

what they have in common with one another will create national solidarity.[35] In both cases, realism is justified by—and confined within—some idea of purpose. Sharon Marcus is one of the few critics to have remarked on the centrality of purpose to Anglo-American realism. Such realism differs from the continental, she notes, in seeking to "communicate a moral vision" according to a "moral purpose."[36] I would add to this formulation that this "purpose" was understood to work along specifically reformist lines. From reformist writings, realist novels had learned how texts can act on readers—and through their readers, the world.[37] In this way, the Anglo-American realist novel can be distinguished from the continental realist novel as described by Georg Lukács. Lukács imagines that the realist depiction of social conditions and their historical determinants will somehow give rise to thoroughgoing social change. The Anglo-American realist novel, by contrast, understands social change to be both gradual and limited, to be reformist rather than revolutionary.

Realism and the novel of purpose predominated until the end of the nineteenth century, when a hitherto unified literary world began to fragment. "One was no longer simply a writer," Stephen Arata has observed, "but a particular kind of writer: decadent, aesthetic, naturalist, socialist, radical, feminist, journalist, romantic."[38] Beneath this apparent pluralism, however, polarizing forces were at work. By the end of the fin de siècle, the literary world was newly divided into the artful and the nonartful, into high, middle, and low. As it happened, there was a resurgence of reformist novels at the

35. I borrow this paraphrase of Howells's arguments from Amy Kaplan's unfolding of the various meanings of "common" in *The Social Construction of American Realism* (Chicago: University of Chicago Press, 1988), 21–23.

36. Sharon Marcus, "Comparative Sapphism," in *The Literary Channel: The Inter-National Invention of the Novel*, ed. Carolyn Dever and Margaret Cohen (Princeton: Princeton University Press, 2002), 267. Marcus seeks to capture the purposefulness of Anglo-American realism by calling it a form of idealism. The category of idealism is present as well in Catherine Gallagher's foundational study of the industrial novel, *The Industrial Reformation of English Fiction: Social Discourse and Narrative Form, 1832–1867* (Chicago: University of Chicago Press, 1980). In her reading of Eliot's *Felix Holt*, Gallagher draws attention to the profound significance of the "is" and the "ought" in Anglo-American realism. But where Gallagher seeks to arrange these two terms in a transcendental relation, asking whether and how the "is" bodies forth the "ought," I seek instead to put them in a temporal relation, asking how the representation of what is makes possible the reality of what should be.

37. In this way, I am arguing that what J. Hillis Miller identifies as the performativity inherent in all realism is instead a feature of Anglo-American realism in particular. The performative dimension of realism is an effect not of language in general but of the particular strategies and expectations of social reform. *The Ethics of Reading: Kant, de Man, Eliot, Trollope, James, and Benjamin* (New York: Columbia University Press, 1987), 61–80.

38. Stephen Arata, "1897," in *A Companion to Victorian Literature and Culture*, ed. Herbert F. Tucker (London: Blackwell, 1999), 54.

same time, including Margaret Harkness's *In Darkest London* (1889), Hamlin Garland's *A Spoil of Office* (1892), Arthur Morrison's *A Child of the Jago* (1896), Jack London's *The People of the Abyss* (1903), and Upton Sinclair's *The Jungle* (1906). And realist novels would continue to be written as well; indeed, they continue to be written in our own day. But the reformist novel was now seen as nonliterary, and the realist novel was now seen as middlebrow. The novel of purpose was no longer predominant.

To summarize: the term "realism" emerged in the context of French artistic debates and was then taken up by British novelists who were less drawn to polemic; it was applied by these novelists to an Anglo-American literary tradition of long standing, which brought together specific reformist commitments with a more general impulse to verisimilitude; a generation later, the term was then taken up by U.S. novelists eager to distinguish themselves from their British predecessors by polemicizing in the manner of the French. This hybrid history has given rise to a great deal of critical confusion in our own day because it has left the canon of Anglo-American realist novels, particularly British novels, necessarily up for debate. Where continental novelists understood themselves as belonging to idealist, realist, and, later, naturalist schools, British novelists only seldom understood themselves in this way. As a consequence, there are no clear limits on how widely the term "realism" should be applied. In the absence of clear programmatic statements like those written by Honoré de Balzac or Emile Zola, critics in our own day have tended to apply the term to all nineteenth-century novels, even those that might otherwise be classified as romantic (Mary Shelley's *Frankenstein*), gothic (Emily Brontë's *Wuthering Heights*), or fantastic (Lewis Carroll's *Alice in Wonderland* and L. Rider Haggard's *She*).[39] Critics have also tended to apply the term retroactively, to novelists writing verisimilarly before realism had even been thought of. Here, too, it is not at all clear how far back the term should be extended—to Austen? to Richardson? to Defoe?[40] For my part, I use the term "realism" only when discussing those authors who were engaged in debates about realism, and I use the term "verisimilitude" to refer to the more general impulse to represent the world accurately.

---

39. These novels have been categorized as realist by George Levine, *The Realistic Imagination: English Fiction from "Frankenstein" to "Lady Chatterley"* (Chicago: University of Chicago Press, 1981), and Nancy Armstrong, *Desire and Domestic Fiction: A Political History of the Novel* (Oxford: Oxford University Press, 1987).

40. Harry Shaw begins with Austen in his *Narrating Reality: Austen, Scott, Eliot* (Ithaca: Cornell University Press, 1999); Elizabeth Deeds Ermarth, with Richardson and Defoe, in her *Realism and Consensus in the English Novel* (Princeton: Princeton University Press, 1983).

This hybrid history calls for two different ways of thinking about realism—and about realism's relation to reform. Insofar as Anglo-American realism derives from the continental, it makes sense to think of it, as many critics do, as a coherent philosophical project, an account of either ontology or epistemology that necessarily entails certain representational practices. For Ian Watt, realism is the literary counterpart to philosophical empiricism and it therefore depends on proper names, precise locations, and concrete detail. For Elizabeth Deeds Ermarth, realism is instead the counterpart of quattrocento perspective and it therefore depends on multiple points of view. And for Caroline Levine, realism is the counterpart to the experimental method and so depends on the suspension of judgment over the course of the narrative.[41] This view of realism as a coherent philosophical project has come under attack by critics who seek to identify the project's contradictions: for poststructuralist critics, the realists are naïve in imagining a reality prior to representation; for Marxist critics, the realists are complicit in mystifying the very social conditions they claim to reveal.[42] Other critics, such as George Levine, have countered these attacks by observing that these contradictions were visible to the realist novelists themselves.[43] What all of these critics nonetheless share is the presumption that realism should be coherent, whether or not they agree that this coherence has been achieved.

When these critics align the realist novel with reformist writing, then, they do so because they believe that both discourses locate reality in the same places and approach it by the same means. In this account, both realism and reformist writing sought to make visible what had been invisible and to draw attention to what had gone unseen—whether it was the conditions inside a factory or on a slave plantation, or the lives of ordinary people and the events of every day. And they sought to do this by using some of the same representational techniques. Having agreed that realism and reform shared the same ends, these critics divide on the question of whether these ends were beneficent or coercive. There is a longstanding debate among historians about whether reform helped to create a more humane and enlightened world or whether it served as a form of discipline and social

---

41. Ian Watt, *The Rise of the Novel* (Berkeley: University of California Press, 1957); Caroline Levine, *The Serious Pleasures of Suspense: Victorian Realism and Narrative Doubt* (Charlottesville: University of Virginia Press, 2003).

42. For the poststructuralist account, see Colin McCabe, *James Joyce and the Revolution of the Word* (London: Macmillan Press, 1978). For the Marxist account, see Rosalind Coward and John Ellis, *Language and Materialism: Developments in Semiology and the Theory of the Subject* (London: Routledge, 1977).

43. Levine, *Realistic Imagination*, 4.

control.[44] The critical debate about literary realism divides in the same way. Generations of critics have taken realism to be progressive. Auerbach, for instance, connected the increasingly "serious treatment of everyday reality" to the progressive "rise of . . . socially inferior human groups to the position of subject matter."[45] And Harry Levin emphasized the political consequences of such a literary project, describing it as the "gradual extension of the literary franchise."[46] Other critics who thought explicitly about the relation between realism and reform tended to share this view of realism as progressive. In the 1980s, by contrast, a new set of critics—Mark Seltzer, D. A. Miller, and Amy Kaplan most prominently—challenged this conception of realism by arguing that knowledge is always bound up with power, that the realist novel, like the reformist investigation, seeks to bring its subjects under control.[47]

There is another way of thinking about Anglo-American realism, however, one that better accounts for the consequences of its hybrid history. This is Peter Demetz's conception of realism as a "syndrome" made up of various features, such as contemporaneous subject matter, events and characters understood as types, and a thick description of the social world. This conception of realism as syndrome has since been taken up by Richard Brodhead, who uses it to emphasize that the features of realism, while tending to manifest themselves together, have no necessary relation to one another. On the contrary, these features were independently developed by various novelists and then imitated by other novelists in turn; it was only through these imitations that a largely accidental conglomeration became recognizable as a single mode.[48] The idea of a syndrome thus offers another way of understanding the relation between realism and reform. In this account, reformist subject matter is simply one of many features that

44. Steven Mintz outlines these positions, and their variants, in his excellent survey of antebellum U.S. reform. He also articulates what is coming to be the new consensus position, that "the realities of antebellum reform are too complex to fit any one formula." *Moralists and Modernizers: America's Pre–Civil War Reformers* (Baltimore: Johns Hopkins University Press, 1995), xvii.

45. Erich Auerbach, *Mimesis: The Representation of Reality in Western Literature*, trans. Willard R. Trask (1946; Princeton: Princeton University Press, 1974), 491.

46. Harry Levin, *The Gates of Horn: A Study of Five French Realists* (Oxford: Oxford University Press, 1963), 57.

47. Mark Seltzer, *Henry James and the Art of Power* (Ithaca: Cornell University Press, 1984); D. A. Miller, *The Novel and the Police* (Berkeley: University of California Press, 1988); and Kaplan, *Social Construction of American Realism.*

48. Peter Demetz, "Zur Definition des Realismus," *Literatur und Kritik* 2 (1967): 333–45. Richard Brodhead draws on Demetz's conception of realism in his discussion of Henry James in *The School of Hawthorne* (Oxford: Oxford University Press, 1984), 141.

got caught up in the consolidation of Anglo-American realism out of continental theorizing and homegrown verisimilitude.

Contemporary novelists recognized that reform had gotten entangled with an emerging realism, as Nathaniel Hawthorne's *Blithedale Romance* (1852) and Anthony Trollope's *The Warden* (1855) make clear. Both novels satirize a world gone mad with reform. *Blithedale* describes the founding of a utopian community along Fourierist lines. The other members of the community are reformers already, committed to such causes as prison reform and women's rights, but their enthusiasm is so infectious that it briefly persuades even an indolent poet, the novel's narrator, to join in what they all believe will be the "reformation of the world."[49] Trollope's *The Warden* (1855) begins with a brash young man, appropriately named John Bold, whose "passion is the reform of all abuses."[50] Bold does not go so far as to invent abuses, but he is quite ready to exaggerate them. He discovers that the property bequeathed to support an almshouse is being used, in large part, to provide a generous sinecure for the guardian of the almshouse, the mild warden of the novel's title. The few inmates of the almshouse all live in comfort, and the warden tends to them faithfully, and yet Bold campaigns for an end to this putative abuse. At the end of both novels, reform is shown to fail. The utopian community at Blithedale dissolves, and its members abandon or betray the other causes they have advocated as well. The warden renounces his position, and the inmates he has cared for are left much worse off than before.

It is hardly surprising that Hawthorne and Trollope take such a dim view of reform—they are opposed to it almost by temperament. Hawthorne's fascination with human fallenness makes him doubt "the world's improvability" (20), while improvement is not even valued by Trollope, who finds old ways, like old buildings, to be the more pleasing for their irregularities. What is more remarkable, however, is the attention each novel devotes to reformist representations. Both novels pause to parody at least one such representation, and, as they do so, they throw into relief their rivalry with reformist writings—specifically, with reformist verisimilitude.

In *Blithedale*, the reformers' representations are visual. The narrator enters a saloon and sees a painting that could have been made by a temperance advocate. It depicts an old man who has passed out from drink, and it leaves the narrator, he tells us, smelling the foul liquor fumes on the drunkard's

49. Nathaniel Hawthorne, *The Blithedale Romance* (1852; London: Penguin Books, 1986), 12. All further references to this edition will be marked in the text.
50. Anthony Trollope, *The Warden* (1855; London: Penguin, 1984), 10. All further references to this edition will be marked in the text.

breath and feeling the headache and tremors that will descend on the drunkard in the morning. "The death-in-life was," the narrator concludes, "too well portrayed" (176). "Too well portrayed," the painting of the drunkard is the novel's prime example of realism. Opposed to this painting are those that are hung next to it, a series of still lifes depicting meats and cheeses. In these paintings, which are more to the narrator's liking, the painter has managed to remove "the grossness from what was fleshiest and fattest," rendering the reality partly ethereal so that what remains is "an indescribable ideal charm" (176). The contrast between these two styles of painting replicates the contrast between a nascent realism and Hawthorne's own representational practices. Again and again in the novel, the real is etherealized by masks and veils, curtain panels and lengths of gauze, fevers, fancies, and champagne, anything that might come between an observer and a reality that would otherwise be too grossly, too immediately real.

In *The Warden*, by contrast, the reformers' representations are not visual but textual. The novel's reformers produce a flurry of texts: first the documents and copies of documents filed against the warden and the church; then the exposés and polemics published in the newspapers; and finally the pamphlets published by cultural critics and the serial published by a reformist novelist. Trollope attacks these various genres of reformist writing by interpolating parodies of them into his own novel. His novel thus reproduces the self-aggrandizing headlines of the London *Jupiter* (a stand-in for the London *Times*), as well as an excerpt from "Modern Charity," a pamphlet by Dr. Pessimist Anticant (Thomas Carlyle). It also summarizes the opening pages of "The Almshouse," a new serial by Mr. Popular Sentiment (the mid-career Charles Dickens).

Of these three, Sentiment comes in for the most extended critique. What Trollope objects to in particular is the exaggerated quality of Sentiment's characters: Sentiment's warden is a demon with a greedy mouth and a leering eye, whose evilness is as unrelieved as the goodness of his victims. "The artist who paints for the million," Trollope's narrator tells us, "must use glaring colours" (137). And yet, while Sentiment's representations are the most extensively critiqued, they are also the only ones to be reproduced through free indirect discourse rather than direct quotation. Sentiment's words come to us through the narrator's voice. The greater intimacy of this technique suggests a troubling closeness between Sentiment's mode and Trollope's own—and the extent to which Trollope must struggle to distinguish his own realism from the reformist realism inaugurated by Dickens.

In *The Blithedale Romance* and *The Warden*, we can see how thoroughly the nineteenth-century literary world was pervaded by reform. And we can also see that at least some novelists were concerned by this. Both Hawthorne and Trollope recognized the entanglement of realism and reformist writings, and Hawthorne rejected both out of hand. Trollope, by contrast, made use of reformist writings by defining his own realism in opposition to them. And other novelists, too, would put reformist writings in the service of their own literary ends. These are the novelists that I focus on in this book.

The Literary Uses of Social Reform

The first generation of novelists to make use of reformist writings did so by borrowing from them not only subject matter but also formal techniques. The formal resources of reformist writings were considerable. Some of their techniques were visual. Benjamin Rush's "Moral and Physical Thermometer" (1790) displays the effects of drinking by arranging various drinks according to their relative strength and then correlating these drinks to the specific "diseases," "vices," and "punishments" to which they give rise. Decades later, John Thompson's *Street Life in London* (1877–78) and Jacob Riis's *How the Other Half Lives* (1890) used photographs to offer readers access to the slums, even to the tenement apartments, that they would otherwise not see.[51] Other techniques were verbal. Henry Mayhew, in his *London Labour and the London Poor* (1861–62), transcribed the vernacular speech of his rat catchers and costermongers, creating in the process a series of working-class soliloquies. Still others were textual. In her *Southern Horrors* (1892) and *A Red Record* (1895), Ida B. Wells gathered and reprinted newspaper reports of lynchings in order to demonstrate how widespread and frequent the practice had become. And antislavery writers, such as Frederick Douglass and Harriet Jacobs, framed their narratives within an elaborate apparatus of authorizing prefaces and explanatory appendices.

Reformist writers also developed specifically fictional techniques, such as new tropes and modes of characterization and, in particular, new plots. The chapters that follow show that Dickens, Anne Brontë, and Elizabeth Stoddard all borrowed plots from the writings of temperance reform. One of these plots is what I call the cautionary temperance tale, which charted the inevitable consequences of drinking, from the first convivial drink, through poverty and sickness, to a horrible death. Temperance reformers used this plot to argue that poverty was a consequence of drinking and prosperity the

51. Benjamin Rush, "Moral and Physical Thermometer" (1790), in *An Inquiry into the Effects of Spirituous Liquors on the Human Body, to Which Is Added a Moral and Physical Thermometer* (Boston, 1790). Jacob Riis, *How the Other Half Lives: Studies among the Tenements of New York* (1890; New York: Penguin Books, 1997).

effect of sobriety, and in this way they helped to make sense of the otherwise bewildering experience of poverty. Without endorsing the ideology behind this plot, Dickens used it to organize the otherwise overwhelming flood of details about urban poverty. Another plot is what I call the plot of doubled promises. This plot begins with the marriage vow and then charts a wife's efforts to save her husband from drunkenness, efforts that are rewarded when he takes the temperance pledge. Female temperance reformers used this plot to articulate a range of otherwise inarticulable complaints about marriage: a husband's drunkenness licensed complaints about his absence, his insolvency, his brutality. Brontë uses this plot in much the same way, to articulate her protagonist's boredom in marriage, while Stoddard uses it to express what other female novelists denied, the fact that her protagonist has loved other men.

In turning reformist techniques to their own representational ends, Dickens, Brontë, and Stoddard unwittingly contributed to the consolidation of a verisimilitude entangled with reform—what would become, in the 1850s, a purposeful realism. The predominance of the novel of purpose meant that the subject of reform offered easy access to the center of the literary field. This was particularly important because the increasing rigidity of gender roles in the nineteenth century made it more and more difficult for women—and, paradoxically, for some men as well—to write. Female novelists struggled with a presumption that the novel was a public genre and thus the proper domain of men. Reform, however, provided a plausible justification for a woman's entrance into print. We can see this in Harriet Beecher Stowe's claim that it was only her outrage about the Fugitive Slave Law that prompted her to set aside her domestic work and take up her pen.[52] For male novelists, particularly those in the United States, the problem was the reverse: the conviction that the novel was a private genre and thus the proper domain of women. Here, too, the claims of purpose redefined novel writing as a properly civic act, as Michael Davitt Bell has shown, and thus made it possible for men to write as well.[53]

So powerful was this conception of the novelist as reformer that it was taken up even by those who had little commitment to a given reform. No-

---

52. Joan D. Hedrick, *Harriet Beecher Stowe: A Life* (Oxford: Oxford University Press, 1994) 207.

53. Michael Davitt Bell has called this the "New England compromise." This antebellum compromise was extended into the postbellum period by William Dean Howells, who argued that the realism he championed was in the service of democracy. Bell, *The Problem of American Realism: Studies in the Cultural History of a Literary Idea* (Chicago: University of Chicago Press, 1993), 31–33.

where is this more clear than in the many writers who began their careers by writing a work of temperance fiction. This fiction ranges from Hawthorne's short story "A Rill from the Town Pump" (1835, 1837), through Walt Whitman's novel *Franklin Evans; or, The Inebriate* (1842), to George Eliot's novella *Janet's Repentance* (1857). To be sure, some of these authors supported temperance in their own lives; certainly, Eliot remained skeptical of drink throughout her career. Others, however, had no commitment at all to temperance reform. The most notorious of these is Walt Whitman, who later claimed that he wrote *Franklin Evans* in a single weekend on the strength of a full bottle of liquor. Hawthorne disavowed his temperance story as well, albeit more obliquely. He prefaced his first serious novel, *The Scarlet Letter* (1850), with a long essay that described his apprenticeship in writing; the essay concluded with the mock serious hope that Hawthorne would one day be memorialized by "THE TOWN PUMP!"[54] What all of these writers demonstrate is that reformist fiction was a subgenre that offered easy access to a literary career. Stoddard states this logic most bluntly when she confesses that she is quite willing to publish "religious lies for Sunday School publishing houses."[55] But many other novelists were willing to do so as well.

Novelists acted as reformers not only through their works but also in their lives. Indeed, reformist activities became the Anglo-American counterpart to the conspicuous bohemianism that was so central, as Pierre Bourdieu has shown, to literary self-presentation in France. French literary figures displayed their status as literary figures by transgressing the rules of ordinary sociability and eschewing money and position; when they did speak out on political issues, as Emile Zola did in the Dreyfus affair, their authority came from their total separation from the political domain.[56] Anglo-American literary figures, by contrast, quite often held governmental positions. Herman Melville sought, and Hawthorne famously held, a position as custom house inspector, while Howells served as the U.S. consul in Venice and Mark Twain was offered positions as secretary to the Nevada secretary of state and as postmaster general of San Francisco. Fewer British literary figures served in governmental positions, largely because it was more possible in Britain for writers to support themselves. Still, Trollope spent his entire professional life in the postal service, and Matthew Arnold was long em-

54. Nathaniel Hawthorne, "The Custom House," in *The Scarlet Letter* (1851; London: Penguin 1983), 43.

55. Quoted in *The Morgesons and Other Writings, Published and Unpublished, by Elizabeth Stoddard*, ed. Lawrence Buell and Sandra Zagarell (Philadelphia: University of Pennsylvania Press, 1984), xv.

56. Bourdieu, *Rules of Art*, 61.

ployed as an inspector of schools—even writing books on how they might be reformed. Many of these positions were largely sinecures, of course, and so do not constitute a serious authorial engagement with political life. Far more significant in this regard are the many novelists who were committed to reform. Dickens established a home for fallen women, while Thomas Hardy campaigned for animal rights. Mark Twain led the fight against U.S. imperialism, and William Dean Howells spoke out on behalf of the Haymarket defendants. In doing so, they differed from Zola in that their actions were seen as continuous with the rest of their literary life.

With so many novelists acting as reformers, reformist action became a legible way of claiming a certain identity as a novelist. Even established novelists, such as Charlotte Brontë at the end of her career and Henry James in the middle of his, felt the need to take a reformer's tour. In her earlier visits to London, Brontë had been a provincial cleric's daughter experiencing the delights of the metropolis for the first time. On her last visit, however, she played the role of the reformer instead. To the considerable surprise of her hosts, she insisted on being taken to altogether more serious places: two prisons, the Foundling Hospital and Bedlam, as well as the post office and the offices of the *Times*. She did all of this even though she had come to recognize, as she had recently confided in a letter to her publisher, that she could not "write books handling the topics of the day—it is of no use trying."[57] Still, her status as a novelist seemed to require that she at least make a show of looking into such topics. James would do much the same thing. In the mid-1880s, he insisted on visiting a prison and taking notes on all that he saw. The notes themselves were not important: they have almost no effect on the novel James went on to write, *The Princess Casamassima* (1885–86). It was the act of taking notes that mattered, and James recorded this act in letters to his friends. "I have been all the morning at Millbank prison (horrible place), collecting notes for a fiction scene," he told one. "You see I am quite the Naturalist."[58] As with Brontë, the prison visit was clearly intended to signal something about James's status as a novelist.

For many novelists, the role of the novelist of purpose was a rewarding one to adopt. I focus, however, on three who chafed against this role. The first of these novelists is George Eliot, who did as much as anyone to establish the realist novelist as a moral teacher and thereby to complete the translation of the reformist novel into the novel of purpose. Setting herself

57. Juliet Barker describes this trip to London in *The Brontës* (London: Weidenfeld and Nicolson, 1994), 714.
58. James to Thomas Sargent Perry, 12 December 1884, in *Henry James Letters*, vol. 3: *1883–1895*, ed. Leon Edel (Cambridge: Harvard University Press, 1980), 61.

up as a moral teacher, she was able to pursue her own unwomanly ambitions while assuaging the objections of her evangelical past. But she found, as she became more and more prominent as a novelist, that she was called on to be a public figure in ways that she found unwelcome. More specifically, she was expected to be an exemplary woman for the woman's movement to make use of, and her depictions of reform in her late novels are shaped by that experience. The second is Mark Twain, who began to write novels of purpose in order to secure a more prestigious, if less profitable, audience. As he made use of reform in this way, he marked the instrumentalization by creating characters who were reformers—but also con men. And the last novelist is Thomas Hardy, who differed from all the others in that he had been explicitly warned away from reformist writing at the beginning and over the course of his career. In his last defiant novel, however, he took up reformist subject matter not to persuade his readers but rather to outrage and disgust them. He sought to reject the idea of the novelist as moral teacher and instead lay claim to the status of artist—that status was secured and confirmed by the opprobrium of his readers.

In the mid-nineteenth century, David Masson and his critical contemporaries understood that novelists took up the subject of reform for a number of different reasons. Twentieth-century critics have lost sight of this fact, and they tend to presume that the presence of reformist subject matter is a certain sign of reformist intention and effect. In doing so, they read *Middlemarch* (1871–72) and *The Adventures of Huckleberry Finn* (1885) as straightforwardly reformist novels, and they fail to recognize that Dickens was not at all a reformer for the first decade of his career. Nor can they account for James's sudden decision to write about slums and suffrage activists. In this way, critics have missed important complexities in the novels I focus on, but they have also missed something crucial about the development of the nineteenth-century novel more generally. Realism emerged by struggling against and learning from reformist writings, while the status of the novel and of the novelist were secured by the prestige of reform. These two developments are the subject of this book.

Chapter 3

Charles Dickens

A Reformer Abroad and at Home

Of all nineteenth-century novelists, Charles Dickens is the one we most often think of as a reformer. Indeed, so thoroughly do we associate his novels with social problems that the mere mention of the Chancery courts conjures up *Bleak House* (1852–53) and the poor laws *Oliver Twist* (1837–39). But while Dickens was the preeminent novelist of reform, the example that all subsequent novelists would either imitate or struggle against, he became such a novelist only slowly. It was only in the 1840s, after he had already written five novels, that Dickens began to identify himself publicly as a reformer, and only sometime after that he began to write in a straightforwardly reformist mode himself.

This is not to say that Dickens's first five novels have nothing to do with reform. On the contrary, they contain many scenes that we would now identify as reformist, such as the debtors' prison in *The Pickwick Papers* (1836–37) and the Yorkshire schools in *Nicholas Nickleby* (1838–39), as well as the workhouse in *Oliver Twist*. Any of these scenes could have been borrowed from contemporary reformist writings. But Dickens himself did not understand these scenes to be reformist at the time that he wrote them, as his prefaces from the time demonstrate. The first preface to *Pickwick*, for instance, describes the novel's composition and defends its form, and the first preface to *Oliver Twist* defends the propriety of writing about thieves. Both ignore what we would take to be the novels' reformist subject matter. The *Pickwick* preface makes no mention at all of debtors' prison, nor does the *Oliver Twist* preface refer to the workhouse or the slums. By the end of the 1840s, however, Dickens had come to think of himself as a reformer and of his novels as doing reformist work. Returning to his earliest novels in order to write new prefaces for the so-called Cheap Edition, he implicitly laid claim to all the reforms that had ensued in the intervening years. Mr. Pickwick, Dickens reminds us in the 1847 preface to *Pickwick*, was harassed by a pair of almost comically rapacious lawyers, but now lawyerly claws have been "pared" by legal reforms. More important, the laws concerning debt have been altered, and "the Fleet Prison [has been] pulled down!"[1] Three years later, in the new preface to the Cheap Edition of *Oliver Twist*, Dickens again neatly paired abuses described with reforms achieved and thereby laid claim to responsibility for the reforms. His novel, he reminds us, described a noisome slum—on "page 267 of this present edition"—and now the Metropolitan Sanitary Association has been established to install new water pipes, toilets, dustbins, and drains.[2]

The difference between the prefaces of the late 1830s and the prefaces of the late 1840s prompts us to ask what happened in the intervening years to transform Dickens into a reformer and a novelist of purpose. A partial answer is readerly response, in particular the response to *Nicholas Nickleby*. Dickens had begun writing the novel with only one definite intention: to satisfy his curiosity about the boarding schools in Yorkshire, which a childhood acquaintance of his had attended.[3] These schools were notoriously a place in which unwanted, often illegitimate children were left to be beaten, neglected, and starved. Dickens took a quick trip to Yorkshire to visit some of them and then began writing. What he wrote, however, suggests that he found a grotesque comedy in the cruel conditions of the schools, a fact that subsequent readers have attempted to explain away. George Gissing, for instance, argues that the novel's comedy was a cunning strategy of reform, that Dickens knew it was most effective to "insist once and once only on the horror" and then to "delight" his readers the rest of the time.[4] Far more likely, I would argue, is that Dickens intended his depiction of the schools to be entertaining and was astonished when they had a reformist effect. While the novel was still being serialized, Dickens's multitudinous readers began demanding that the Yorkshire schools be shut down. And many were. Dickens would later take credit for this reform. In the preface to the 1848 Cheap Edition, he begins by observing that when the novel was written there were "a good many cheap Yorkshire schools in existence. There are very

1. Charles Dickens, *The Posthumous Papers of the Pickwick Club* (1837; London: Penguin, 1986), 46. All further references to this edition will be marked in the text.

2. Charles Dickens, *Oliver Twist* (1839; Oxford: Oxford University Press, 1966), 351.

3. Philip Collins provides this background in his *Dickens and Education* (London: Macmillan, 1963), 110.

4. George Gissing, *The Immortal Dickens* (London: Cecil Palmer, 1925), 98–99.

few now."[5] But he had not conceived of this possibility while he was writing the novel. It was only from the responses of his readers that he learned that a novel might ameliorate the abuses it described.

Having made this discovery, Dickens did not act on it quickly. He instead returned, in *The Old Curiosity Shop* (1840–41), to the sentimental mode he had perfected in *Oliver Twist* and then attempted to write, in *Barnaby Rudge* (1841), in the historical mode most famously exemplified by Sir Walter Scott. The crucial turn in Dickens's career came, I believe, with his 1842 tour of the United States. It was during this tour that Dickens first took on the role of the reformer, inspecting schools, prisons, and poorhouses in the various cities that he visited. Upon his return to Britain, he engaged himself for the first time in reform movements there as well. He wrote open letters in favor of ragged schools and against capital punishment, and he also involved himself more directly with reform. He helped to establish Urania Cottage, a home for fallen women, and remained its inspector, visiting once a week, for the next ten years. In the 1850s, his interest shifted to sanitary reform, and he commissioned a number of articles on public health for the magazine he was then editing, *Household Words*.[6] As Dickens became a reformer, he became a reformist writer as well, with the Christmas books of the mid-1840s being followed by his great novels of reform, most famously *Bleak House* and *Little Dorrit* (1855–57).

The chapter that follows asks two questions about the transformation that took place between the 1830s and the 1840s. First, if Dickens was not a reformer early in his career, if he did not imagine that his novels could alter the abuses they described, then why did he borrow both subject matter and narrative structures from contemporary reformist writings? Second, why was it a visit to another nation that prompted Dickens to become a reformer in his own? How did his time in the United States paradoxically turn Dickens into one of the few nineteenth-century novelists to argue for an exclusively national conception of reform?

From Charity to Reform: *Sketches by Boz*

Dickens's first book, *Sketches by Boz*, was made up of the short texts he had written for various newspapers over the preceding two years. When he republished these texts in a single volume, he did not arrange them chronologically but instead divided them into four sections. The first of these sections,

5. Charles Dickens, *Nicholas Nickleby* (1839; London: Penguin, 1978), 47.
6. Fred Kaplan catalogues Dickens's reformist activities in *Dickens: A Biography* (1988; Baltimore: Johns Hopkins University Press, 1998), 148, 200, 150, 228, 268.

"Seven Sketches from Our Parish," is a nostalgic tribute to a way of life that the narrator, like Dickens himself, will soon abandon. By the beginning of the second section, the narrator has already left the village for the city, and there Dickens will remain for the rest of his career. *Boz* is organized, then, around the opposition between rural and urban, between past and present, with the parish sketches serving as one pole in both of these oppositions. But the parish sketches are themselves internally divided by a less obvious distinction: the distinction between charity and social reform.

That the differences between charity and reform are of interest to Dickens is made clear on *Boz*'s first page. In the first of the parish sketches, the narrator imagines a poor man with a large family, whose debts are increasing, whose wife is growing ill, whose children are suffering from hunger. "What can he do?" the narrator asks. "To whom is he to apply for relief? To private charity? To benevolent individuals? Certainly not—there is his parish."[7] The narrator is here referring to the recent passage of the Poor Law Amendment Act of 1834, which used the parish as the conduit for newly standardized and rationalized efforts to aid the poor. The poor had been assured, since Elizabethan times, of poor relief as an ancient and customary right, but now they were subject to new rules as a condition of receiving it. Workhouses were built in those parishes that did not yet have them, while existing workhouses were reorganized according to severe disciplines. Only when paupers suffered more than the hardest-pressed of workers, argued the Benthamite proponents of poor law reform, would labor be a more appealing choice than idleness.[8] Dickens's objections to the New Poor Law are well known, and he would detail the suffering inflicted by the workhouse regime most famously in *Oliver Twist*. In *Boz*, however, it is not the poor law itself that concerns Dickens so much as the era of social reform that this law ushered in. The poor law is significant here only as the most obvious instance of a reform that severs the customary ties of obligation and entitlement and thereby dissolves communities that have long been knit together by the generosity of "benevolent individuals" and their acts of "private charity."

The rest of the parish sketches are devoted to anatomizing the differences between this superseded charity and this emergent reform. Dickens's intentions here are more speculative than polemical, and it is for this reason that he abandons the inflammatory subject of the New Poor Law and instead creates mildly comic figures to personify both charity and reform. Charity

7. Charles Dickens, *Sketches by Boz* (1836; New York: Penguin, 1995), 17. All further references to this edition will be marked in the text.

8. David Englander offers a full account of the history and provisions of the New Poor Law in *Poverty and Poor Law Reform in Britain: From Chadwick to Booth, 1834–1914* (London: Longman, 1998).

is represented by the so-called Old Lady, whose "name always heads the list of any benevolent subscriptions," who donates twenty pounds toward the purchase of a new church organ and makes annual gifts of coal and soup to the parish poor (27). The alternative to charity is represented by the famous London reformer invited to the parish to speak. And speak he does, of "green isles—other shores—vast Atlantic—bosom of the deep—Christian charity—blood and extermination—mercy in hearts—arms in hands—altars and homes—household gods" (57). That the representative of reform should be an orator rather than a poor law authority marks the contemporaneous shift from an early period of utilitarian reform, under the control of an administrative elite, to the more popular reform that would characterize the rest of the nineteenth century. Through the opposition between the London orator and the Old Lady, Dickens distinguishes reform from charity on two grounds. Reform concerns itself with what is far away ("other shores—vast Atlantic"), while charity attends to what is near at hand; and charity involves the direct provision of concrete aid (twenty pounds, coal and soup), while reform works more indirectly, through the mediations of speeches and other texts.

These distinctions held steady over the course of Dickens's career. In *Pickwick*, reform is represented by the people of Muggleston, who write one thousand petitions opposing plantation slavery abroad and another thousand supporting the factory system at home. And in *Bleak House*, more famously, it is represented by Mrs. Jellyby, who dictates scores of letters in a single sitting and once mailed five thousand circulars in a single day. But all of this writing is, the narrator tells us, little more than waste paper. Set against these ineffectual reformers are two exemplars of charity, Mr. Pickwick and Mr. Jarndyce, each of whom is quick to respond to the suffering he encounters with a useful something from his waistcoat pocket. Again and again, reform is opposed to charity, and this opposition reveals Dickens's view that reform is prone to overlook social problems near at hand—and helpless to remedy those problems it does identify.

Or so Dickens's satire of reformers would suggest. But while he invariably ridicules the reformers he depicts, Dickens often acts much like a reformer himself. In his own novels, he too circulates representations of suffering among those who cannot see the suffering for themselves; he too substitutes mediating texts for direct and local acts of charity. Here is the first passage in which he does so:

> That wretched woman with the infant in her arms, round whose meagre form the remnant of her own scanty shawl is carefully wrapped, has been attempting to sing some popular ballad, in the hope of wringing a few pence from the

compassionate passer-by. A brutal laugh at her weak voice is all she has gained. The tears fall thick and fast down her own pale face; the child is cold and hungry, and its low half-stifled wailing adds to the misery of its wretched mother, as she moans aloud, and sinks despairingly down, on a cold damp doorstep.

Singing! How few of those who pass such a miserable creature as this, think of the anguish of heart, the sinking of soul and spirit, which the very effort of singing produces. Bitter mockery! Disease, neglect, and starvation, faintly articulating the words of the joyous ditty, that has enlivened your hours of feasting and merriment, God knows how often! (77)

This passage comes from "The Streets—Night," one of a pair of sketches that marks *Boz's* move from the parish to the city. With this move, the culture of charity comes to an end. Charity consists of concrete assistance offered face-to-face, and here no "passer-by" views the "wretched woman" with "compassion" and no one comes to her aid. The narrator recognizes that there is no possibility of reconstituting the parish on the anonymous city streets, and so he attempts to create a new kind of community to replace it. To do this, he must address those who have not seen the woman for themselves, and he can do so only through a mediating text. He offers us a few paragraphs because no one offered the "wretched woman" a "few pence," and he demands of us something more complex than "compassion." He demands, that is to say, something closer to reform.

What is required by this passage, and what is required by reformist representation more generally, is a specific way of thinking about the poor. It involves, first of all, our recognition that any particular instance of suffering is not an isolated instance but rather part of a general phenomenon; the narrator prompts this realization when he moves from the single "wretched woman" to the category of all "such miserable creatures." And it involves as well our acknowledgment that the existence of such phenomena entails certain responsibilities for those who remain unaffected by them. In this passage, the precise terms of responsibility might seem remarkably inadequate to the suffering described: "thinking" of a woman's "anguish of heart" as she tries and fails to secure food for herself and her child will do little to save either of them from starvation. But the content of this responsibility is less important than its structure. The obligations of charity were discharged through a familiar, indeed time-honored, circle of relations: the Old Lady helps the poor of her parish, whom she sees in church every Sunday bowing their thanks from the side aisle. The responsibilities entailed by reform, however, establish a new circle of relations among persons who are not yet identified—and who may never be known to one another. Where charity expects that we will feel compassion for the single "wretched woman" standing before us, reform calls upon us to encompass in our minds all "miserable creatures," whether we ever see them or not. In this way, reform brings each of us in turn into an imagined relation with all of the urban poor.

These relations are capable of infinite expansion, until a single person is made to feel responsible for all the suffering in the world. Such a feeling can lead only to paralysis, and the emergence of nineteenth-century reform as a cognitive mode was therefore made possible by the simultaneous emergence of other modes that seem to compete with, but actually complement, reform. They do so by variously limiting the imagined connections that reform was busily calling into being. Wai Chee Dimock has identified one such mode in the legal structures that attend capitalism, such as limited liability and tort law; she argues that these structures limited connections by distinguishing between those sufferings that are worthy of consideration and those that are not.[9] Bruce Robbins has identified professionalism as another such mode; he argues that one's professional identity not only selects the specific sufferings that are one's proper concern but also, and more importantly, reduces the affective intensity of that concern.[10] But the most common cognitive mode for managing a potentially global responsibility is the one that Mary Poovey has identified, the rise of national thinking. Taken together, social reform and nation formation taught persons that their concern should encompass everyone within and no one beyond the borders of the nation.[11] This well describes Dickens's own thinking in mid- to late career. I will show, at the end of the chapter, how he came to such a position after his involvement with reform movements that were conceived of as Anglo-American. But first I will explore Dickens's early relation to one reform movement in particular, namely, temperance reform.

In "The Streets—Night," Dickens demonstrates why reform is necessary in a world no longer confined to the parish, but this does not mean that his own writings become reformist. On the contrary, he struggles in subsequent sketches to distinguish his own representational practices from those of the reformers. His competition with reformist writings is most straightforward in "A Visit to Newgate." The narrator begins by announcing that his sketch of Newgate Prison will differ from the "numerous reports" that "numerous committees" have already made (235). These reports rely on quantification and measurement, modes of description that the narrator dismisses out of

9. Wai Chee Dimock, *Residues of Justice: Literature, Law, Philosophy* (Berkeley: University of California Press, 1997).

10. Bruce Robbins, "Telescopic Philanthropy: Professionalism and Responsibility in *Bleak House*," in *Nation and Narration*, ed. Homi K. Bhabha (London: Routledge, 1990).

11. Mary Poovey, *Making a Social Body: British Cultural Formation, 1830–1864* (Chicago: University of Chicago Press, 1995), 8.

hand: "We took no notes," he announces, "made no memoranda, measured none of the yards, ascertained the exact number of inches in no particular room; are unable even to report of how many apartments the jail is composed" (235). Against the objectivity of numbers, the narrator sets his own subjective impressions: "[W]e saw the prison, and saw the prisoners; and what we did see, and what we thought, we will tell at once in our own way" (235). Dickens is here distinguishing his own work from the vast body of social-scientific reformist writing that would include Edwin Chadwick's *Report on the Sanitary Condition of the Labouring Poor* (1842), Henry Mayhew's *London Labour and the London Poor* (1861–62), and Charles Booth's *Life and Labour of the People of London* (1891), as well as a host of other, now-forgotten statistical surveys and parliamentary reports.

But not all reformist writing was of this kind. Much, in fact, was indistinguishable from "A Visit to Newgate," offering firsthand accounts of suffering that relied on specifically literary strategies of description. Many reformers found, as the examples of Harriet Beecher Stowe and Elizabeth Gaskell remind us, that literary forms were more effective than social-scientific ones in creating sympathy or, in the case of temperance, identification. And while it was easy for Dickens to distinguish his own work from the social-scientific "committee report," it was much more difficult for him to distinguish himself from this other body of reformist writing. This difficulty emerges most clearly with respect to the temperance movement. For nineteenth-century temperance was quite simply the storytelling reform. Earlier generations of temperance reformers had relied on putatively scientific discourses, such as Benjamin Rush's "thermometer" or Joseph Livesey's chemical demonstrations that there was no nutritious content to alcohol.[12] But temperance became an influential social movement only after it was reconceptualized in terms of narrative, specifically in terms of a narrative that unfolded the inevitable consequences of drink: starting with the first occasion of drunkenness, the first exposure to spirits, even the very first taste of alcohol, the narrative follows an unyielding trajectory of moral, physical, and economic decline. The narrative's innocuous beginnings invited readers to identify themselves with characters tempted to take their first sip, while its hideous conclusions warned them to stay abstinent.[13] This narrative, which I call the cautionary temperance tale, percolated in Victorian fiction over the course of the century, rising from the anonymous tracts circulated by reformers; through the

12. Benjamin Rush, *An Inquiry into the Effects of Spirituous Liquors on the Human Body, to Which Is Added a Moral and Physical Thermometer* (Boston, 1790).

13. John W. Crowley offers the richest formal analysis of such narratives in his *Drunkard's Progress: Narratives of Addiction, Despair and Recovery* (Baltimore: Johns Hopkins University Press, 1999).

didactic short stories written by such authors as Sarah Stickney Ellis, better known for her conduct books; and into the works of such canonical authors as George Eliot and the Dickens of *Hard Times* (1854). As early as *Boz*, however, Dickens was already making use of it.

In order to understand why Dickens might need the cautionary temperance tale, we first must understand what he is trying, in *Boz*, to achieve. Nearly all of the sketches that make up *Boz* were first published independently, in a number of different magazines. It was only when Dickens was preparing them for their reissue in volume form that they were arranged in their present order. In doing so, Dickens imposed on the vagaries of biography and the contingencies of history an arc of literary development. This arc is visible in the section titles. After "Seven Sketches from Our Parish," *Boz* moves to the city. The titles of the subsequent sections reduce the sketch form to its component parts, as if to demonstrate that the city requires new techniques of description ("Scenes"), characterization ("Characters"), and plotting ("Tales"). Critics have long recognized that Dickens's formal innovations emerged out of his efforts to represent the modern city. Raymond Williams argues, for instance, that the hidden connections revealed over the course of Dickens's plots reflect an urban experience of seeming randomness and underlying order, while Alexander Welsh attributes the thinness of Dickens's characters to an urban emphasis on surface rather than depth.[14] I would like to extend this line of argument by focusing on that aspect of city life that most concerns Dickens in *Boz*, namely, the stark disparities of poverty and wealth.

That these disparities exist is something Dickens everywhere acknowledges; how they might be represented is the subject of "Meditations in Monmouth-street," one of *Boz*'s early city sketches. The narrator visits the secondhand clothing shops that line Monmouth Street in order to indulge in the pleasures of imagining the persons whom the castoff pieces of clothing metonymically conjure up. The narrator does this awhile and then turns to the more difficult task of imagining the possible relations among the people he has invented. Where imagining the individual people required him to infer economic status, imagining the relations among them now requires him to account for economic difference. He experiments with two strategies for doing so, the first temporal, the second spatial. The temporal strategy is prompted by an array of suits, some that have been worn by boys and some by men; some that are respectable; some gay; and some degraded. The

---

14. Raymond Williams, *The Country and the City* (1973; Oxford: Oxford University Press, 1975), 155; Alexander Welsh, *The City of Dickens* (1971; Cambridge: Harvard University Press, 1986), 1.

narrator connects these suits to one another by imagining them all belonging to the same man at various moments in his life, a life that begins in the safety of his mother's home and then descends through increasing degradation and crime to an ignominious sentence of death. What connects all of these stages is the cautionary temperance tale. The crucial turn in the young man's life came when he fell under the wayward sway of new acquaintances and "swaggered" with them into "the public house" (100). From this, the rest surely follows. The narrator sketches in a few strokes the "bare and miserable room, destitute of furniture," the wife and children, "pale, hungry, and emaciated," and the man himself "cursing their lamentations, staggering to the tap-room, from whence he had just returned," and finally striking the wife who has followed him to plead for a little money with which to buy bread (101).

The ideology of the cautionary temperance tale is clear. It transforms the present fact of economic inequality into a prior history of individual choices unwisely made. The sight of rich and poor suits hanging next to one another on a rack, like the sight of rich and poor persons passing one another on the street, need not serve as a critique of the existing economic order so long as poverty can be explained as the just consequence of drinking. But Dickens is not interested in the ideology of the cautionary temperance tale, at least not in "Monmouth-street." Instead, he is interested in its form. It is, for him, a narrative capable of organizing the facts of economic disparity, one that offers itself up quite readily to his use.

Having taken up the cautionary temperance tale, Dickens then relinquishes it with ease. He replaces the temporal structure of narrative with the spatial structure of a dance. Distracted from the array of suits by a miscellaneous collection of shoes, the narrator brings the shoes into relation with one another by imagining people dancing. Here, the differences between the sturdy boots of the workers, the faded shoes of the shabby genteel, and the elegant pumps of the dandy are largely forgotten, subordinated to a vision of harmony that dance can achieve, if only briefly and through obvious artifice. But the artifice of the dance reminds us that the cautionary temperance tale is similarly conventional. And indeed the tale will appear again in *Boz*, in a story entitled "A Drunkard's Death." Once more, the cautionary temperance tale serves as one narrative resource among many capable of accounting for otherwise unaccountable economic transitions. It emplots a sudden fall in fortune, just as a sudden rise in fortune has been plotted, in "The Boarding-House," by an impulsive marriage between servant and master or, in "The Tuggs at Ramsgate," by an unexpected inheritance. The juxtaposition of these stories suggests that the temperance narrative is for Dickens no more real than any other fairy tale.

But while Dickens ignores the ideology of the cautionary temperance tale in "Monmouth-street," he confronts it in another sketch, "Gin-shops." This sketch begins with the observation that gin shops are "numerous and splendid" in proportion to the "dirt and poverty of the surrounding neighborhood" (217), and the narrator devotes the rest of the sketch to elaborating the two terms of this equation. He depicts both the tawdry glamour of the gin shop and what he knows his readers will find even harder to imagine, the filth and wreckage of the poor neighborhoods and the degraded behavior of the people crowded in them. Throughout the sketch, the conditions of poverty and the act of drinking are represented as coexistent. Only in the conclusion does the narrator attempt to establish a causal relation between them, and the relation he establishes is explicitly opposed to the one that would be offered by temperance reform. Addressing the "gentlemen" and "ladies" who advocate temperance, the narrator insists that "gin-drinking is a great vice in England, but poverty is a greater" (220). Until poverty is eradicated, "gin-shops will increase in number and splendor" (220). That is to say, it is not drinking that leads to poverty, but rather poverty that leads to drinking. In arguing that drinking is an effect rather than a cause, Dickens is challenging the fundamental premise of temperance reform, and this challenge has formal consequences. For "Gin-shops" describes a night's worth of customers without attempting to imagine the life story of any one of them. This, the one sketch explicitly critical of temperance reform, is also the one sketch that does not borrow from temperance reform any of its familiar narrative structures. And indeed throughout *Boz* Dickens keeps his appropriations separate from his critiques. It is not until *Pickwick* that he will attempt to bring these two impulses together, to critique the ideology of temperance even as he makes use of its characteristic narratives.

The Pickwick Papers and the Limits of Reform

The cautionary temperance tale appears twice in *Pickwick*, first as "The Stroller's Tale," the first of the nine interpolated tales that punctuate *Pickwick*'s main plot, and later as an episode within the main plot itself. "The Stroller's Tale" resembles Boz's "Monmouth-street" imaginings in many ways, moving from poverty and sickness to delirium and death. But while the progress through these stations is familiar, the narrative itself is made grotesque by the fact that this particular drunkard is a circus clown. The deformities of his body are magnified by his motley, and his glassy eye stares all the more blankly for the surrounding greasepaint. There is horror in this, but there is also dark comedy, and Dickens's choice of a clown is the first sign that the cautionary temperance tale is here being parodied. A more obvious sign is the context in which the tale is told. Mr. Pickwick returns to his rooms one evening to find his friends waiting there with a stranger, who has offered to tell them the story of a man who died of drink. Pickwick listens to the story in silence and, after hearing its harrowing conclusion, puts down his brandy and water and opens his mouth to speak. The logic of temperance reform presumes that Pickwick will then renounce alcohol in words, as he has already set it aside in fact, but this is not what happens. Instead, some visitors arrive before Pickwick says anything, some confusions ensue from their visit, and the adventures of the Pickwickians resume as a result. The evening concludes, the narrator tells us, "with the conviviality with which it had begun" (115).

That Pickwick is not converted to sobriety by this story is not surprising, for the man who tells the story is not a reformer but a con man. More precisely, he is, in the words of another con man, a "Rum fellow—does the heavy business—no actor—strange man—all sorts of miseries—Dismal Jemmy, we call him on the circuit" (104). Dismal Jemmy's con artistry estranges the cautionary temperance tale in two crucial ways. With respect to the narrative's performative dimension, con artistry disables its reformist effects. Taking a glass of brandy and water before starting to speak, Dismal Jemmy presents the "miseries" of his tale as a kind of theater piece and in doing so ensures that his audience will be entertained but not transformed. In this way, Dismal Jemmy resembles no one so much as Dickens himself. Like Dismal Jemmy waiting for Pickwick's return, Dickens relies on the "miseries" of drunkenness to sustain an audience's desire across a period of delay: the preamble to "The Stroller's Tale" concludes *Pickwick*'s first number, and the tale itself begins the second. And like Dismal Jemmy expecting to be paid for his story, Dickens hoped to profit from the contemporary interest in reform: "The Stroller's Tale" was written before *Pickwick* was even conceived of, intended to be yet another sketch by Boz. But if Dismal Jemmy's con artistry throws into relief all that is most cynical in Dickens's use of the cautionary temperance tale, it also enables what will be productive in this use as well. Con artistry does the work of defamiliarization. Dismal Jemmy reveals the temperance narrative *as* a narrative, isolating its constitutive elements and thus making them available for Dickens's use. Two of these elements are particularly significant: the disciplined structure of the narrative itself and the license it provides for verisimilar detail.

Pickwick everywhere bears the marks of Dickens's efforts to transform the text into something more verisimilar and more disciplined. That this was his aspiration is demonstrated by *Pickwick*'s publication history. *Pickwick* began when a publishing firm, Chapman and Hall, commissioned a series of sporting sketches from a celebrated illustrator, Robert Seymour, and then looked for someone to write the accompanying text. They settled on the promising young author of *Sketches by Boz*. In securing the illustrator before the writer, the publishers were following the contemporary practice of subordinating serial text to serial illustration, but Dickens famously challenged this subordination. His challenges reveal the novelistic ambition that was growing within him, and they also help us to specify what he understood a novel to be. From the beginning, Dickens insisted that he, and not the illustrator, be the one to choose the topics *Pickwick* would take up. In practice, this meant that *Pickwick* would focus on something other than hunting and shooting, specifically on the London Dickens knew so well. Dickens struggled over this with the illustrator, who finished three of the four illustrations for the second number and then shot himself through the heart. The publishers wanted to cancel the serial, but Dickens persuaded them to continue on very different terms. He insisted that he be allowed to choose the next illustrator, further securing his own predominance, but he also insisted that the number of pages per serial part be increased by a third while the number of illustrations be halved. In practice, this meant that Dickens was now free to develop two rather long episodes per serial part rather than four very brief ones, and this new expansiveness made it possible for him to imagine episodes extending the length of a part or even from one part to the next.[15]

Over the course of *Pickwick*, we can see Dickens exercising his new prerogatives more and more, as he works to transform the comic serial into a serial novel. In *Boz*, we see the story of Dickens's apprenticeship in city writing because of the retrospective reorganization of the sketches. In *Pickwick*, by contrast, his apprenticeship in novel writing is inadvertently recorded by the unforgiving nature of serial publication itself. Rendering revision impossible, the serial preserves within itself the history of its own false starts, failed experiments, and new beginnings. It enables us to see Dickens aspiring to narrative discipline and verisimilar detail.

Pickwick begins in the most undisciplined of ways. Mr. Pickwick calls a meeting of the Pickwick Club and proposes that a Corresponding Society be formed to travel through England and report back on the adventures that befall them. Pickwick and his young friends thus begin their travels free to go almost anywhere and do almost anything, and *Pickwick*'s early chapters are remarkable for the abundance and variety of the adventures they contain. The adventures are connected by a narrative as capacious as Pickwick's proposal: the picaresque. The picaresque is punctuated, however, by nine in-

---

15. Robert L. Patten offers the most thorough and thoughtful discussion of *Pickwick*'s composition ("*Pickwick Papers* and the Development of Serial Fiction," *Rice University Studies: Studies in English* 61, no. 1 [Winter 1975]: 51–74).

terpolated tales, stories that the Pickwickians hear or find during their travels. These tales serve as a model of what *Pickwick* itself would become. They stand out, brief and self-sufficient, among Pickwick's wanderings from part to part and from place to place, exemplifying the kind of narrative discipline that Dickens was trying to bring to *Pickwick* as a whole. Gothic in mode, the early tales take up topics (crime, poverty, madness, disease) that herald Dickens's growing commitment to verisimilitude. And in doing so, they reveal that the picaresque main plot, with all its freedom and joy, depends on the denial of troubling social facts. As *Pickwick* goes on, it is interrupted by these interpolated tales less and less often, and the ones that do appear are increasingly fantastic: hot springs are formed from the tears of a heartbroken prince, and a man falls in love with a ghost. This change occurs because the tales have done their formal work. The protorealism of their content and the more disciplined structure of their form have been transferred from the tales into the main plot of *Pickwick*.

The crucial conduit for this transfer is another temperance narrative. Temperance reform is brought into the main plot by a second con man, the Rev. Mr. Stiggins. He is identified in the introductory list of characters as "*the red-nosed 'deputy shepherd'*" (66), a description that records both the rhetoric of his self-announcing piety and the physical signs of his barely concealed love of drink. Stiggins is preying on the new wife of Toby Weller, a widow who owns a public house. A happy drinker himself, Toby is dismayed to find his wife succumbing to the influence of temperance reform. In a neat inversion of the stories that temperance reform tells about rescue from drink, Toby tries, throughout the novel, to save his wife from Stiggins's influence and thus to restore peace to his public-house home. The climax of Toby's efforts comes when he arranges for two friends to ply Stiggins with rum and water and then send him on to the temperance meeting he has been invited to address.

This meeting is what the nineteenth century would have called an "experience meeting." Experience meetings belonged to the third wave of British temperance reform; they followed the free licensing movement of the 1820s, which had sought to make alcohol less desirable by making it more readily available, and the antispirits movement of the 1820s and 1830s, which had sought to end the consumption of gin. In the 1830s, a third movement, the teetotal movement, emerged and radicalized temperance reform in two ways. Where antispirits had limited its attacks to gin and whisky, teetotalism prohibited all forms of alcohol; and where earlier temperance reformers had directed their energies to preventing the sober from becoming drunkards and to controlling the damage that drunkards could do, teetotalism sought to reclaim drunkards to a life of sobriety. As a result, teetotalism challenged what had been the middle-class dominance of temperance reform, in part by proscribing characteristically middle-class, as well as working-class, drinks, but more importantly by transforming the temperance meeting into a forum in which working-class men and women could narrate their own experiences of drunkenness. These "experience meetings" were organized around the recitation of stories that took their structure from the Puritan tradition of personal witness: reformed drunkards would recount the sufferings they had endured because of their drinking, the moment of their conversion to sobriety, and the rewards that had come with abstinence. And their listeners, persuaded by these stories to sign the temperance pledge, would then go on to recount the stories of their own rescue in the hopes of saving other drunkards in turn.[16] The result was a narrative that I call the narrative of temperance conversion.

Because these narratives were performed orally, most of them have been lost. But a few of the most prominent speakers did record their oral narratives in written form as well. The most influential of these was John Gough's *Autobiography* (1845); Gough made a sensational career, in the United States as well as Britain, out of his redemption from drunkenness. Just as oral narratives were central to temperance meetings, so written narratives were central to the temperance press: a number of journals published them, and the *Commonwealth* even sponsored a competition and awarded prizes to the best. Although she does not explicitly discuss it, Reginia Gagnier predicts the form that this narrative takes in her study of nineteenth-century life writing. One of Gagnier's central arguments is that the contingencies of working-class life made it difficult for workers to narrate their lives according to the model set by middle-class autobiography; the individual autonomy presumed by the middle-class progress from childhood and schooling, through separation from family and crisis, to the "recovery or discovery of a new self" was simply not part of working-class life.[17] But Gagnier does note a single exception: those workers with access to conversion narratives were able to conceive of their lives in terms that resembled recognizably middle-class narratives and were thus able to lay claim to middle-class subjectivity. Gagnier understands conversion to be religious, but her argument can easily be

---

16. Brian Harrison (*Drink and the Victorians*) has given the definitive account of temperance narratives and their indebtedness to Puritan tradition. It is worth noting that the narratives Harrison describes persist in our own day. Alcoholics Anonymous differs from the nineteenth-century temperance movement in its insistence that a single pledge is not sufficient, in its emphasis on "one day at a time," but its meetings are nonetheless structured around the recounting of similar narratives of conversion, as Klaus Makela et al. demonstrate in their *Alcoholics Anonymous as a Mutual-Help Movement* (Madison: University of Wisconsin Press, 1996).

17. Reginia Gagnier, *Subjectivities: A History of Self-Representation in Britain, 1832–1920* (Oxford: Oxford University Press, 1991), 150.

extended to account for the secular conversion narratives that lie at the heart of temperance reform.

These narratives rely on the conversion to sobriety to structure the experience of working-class life. In *The Life and Adventures of Colin* (1855), it is the editor of the *Bristol Temperance Herald* who has divided the autobiography into chapters that reflect teetotal values, but in *Incidents in the Life of Robt. Henderson; or, Extracts from the Autobiography of "New-cassel Bob" (A Tyne-Side Rake)* (1869), it is Henderson himself who has chosen to divide the story of his life into two halves, "The Old Man" and "The New Man," around his simultaneous conversion to Christianity and sobriety.[18] Moreover, John Vine Hall's *The Author of "The Sinner's Friend": An Autobiography* (1865) and William Farish's *The Struggles of a Hand Loom Weaver* (1889) both reiterate a narrative whose arc is best captured in the title of a third text, *A Sketch of the Life of Miles Watkins, of Cheltenham; wherein is related the particular incidents connected with his history . . . and the ultimate happiness enjoyed by him, since adopting the Total Abstinence Pledge: Written by Himself* (1841).

The "ultimate happiness" achieved by Miles Watkins was importantly economic, and he was far from alone in that. The signing of the temperance pledge not only articulated a worker's ambition to raise his or her class status but also often served as the first step toward achieving that end. No one demonstrates this better than Joseph Livesey, the founder of British teetotalism; his own life, as related in his *Autobiography* (1881), dramatizes the rise from handloom weaver to factory owner, and through his reformist labors he advocated that others follow the same path. But while the temperance conversion narrative offered a structure capable of organizing the facts of working-class life, it did so by presenting those facts as the consequences of individual choices. Poverty, disease, crime, imprisonment, and death are all described as the effects of drinking, while health, happiness, prosperity, and salvation can be described as the effects of sobriety. In this way, the bewildering and often brutal changes brought about by industrialization and urbanization could be organized around, and simplified through, the story of an individual drunkard's progress from the sufferings caused by drinking to the "ultimate happiness" achieved by abstinence.

Dickens shows the dangers of this simplification in *Pickwick* when he describes the temperance meeting that the drunken Stiggins attends. The meeting begins with the recounting of temperance conversion narratives,

18. While the temperance narratives I cite were published over a broad span of time, they all recount conversions that took place in the late 1830s or early 1840s, in the midst of the teetotal moment that Dickens is describing.

which are recorded in summary fashion by the secretary of the temperance society. Here is one:

> Walker, tailor, wife, and two children. When in better circumstances, owns to having been in the constant habit of drinking ale and beer. . . . Is now out of work and penniless; thinks it must be the porter (cheers) or the loss of the use of his right hand; is not certain which, but thinks it very likely that, if he had drank nothing but water all his life, his fellow work-man would never have stuck a rusty needle in him, and thereby occasioned his accident (tremendous cheering). (547)

H. Walker is followed by Betsy Martin, who attributes the fact that she was born with one eye to her mother's drinking of bottled stout; she has joined the temperance society in the hope that abstaining from drink will cause a second eye to grow. Then comes one-legged Thomas Burton, who found that his wooden legs wore out quickly when he bought them secondhand and drank gin and water; now that he buys new wooden legs, they last twice as long, a difference he attributes to having given up gin. What makes these stories comic is, of course, their false account of causation, but false causation is, as Dickens emphasizes, more than just a joke. Here, the problem is the substitution of false causes for true ones (porter for a workplace injury), while in "Gin-shops," the problem was the inversion of cause and effect (poverty and drinking). In both cases, however, temperance narratives distort the very phenomena they are intended to address.

This misrepresentation was all the more disappointing because what drew Dickens to temperance reform was precisely the representational license it seemed to convey. On the one hand, reform justified an attention to what had hitherto been excluded from the domain of representation. "Gin-shops" makes this claim directly. The slums "can hardly be imagined" and are only rarely seen (217), and so the narrator is therefore permitted, indeed obligated, to circulate representations of what would otherwise go unperceived. In *Pickwick*, too, reform serves as a conduit for verisimilar detail. Just as it was the cautionary temperance tale told by Dismal Jemmy that first introduced the topic of poverty in *Pickwick*, so it is the temperance meeting that first brings poverty into *Pickwick*'s main plot: a prosperous procession of established landowners, successful professional men, and well-tended servants is interrupted by the poor people described in the temperance secretary's report. On the other hand, temperance narratives confine perception, and thus representation, within the limits of their own ideology. Reformers see, as Dickens points out in "Gin-shops," the narrow circumstances of drinking but not the broader conditions of poverty. Pushed to the periphery of the temperance narrative are troubling social facts, and Dickens attempts, in *Pickwick* as well as "Gin-Shops," to bring these facts back into view. H. Walter is "out of work and penniless," Henry Beller, too, is "out of employ now" (548), and Betsy Martin is only slightly better off, a widow struggling to support her child by "charring and washing" (546). Their poverty has outlasted their drunkenness, and Dickens, in drawing attention to the suffering that persists even in sobriety, implicitly condemns temperance narratives for failing to see that.

In this way, Dickens shows what Dimock, Robbins, and Poovey argue: that reform depends not only on the forming, but also on the denying, of certain connections. The narratives of temperance reform make it possible for us to sympathize with some suffering people (the sober poor) by also making it possible for us to ignore or even condemn others (the poor who drink). Having shown the limits of the temperance narratives, Dickens then tries to represent all of the poor, without mediation. He attempts this when Mr. Pickwick is sentenced, on a matter of principle, to debtors' prison. In the Fleet Prison, Pickwick encounters for the first time that poverty of which the narrator has always been aware. Hearing a reference to the so-called poor side of the Fleet, he immediately resolves to visit it. He embarks on a tour of the prison's courtyard, which is filled with screaming children, lounging men, and harassed and dirty women. So overwhelming is this experience that Pickwick's perceptions become deranged. He recognizes the disreputable men with whom he briefly shared a cell, but those men multiply before his eyes:

> The great body of the prison population appeared to be Mivins, and Smangle, and the parson, and the butcher, and the leg, over and over, and over again. There were the same squalor, the same turmoil and noise, the same general characteristics, in every corner; in the best and worst alike. The whole place seemed restless and troubled; and the people were crowding and flitting to and fro, like the shadows in an uneasy dream. (737)

This is poverty without drinking; this is representation that does not depend on individualizing narratives. Dickens refuses to distinguish Mivins and Smangle from the "great body of the prison population." And he refuses to place them on the downward path of the cautionary temperance tale, which would reassure us that their imprisonment was caused by drinking, or on the upward path of the temperance conversion narrative, which would reassure us that sobriety will lead to gainful employment. But as a result of these refusals, he leaves Mivins and Smangle and all of the rest with quite literally nowhere to go. They can do nothing but "flit to and fro," "over and over, and over again." And if there is nowhere for them to go, there is nothing for Pickwick to do. The suffering he sees does not admit of obvious solutions, and Pickwick makes his famous announcement that he has seen enough and will henceforth confine himself to his cell.

Pickwick confined in his cell figures *Pickwick*'s inability to move forward until Dickens finds an alternate way to delimit the experience of poverty. He finds a way in a narrative of his own devising, what I will call the charitable picaresque. On the "poor side" of debtors' prison, Pickwick encounters two of his old antagonists, the con man Arthur Jingle and Jingle's servant, Job Trotter. The two have appeared in the serial from time to time, first befriending the Pickwickians, then duping them, then eluding Pickwick and Sam Weller's efforts to exact revenge. Such recurrent encounters are typical of the picaresque, whose protagonists often meet their opponents again and again. And indeed Jingle accounts for his imprisonment so elliptically—"deserved it all," he says (690)—that he might as well be referring to deceptions imposed as to debts run up. His presence in the Fleet, that is to say, might as well be connected to the conventions of the picaresque as to the realities of poverty. These picaresque conventions are significant because they create a kind of traveling community, a parishlike world in which charity is still possible. And it is for this reason that Jingle and Job are the only debtors whom Pickwick assists, the only ones to receive "something" from his "waist-coat pocket" (691). The circumstances of poverty are always overwhelming, as Dickens is finding and temperance reformers have long known, but the return of Jingle offers a nostalgic strategy for delimiting poverty's depiction. Where temperance reform attends only to what fits into a particular narrative—drunken suffering, sober reward—the charitable picaresque attends only to what belongs to a particular character. Because everything is done to help Jingle and Job, nothing need be done to help anyone else. In Jingle, then, we can see the origins of a character like Little Dorrit, whose presence in and immunity to the degraded world of the Marshalsea Prison ensure that we can sympathize with some debtors without being overwhelmed by sympathy for all. We can see, too, the origins of the strategy by which Dickens, in his later urban novels, will transform the unfathomable city into a knowable community.

Anglo-American Reform: *American Notes*

When Dickens arrived in the United States, in 1842, he claimed that he had come as a private traveler on a pleasure tour. It soon become clear, however, that he had come to campaign for an international copyright law.

At the first of the public dinners held in his honor, Dickens offered a toast to the day when U.S. authors would profit from the sale of their works in Britain—and British authors, from the sale of their works in the United States. At the second dinner, he rose and asked "leave to whisper in your ear two words: *International Copyright*."[19] This campaign was obviously ill-advised, alienating those readers who had gathered in the thousands to greet Dickens's steamer or follow his railway car and who lined up in the hundreds to shake his hand.[20] But the campaign was also at odds with the writing that Dickens was about to do. The book that he published about his U.S. travels, *American Notes* (1842), borrowed extensively from the writings of two U.S. reformers, Samuel Gridley Howe's annual reports for the Perkins Institution and Theodore Weld's antislavery pamphlet *American Slavery As It Is* (1839). Dickens reprinted portions from both of these texts without asking their authors for authorization or offering them compensation. My purpose in noting this is not to accuse Dickens of hypocrisy but rather to draw attention to what these borrowings show us about his involvement in an Anglo-American culture of reform.

Dickens's involvement with this culture began with the reading that he did before he went on his tour. A contemporary reporter describes him as surrounded by the books written by previous British travelers, among them Frances Trollope's *Domestic Manners of the Americans* (1832), Frederick Marryat's *A Diary in America, with Remarks on Its Institutions* (1839), and Harriet Martineau's *Society in America* (1837).[21] That Dickens read these other books is significant because the genre is an unusually standardized one, with conventional topics and even a conventional itinerary. The most common topic was national difference, and the most obvious way in which this difference was articulated was in terms of manners. Indeed, the discussion of manners in these travel books did much to establish the terms through which transatlantic differences would continue to be described: U.S. intrusiveness and British reserve; U.S. hustle and British leisure; the U.S. merchant and the British gentleman.

The conventional itinerary included the principal cities of the United States (Boston, New York, Philadelphia, and Washington, DC) and the principal natural sites (the Mississippi River, the prairies of the West, and,

19. Quoted in Edgar Johnson, *Charles Dickens: His Tragedy and Triumph*, 2 vols. (New York: Simon and Schuster, 1952), 1:381.

20. Meredith McGill notes that Dickens does not seem to have realized that his extraordinary popularity was made by possible by the reprinting he had come to campaign against. McGill unfolds the further ironies of Dickens's U.S. tour in *American Literature and the Culture of Reprinting*, 113–30.

21. Johnson, *Charles Dickens*, 1:360.

above all else, Niagara Falls) but also, and more surprisingly, institutions of reform: the poorhouses of Boston, the asylums of Long Island, the prisons of Philadelphia. So conventional was this itinerary that it was followed not only by those travelers we now think of as reformers, such as Martineau and Dickens, but also by those travelers who had little to do with reform at all. The naval explorer Basil Hall may have paid his first New York visit to the Brooklyn Navy Yard, but he paid his second to the juvenile Home of Refuge.

As a consequence of this itinerary, British travelers ended up contributing, whether they intended to or not, to Anglo-American reform. They did so most obviously through face-to-face exchange, as when Hall lectured New York firefighters on recent innovations in fire hoses. These exchanges, which were made possible by travel, were then preserved and disseminated through the subsequent travel books. We can see this process at work in *American Notes*. At times, Dickens records his impressions of various reformist institutions because he thinks that aspects of them should be adopted in Britain: he particularly admires the child-sized furniture used in the Boston orphanages or the few small comforts that the inmates of Boston almshouses were permitted to retain. At other times, Dickens records his impressions so that the people of the United States will see what is still in need of reform, such as the provisions for black children in the juvenile prisons of Philadelphia. The extensive exchanges possible within a shared culture of reform are most clear with respect to prisons. When Dickens describes the Boston House of Corrections, he notes that the United States invented the work regime now used in London prisons. He then goes on to remark, in a footnote, that the system has since been perfected in two particular London prisons, which he identifies and whose governors he explicitly names. More generally, Dickens urges the United States not to be so quick to rely on prison labor, which allows prisoners opportunities to conspire with one another, as well as driving noncriminal laborers out of work. At the same time, he holds up the panopticonlike arrangement of the new prison in Boston as a model for all future British prisons. And his description of reformist institutions culminates in an impassioned attack on the solitary confinement pioneered at Philadelphia's Eastern Penitentiary, which isolated the prisoners in solitary cells for the entire length of their term.

The reformism of travel books was not limited to those moments when they describe obvious sites of reform. These books also, and more importantly, engaged with the two most highly contested reform movements of the era, suffrage reform and the antislavery campaign. Some travelers engaged these questions deliberately. Martineau, for instance, came to the United States fully committed to the abolition of slavery abroad and to radical politics at home. She therefore gathered evidence in support of these positions during her travels and disseminated this evidence through her travel books once she returned to Britain. But, as I suggested in my preface, all travel books ended up contributing to those reformist debates. This is because any reference to U.S. manners touches on status, as defined by race and class, and therefore on questions of slavery and democracy. It was impossible for a British observer to praise, for instance, the self-respect of American servants or to condemn the too-promiscuous mixing of classes, to praise the graciousness of plantation culture or to condemn the indolence of poor southern whites, without entering into a debate about whether suffrage should be expanded in Britain and slavery abolished in the United States. Indeed, so many attacks on U.S. democracy took the form of attacks on American manners that the *Westminster Review*, which supported suffrage reform, mocked the strategy for its inconsequence: "When I exclaim, 'This is a noble, an extraordinary country!' I am answered in Abigail phrase—'But, shocking, the people eat with their knives.'"[22]

Dickens was no exception. He came to the United States fully alive to the reformist possibilities of the tour and the travel book, and he was committed to writing in support of the nation's experiment with democracy and in condemnation of its acceptance of slavery. Dickens saw in the nation's republicanism a peaceful alternative to what he took to be the violence of the Chartists. And the people of the United States in turn saw in Dickens their own rebellion against British authority; for them he was, as John Forster later described him, an "embodied protest" against the British institutions that the United States had rebelled against.[23] But Dickens's experience of U.S. manners famously turned him against democracy. The letters that he wrote during his tour are increasingly filled with complaints about the ignorance and the touchiness of the people around him, their taciturnity and their brag, their lack of cleanliness and, above all else, their habit of spitting. He went on to record many of his complaints about U.S. manners in *American Notes*, and in doing so he ended up contributing to the discourse opposing suffrage reform.

But while Dickens's faith in democracy was shaken, his abhorrence of slavery only grew stronger. He became more and more committed to writing against it, but he was also redefining what writing against it would require. In *American Notes*, he confessed to a fear that he would not be able to reveal any of its horrors. In particular, he feared that he would be unable to see beneath "the disguises" in which slavery would surely be "dressed," and, indeed, he was not permitted, during his visit to a Virginia plantation, to witness the slaves at their noontime meal or to inspect their cabins.[24] But if Dickens doubted his ability to gather evidence, he also doubted that more evidence was needed. Referring to the "host of facts already heaped together on the subject" (174), Dickens implicitly suggests that these facts have done nothing to abolish slavery.

What is needed, Dickens recognizes, are not only texts that seek to reveal but also texts that seek to defamiliarize. And it is the latter that he intends *American Notes* to become. In this way, *American Notes* differs from Dickens's great reformist novels, such as *Bleak House* and *Dombey and Son* (1846–48). Those novels devote themselves to revelation: to the realist representation of what often goes unseen (Tom All Alone's) and the metaphorical representation of what cannot be seen at all (the Circumlocution Office). Such representations are capable of persuading persons who have never encountered a given social problem; they are useful, for instance, in persuading northerners and Englishmen to oppose slavery. But they are not at all capable of persuading those persons who are responsible for the problem itself—in this case, the slaveholders. Revelation is of no use to those who know the realities of slavery all too well, who are surrounded by those realities in every plantation house, in every field, in every public square. Where slavery is familiar, it no longer shocks, and Dickens recognizes that to live in the southern states is to have one's "senses blunted to its wrongs and horrors in a slave-rocked cradle" (184). What will be valuable about his perspective, then, is not its capacity to reveal what slavery would hide (the interior of the slave cabin, the contents of the daily meal) but rather its capacity to be horrified by what everyone else has too often seen. What will be valuable about his perspective is its capacity to defamiliarize, a capacity that Dickens identifies as specifically British. When a southern man told Dickens that the British were ignorant of the reality of slavery, Dickens replied that the British were, on the contrary, much more "competent to judge of its atrocity and horror than those who have been reared in its midst."[25]

But Dickens never became the kind of witness he had intended to be. He had intended to travel through the slaveholding states as far south as Charleston, but he ended up limiting his southern tour to a few days in Virginia and then traveling through the western states instead. He gives conflicting accounts of this change of itinerary. In his letters home, he explains

24. Charles Dickens, *American Notes for General Circulation* (1842; London: Penguin, 1972), 174. All further references to this edition will be marked in the text.
25. Quoted in Forster, *Life of Charles Dickens*, 251.

the decision by saying that a southern acquaintance, Senator Henry Clay, told him that the roads were bad, that the fever season was arriving, and that there was nothing to see in South Carolina anyway. In *American Notes*, by contrast, Dickens implies that it was his own sensitivity to the evils of slavery that kept him away. Throughout the text, he has presented himself as haunted by the thought of slavery. As far north as Boston, the subject of churches leads Dickens to think of one of the city's most prominent ministers, William Ellery Channing, which leads him to think of Channing's antislavery activism and "that most hideous blot and foul disgrace—Slavery" (76). As he travels south, his dread increases. In Baltimore, he is waited on by a slave for the first time and is filled with "a sense of shame and self-reproach" (161). Pausing in Washington, DC, he balances his desire to witness plantation realities against "the pain of living in the constant contemplation of slavery" (174). It is at this point that he decides to alter his itinerary. The alteration of the itinerary is thus presented as the ultimate proof of Dickens's sensitivity. Whereas slave owners live with "senses blunted" to the suffering around them, Dickens cannot even bear to see. In this way, the lack of any extended southern descriptions are the most defamiliarizing descriptions of all.

But while Dickens's own descriptions of slavery are therefore limited to a few brief pages on Virginia, he nonetheless manages to append a full chapter on slavery to the end of *American Notes*. The rest of the book is structured by the order of Dickens's tour, moving from north to south, then west, then north again; the "Slavery" chapter is the only one to appear out of place. The book's penultimate chapter, it is placed between "The Passage Home" and "Concluding Remarks," a location that emphasizes the fact that it could have been written anywhere. And indeed it draws not on Dickens's own experiences of the United States but rather on his reading of U.S. texts—and on his unauthorized borrowing of them. It is this chapter that Dickens takes, without permission or even attribution, from Weld's *American Slavery As It Is*. In doing so, Dickens commits piracy as well as plagiarism, but the result is one of the richest contributions to the writings of Anglo-American antislavery.

Dickens's act of reprinting was surely at odds with his own copyright campaign, but it was not at all a violation of the norms of contemporary reformist writing.[26] On the contrary, reformist reprintings were quite common. Weld was not the only author whom Dickens reprinted in *American Notes*: his description of the education of deaf and blind children is taken

26. It is here that I depart from McGill's discussion of Dickens's reprinting of Weld, by recovering a context, the reformist community, in which authors did not object to being reprinted.

directly from Howe's annual reports. Nor was Dickens the only author to reprint Weld. A decade later, Harriet Beecher Stowe borrowed some situations from Weld's pamphlet in her plotting of *Uncle Tom's Cabin* (1851–52), and she reprinted portions of it in her subsequent *Key to Uncle Tom's Cabin* (1853). All of these reprintings were viewed with total equanimity, even indifference by those concerned. In the biography they wrote of their father, Howe's daughters quote excerpts from *American Notes* to describe Dickens's visit to their father's school, and they interpolate into these excerpts a bland reference to Dickens's reprinting, "[Here follow extracts from Dr. Howe's Reports]."[27] As for Weld, there is no record of his ever protesting, or even remarking upon, the use that Stowe and Dickens made of his pamphlet. And it makes sense, of course, that these reformers would not protest, since reprinting disseminated their writings more widely. *American Notes* extended the geographic circulation of Weld's and Howe's writings, just as *The Key to Uncle Tom's Cabin* would later preserve text from a pamphlet that had otherwise gone out of print.

But if reprinting was a common practice in reformist circles, Dickens and Weld were nonetheless rare in recognizing that it had rhetorical possibilities as well. Weld's pamphlet is divided into two parts: a description of the realities of slavery; and a rebuttal to the objections of those who insist that slavery cannot possibly be that bad. The first half describes the food given to the slaves to eat; the labor they are made to do; the clothing they are given to wear; the housing they are given to live in; and the "privations and inflictions" they endure.[28] Interspersed between these sections are more narrative testimonies, which touch on all of these topics. The second half of the pamphlet, the rebuttal to the objections, takes up seven different objections in turn, from the claim that such cruelties are simply incredible to the claim that they are surely prohibited, if not by law, then certainly by public opinion.

Weld's method of description is announced in his pamphlet's subtitle: "With testimony from a thousand witnesses." These witnesses can be divided into two groups. The first group is made up of firsthand witnesses to slavery, a group that includes travelers as well as southerners who left the southern states because they opposed slavery, such as Weld's own wife and sister-in-law, Angelina and Sarah Grimké. The second group is made up of those who know slavery even more closely, namely, the slaveholders

27. Maud Howe and Florence Howe Hall, *Laura Bridgman: Dr. Howe's Famous Pupil and What He Taught Her* (Boston: Little, Brown, 1903), 107.
28. Theodore Weld, *American Slavery As It Is* (New York: American Anti-Slavery Society, 1839), 10. All further references to this edition will be marked in the text.

themselves. These witnesses are made to testify against themselves unwittingly, through the advertisements they post in southern newspapers for the return of their runaway slaves. At Weld's request, the Grimké sisters spent months reading these newspapers and culling advertisements for him to excerpt, and what they found is evidence such as this, which Weld organized in the following chart:

WITNESSES	TESTIMONY
Mr. Micajah Ricks, Nash County North Carolina, in the Raleigh "Standard," July 18, 1838.	"Ranaway, a negro woman and two children; a few days before she went off, *I burnt her with a hot iron*, on the left side of her face, *I tried to make the letter M.*"
Mr. Asa B. Metcalf, Kingston, Adams Co, Mi. in the "Natchez Courier," June 15, 1832.	"Ranaway Mary, a black woman, has a *scar* on her back and right arm near the shoulder, *caused by a rifle ball*."
Mr. William Overstreet, Benton, Yazoo Co. Mi. in the "Lexington (Kentucky) Observer," July 23, 1838.	"Ranaway a negro man named Henry, *his left eye out*, some scars from a *dirk* on and under his left arm, and *much scarred* with the whip."

(77, emphasis in the original)

These are the first three entries in a subsection of "Punishment" entitled, "Brandings, Maimings, Gun-Shot Wounds, &." One hundred sixteen more entries follow these three, before a new subsection begins: "The Mutilation of Teeth" (83). Through excerpting and reprinting, Weld transforms southern newspapers into a grim catalogue of injury.

There is a nice irony in making slave owners bear witness against themselves, but that is not the most important reason for Weld's reprintings. His primary concern, evident in the pamphlet's opening pages, is with confirming the veracity of his claims. The pamphlet is framed by a "Note" from its publishers, the American Anti-Slavery Society, announcing their intention of publishing more such pamphlets and inviting readers to submit new testimony. They caution, however, that any testimony must be certified. Those witnesses not known personally to the society should submit their testimony with an affidavit from "some person or persons of respectability" (iv). And indeed the narrative testimonies that punctuate the first half of the pamphlet are invariably certified by an entire committee of ministers, town clerks, and justices of the peace. Prior to the publishers' note, however, comes Weld's own "Advertisement to the Reader," which notes the superiority of the slave owner's unwitting testimony even to testimony with affidavit. It is highly improbable, he dryly observes, that such men would lie or exaggerate in order to "proclaim their own infamy" (iii). Reprinting thus functions as a technique of veracity. It enables Weld to remove statements from a context (an advertisement) in which slave owners have every motivation to tell the truth (so that their runaway slaves will be properly identified) and to place them in a context (an antislavery pamphlet) in which slave owners have every motivation to lie (so as to minimize the brutality of slavery).

In his "Slavery" chapter, Dickens excerpts many of the same passages from Weld in turn, including two of the ones quoted above. But for him, the passages function somewhat differently. Whereas Weld uses them to confirm the violence of slavery, Dickens uses them to confirm the failure of public opinion. Weld, too, takes up the question of whether public opinion is capable of limiting the abuses of slavery, but Dickens focuses on this question almost exclusively. Public opinion, he observes, is not always benevolent, as a quick glance at the southern newspapers confirms. Here are these newspapers, as Dickens describes them:

> "Cash for negroes," "cash for negroes," "cash for negroes," is the heading of advertisements in great capitals down the long columns of the crowded journals. Woodcuts of a runaway negro with manacled hands, crouching beneath a bluff pursuer in top boots, who, having caught him, grasps him by the throat, agreeably diversify the pleasant text. The leading article protests against "that abominable and hellish doctrine of abolition, which is repugnant alike to every law of God and nature." The delicate mamma, who smiles her acquiescence in this sprightly writing as she reads the paper in her cool piazza, quiets her youngest child who clings about her skirts, by promising the boy "a whip to beat the little niggers with."—But the negroes, little and big, are protected by public opinion. (273)

The child promised a whip by his "delicate mamma" recalls the "slave-rocked cradle" of hardened sensibility, and it is clear that Dickens takes the southern newspapers to be one of the texts that his own writings must defamiliarize.

These newspapers constitute a public sphere that has been deformed by a too-familiar violence. What shocks Dickens about the slave advertisements is not so much the scar on the "negro woman's" cheek as the fact that the woman's owner is willing to publish under his own name the statement, "I burnt her with a hot iron. . . . I tried to make the letter M." The fact that he would have no compunction about announcing this is a sign that public opinion has grievously failed. And yet Dickens himself does not reprint the man's name. On the contrary, he strips away the local identifications that Weld was so careful to preserve. There is no reference, in *American Notes*, to Mr. Micajah Ricks, or Kingston, Mississippi, or the *Lexington Observer*. There are only references to brandings and shootings and dirkings, acts that could have taken place in any slaveholding state, and the local is thereby regionalized.

In this way, Dickens suggests that public opinion has failed across the southern states. But he does more than that: he also attempts to constitute a new, larger public to take its place. He does so by embedding the public sphere of the southern states in the broader public sphere of Anglo-America through a series of reprintings so complex that it is worth pausing to reiterate their sequence. "Slavery" is a chapter composed by an author who has recently returned to Britain, which reprints a pamphlet that was first printed in New York, whose author himself reprinted excerpts of articles drawn from newspapers and magazines across the southern states. And with the publication of *American Notes*, this transatlantic circuit is made complete. For Dickens's huge popularity ensured that *American Notes* would be reprinted at once by publishers all over the United States—even in the southern states, which had outlawed the circulation of antislavery texts. In this way, the "Slavery" chapter returns the slave owners' words back to the southern states, but only after passing them through the defamiliarizing perspective of a quite different public, the non-slave-owning public of the northern states and of Great Britain. And this perspective did its work. Southern readers were shocked to see what their own newspapers looked like through unfamiliar eyes, as their indignant reviews of Dickens's book made clear. Reprinting proved to be a powerful technique of defamiliarization.

Martin Chuzzlewit and the Retreat from the Anglo-American World

Although *American Notes* bitterly attacked the United States, its reception did not divide along national lines. To be sure, many U.S. citizens were outraged by the book, and some British subjects were amused. But working-class readers in Britain, who had hoped that Dickens would champion the suffrage cause, were very disappointed by his conclusions, and the book was quite critically reviewed in a number of liberal British magazines.[29] At the same time, U.S. publishers were leery of voicing their criticisms of the book, for fear that they would be punished when it came time for Dickens to make an informal arrangement about the reprinting of his next novel. And so some of them waited to reprint critical reviews from Britain, rather than issuing their own. As so often, transatlantic ties, in this case political sympathies and publishing relations, proved more potent than national affiliations.

But not for Dickens. Over the course of his tour, he had grown more and more disillusioned with the United States, until he famously proclaimed, "this is not the country that I came to see; this is not the republic of my imagination."[30] His disillusionment was increased and made bitter by the many hostile reviews of his travel book. As a consequence, Dickens began to withdraw from the very Anglo-American networks that his tour and travel book had exemplified. He first withdrew as much as he could from the Anglo-American literary marketplace, refusing to negotiate anymore with U.S. publishers over the terms of reprinting. He also withdrew from Anglo-American reform. He abandoned his commitment to suffrage and became even more hostile to Chartism. And he became quite skeptical of the antislavery campaign as well, so much so that he failed to support the Union during the U.S. Civil War.

The withdrawal from Anglo-America structures Dickens's next novel, *Martin Chuzzlewit* (1843–44). *Martin Chuzzlewit* was advertised as a story of "English Life and Manners," but the very weak sales of its first numbers prompted Dickens to send its eponymous hero to the United States. The novel's U.S. sections draw heavily on *American Notes*. But while these sections repeat many of the criticisms Dickens already made of the United States, they repeat them with a difference. The novel posits an absolute separation between the two nations that, as Dickens's own experience of the United States showed, simply did not exist. It denies the very Anglo-American networks that his own tour and travel books had relied on and thrown into relief.

Dickens attacks the U.S. press, for instance, without acknowledging what he well knew, that it was embedded in a print culture that was importantly Anglo-American. The first voices that Martin hears in the United States are

---

29. Philip Collins notes, in his survey of the contemporary reviews, that the more prestigious British magazines dismissed *American Notes* for its sloppiness, its superficiality, and the intemperance of its attacks on the United States (*Dickens: The Critical Heritage* [London: Routledge, 1971], 118).

30. Quoted in Johnson, *Charles Dickens: His Tragedy and Triumph*, 1:404.

the voices of the newsboys, who are hawking the "New York Sewer," the "New York Stabber," the "New York Family Spy," the "New York Private Listener," the "New York Peeper," the "New York Plunderer," and the "New York Keyhole Reporter."[31] The joke is clear. Dickens, who was harassed by U.S. newspapers at every turn, now accuses them of being intrusive (the private listener, the keyhole reporter, the family spy, the peeper), as well as lurid and sensationalistic (the stabber, the sewer), and rapacious (the plunderer). So much we would expect. But Dickens also denies the many connections between the British and U.S. literary marketplaces, even those connections that he protested and those he made use of himself. No reprinting happens in the United States he describes, nor is there much reading of texts from the other nation. Indeed, the novel mocks a U.S. newspaper editor for imagining that his articles are read in London, and it also mocks a man who claims to have visited Britain extensively, if only through his reading, and who then insists that Queen Victoria lives in the Tower of London.

In much the same way, Dickens attacks U.S. slavery but does not acknowledge what he himself participated in, the Anglo-American campaign for its abolition. On the contrary, he suggests that there can be no fellowship between antislavery activists in Britain and the United States. Martin is strongly opposed to slavery, and his manservant has an instinctive resistance to it as well. Indeed, Martin must keep the manservant away from all slaves for fear that he will foment some kind of rebellion. Martin is at first pleased, then, to be introduced to some U.S. abolitionists, but he is quickly shocked by the lightness with which they speak of slavery. One abolitionist tells him that "the negroes were such a funny people" that it was impossible "to associate any serious ideas with such a very absurd part of the creation" (246), and all the other abolitionists agree. The scene stands in striking contrast to Dickens's tribute, in *American Notes*, to the American antislavery activist William Ellery Channing.

Dickens also ignores the Anglo-American scope of reform by denying that the political rhetoric of the United States might ever serve as a resource for reformers in Britain. Instead, Dickens joins other conservative British observers in mercilessly parodying that rhetoric. Twice, the narrator imitates the high-flown celebration of democracy only to have it fall flat in a reference to slavery. As Martin's ship approaches the New York harbor, the narrator describes the passengers as breathing "the air of Freedom which carries death to all tyrants, and can never (under any circumstances worth mentioning) be breathed by slaves" (218). Later, the narrator will inaugurate

---

31. Charles Dickens, *Martin Chuzzlewit* (1843–44; Oxford: Oxford University Press, 1998), 220. All further references to this edition will be marked in the text.

a new number by apostrophizing those who "dreamed of Freedom in a slave's embrace, and waking sold her offspring and his own in public market" (293). Worst of all, in the novel's view, is the fact that the people of the United States often make similar pairings of freedom and slavery without even realizing that such pairings might sound odd. When a newspaper editor starts to boast that the free press is "as much one of the ennobling institutions of our happy country as—" and then pauses for the best possible comparison, his companion quickly provides: "As nigger slavery itself" (227). Passages like these admit no possibility that the language of freedom may be appropriated by antislavery activists, British and U.S. alike, in order to argue for a more perfect freedom, even though such appropriations had long been a staple of antislavery reform.

This withdrawal from the Anglo-American world is thematized in the novel's plot. Martin and his manservant remain isolated from the people of the United States. The elite shun the pair for their lack of money, while the manners of the rest are more than Martin can bear. Their only friend is a cultivated old gentleman who conveniently voices Dickens's own criticisms of the United States even more vehemently than Martin himself. But while Martin is isolated in the United States, he is nonetheless changed by it. It is in the United States that Martin is transformed from a monster of selfishness to a paragon of generosity. In this transformation, however, the United States functions only as a site of ordeal: it has nothing to teach; it offers much to endure. After Martin has lost all his money on a parcel of swampland, after he has wrecked his health by fever, at the moment when he fears that his only companion, the manservant, is about to die and leave him alone in the wilderness—at that moment, Martin is transformed. Once he has done so and his manservant has recovered, he immediately arranges for the two of them to return home. Before they leave, however, Martin makes sure to gather up the emigrants he met on the passage to the United States, all of whom are suffering, and shepherd them back home as well. And, as he does so, he carries with him the Dickensian novel of reform.

The biographer Peter Ackroyd has argued that it was in the United States that Dickens learned he was an Englishman.[32] He learned other things as well. He learned that he could present himself publicly as a reformer, which he would begin to do as soon as he returned to Britain. And he learned that he could be a reformist writer. But through his involvement with Anglo-America, Dickens developed a vision of reform that was profoundly national. Indeed, his focus on the national distinguished him from many of his Anglo-American contemporaries, including one who otherwise resembled him quite closely, Harriet Beecher Stowe.

32. Peter Ackroyd, *Dickens* (New York: HarperCollins, 1990), 365.

Stowe's 1853 tour of Great Britain was in many ways the complement to Dickens's tour of the United States a decade before. She was just as popular as he had been. When she landed in Liverpool, she found the docks thronged with people eager to be the first to catch a glimpse of her, and her subsequent travels toward London confirmed that she could go nowhere in public without attracting crowds who would call out her name and cheer. She had suffered just as much from unauthorized reprinting. But where Dickens complained about such reprinting, Stowe calmly received compensation. Her readers arranged a so-called Penny Offering in her name, which yielded, along with other gifts, more than twenty thousand dollars.[33] And Stowe also served, as Dickens had done, as a conduit for the transatlantic circulation of antislavery texts. A group of female antislavery activists organized a petition entitled "An Affectionate and Christian Address of Many Thousands of Women of Great Britain and Ireland to Their Sisters the Women of the United States of America" (1853), which protested slavery, in particular, the destruction of slave families and the denial of religious education to the slave. Lacking any other way of making their political will known, half a million women signed this petition. When complete, the signatures filled twenty-six thick volumes.[34]

When Stowe arrived in London, a dinner was given in her honor by the Lord Mayor. Dickens was invited as well. One dinner guest proposed a toast to "the literature of England and America" and praised both Stowe and Dickens for having used "fiction as a means of awakening the attention of the respective countries to the condition of the oppressed and suffering classes." In response, Dickens offered a revealing toast to Stowe. Calling her the "authoress of a noble book, with a noble purpose" and assuring her of a "welcome in any English home," he then went on to discuss not her book, *Uncle Tom's Cabin*, but rather one of his own, the recently published *Bleak House*.[35] In doing so, he turned the attention from the campaign against slavery, in which both persons from both nations were involved, to the more parochial reform that *Bleak House* was advocating, the reform of London's Chancery courts.

To juxtapose *Bleak House* and *Uncle Tom's Cabin* is to see the difference between national and transnational reform. *Uncle Tom's Cabin* focuses on

33. Joan D. Hedrick notes, in her excellent discussion of Stowe's tour, that many gave these gifts intending them to further the work of antislavery reform, not compensate Stowe for the losses of reprinting (*Harriet Beecher Stowe: A Life* [Oxford: Oxford University Press, 1994], 240).

34. Hedrick offers a full account of this in *Harriet Beecher Stowe*, 244–45.

35. Harry Stone describes this exchange in "Charles Dickens and Harriet Beecher Stowe," *Nineteenth-Century Fiction* 12, no. 3 (December 1959): 198.

the United States, but it imagines that the problem of U.S. slavery will find its resolution in other nations. Its noble mixed-race characters escape first to the northern states and then to Canada. After some time in Canada, they go on to France for further education, after which they plan, the narrator tells us, to settle permanently in Liberia. One of its comic black characters is rescued from slavery and taken to New England, where she, too, prepares to go to Africa as a missionary. Africa, then, is the place to which the novel's antislavery reform is tending. In *Bleak House*, by contrast, Africa is the place where reform fails. The novel sets the properly local concerns of its good characters, such as Esther Summerson, against the ludicrously global imagination of Mrs. Jellyby, with her focus on an Africa that the novel names Booriboola-Gha. The modest local actions of women like Esther (visiting one poor family, taking in one abandoned child, keeping house) will radiate outward, the novel implies, until they remake the entire nation. But the global imagination of reformers like Mrs. Jellyby does not enable a complementary concern with the local. Her "telescopic philanthropy" famously permits her to see "nothing nearer than Africa," certainly not the distress of her own family and the disorder in her own home.[36]

Dickens was not alone in expressing skepticism about African entanglements; the failure of the 1842 Niger Expedition had persuaded many British reformers to abandon their dreams of educating and civilizing the Africans.[37] But Dickens's response to Stowe reveals something more. In setting *Bleak House* alongside *Uncle Tom's Cabin*, in setting the Chancery courts against slavery, Dickens draws attention to his rejection of Anglo-American reform more generally. He had learned to be a reformer in the United States, and he had done his first reformist writings there, but he had since turned away from the reformist culture that had formed him. He did so in part because he was disillusioned by U.S. manners and in part because he was outraged by U.S. reprinting. But he also did so because national boundaries offered what he had been looking for since the earliest *Sketches by Boz*, a way of delimiting connections that could otherwise ramify beyond action or even comprehension. For Dickens, the withdrawal to the nation was what enabled reform.

36. Charles Dickens, *Bleak House* (1851–53; London: Penguin, 1996), 52.
37. Brahma Chaudhuri discusses Dickens's response to this in "Dickens and the Question of Slavery," *Dickens Quarterly* 6, no. 1 (March 1989): 4.

Chapter 4

Anne Brontë and Elizabeth Stoddard
Temperance Pledges, Marriage Vows

Charlotte Brontë and Elizabeth Stoddard constitute one of the standard pairings of transatlantic literary studies, and it was through this pairing that Stoddard was restored to the canon of American literature. Relatively well known in her own day, Stoddard wrote a number of short stories and a series of newspaper columns, as well as three novels. The first of these novels, *The Morgesons* (1862), was a succès d'estime, but it would soon be forgotten. It remained out of print through much of the twentieth century in large part because it did not fit into either of the genres commonly invoked in the canonization of antebellum U.S. fiction, being neither a (feminine) sentimental novel, nor a (masculine) romance. In order to argue for its literary value, then, the critics who rediscovered *The Morgesons* in the 1980s, Sandra Zagarell and Lawrence Buell, needed to find an alternate literary context in which it could be placed. They found such a context in the British novel. Observing Stoddard's personal affinity for the Brontës and the many inter-textualities between *The Morgesons* and *Jane Eyre* (1848), Zagarell and Buell argued that *The Morgesons* revises the female bildungsroman in the largely British mode of the female gothic.[1] As a consequence, *The Morgesons* is one of the few novels to have entered the canon under transatlantic auspices.

---

1. Lawrence Buell and Sandra Zagarell, "Biographical and Critical Introduction," *Morgesons and Other Writings*, xviii–xix. See also Anne-Marie Ford, "Gothic Legacies: *Jane Eyre* in Elizabeth Stoddard's New England," in *Special Relationships: Anglo-American Affinities and Antagonisms, 1854–1936*, ed. Janet Beer and Bridget Bennett (New York: Palgrave, 2002).

Significantly, this transatlanticism was of a particular moment, the moment when critics like Buell and Robert Weisbuch were seeking to theorize the felt dependency of U.S. literature on the British tradition.

Stoddard herself had much to say about transatlantic literary relations—both in the reviews she wrote for the *Daily Alta California* and in her own fiction. At times, she rejects the idea of British cultural preeminence. Charles Dickens intrudes on the world of *The Morgesons* in the course of making his famous U.S. tour, but the novel's characters respond to his visit with nothing but contempt. When the protagonist learns that they are staying in the same hotel as Dickens, one of her traveling companions exhorts her "not to look" at him. The protagonist complies, sardonically lamenting that she will thereby lose her chance of being "immortalized" along with all the other things that Dickens would find to criticize in the United States.[2] At other times, however, Stoddard claims that U.S. literature has not progressed as far as British or continental. In a review essay in the *Daily Alta California* devoted to women's writing, for instance, she sadly concludes that "we have no Elizabeth Browning, Brontë, George Sand or Miss Bremer, to offer to our enemies, the critics."[3]

Here, Stoddard places herself in a dependent, or at least belated, relation to Charlotte Brontë, but she more commonly describes that relation in terms of mourning. Stoddard mourns for the early deaths of Brontë and her sisters, and she mourns, in doing so, for the premature death of her own career. On the occasion of Charlotte Brontë's death, in 1855, Stoddard wrote a column that paid tribute to all three sisters. Praising *Wuthering Heights* (1847) and *The Tenant of Wildfell Hall* (1848) as "singularly original novels," she singles out *Jane Eyre* for praise as a "daring and masculine work." She goes on to describe their lives with such pathos that she ensures that her readers will share her "interest and sorrow" at the news that Charlotte Brontë is dead.[4] This mourning continues in the last of Stoddard's major short stories, "Collected by a Valetudinarian" (1870). The story describes the growing friendship between two middle-aged women, each suffering from an undefined melancholy, who are brought together by their shared interest in a third woman, an unpublished writer, now dead of tuberculosis. This writer is explicitly compared to Charlotte Brontë. Eventually, the two friends find the writer's diaries, in which descriptions of nature and musings on death are interspersed with commentary on her own writing: "Shall

2. Stoddard, *Morgesons and Other Writings*, 161.

3. Stoddard, "Our Lady Correspondent," *Daily Alta California*, 22 October 1854, reprinted in *Morgesons and Other Writings*, 314.

4. Stoddard, "Our Lady Correspondent," *Daily Alta California*, 2 June 1855, reprinted in *Morgesons and Other Writings*, 317.

I dare tell the truth about men and women?" one entry asks. "Can any wild invention excuse me for bringing to light that which exists with reason and with passion? Who may speak if I can not? I fear not my unborn publisher."[5] The implication is clear: Brontës do exist in the United States, and perhaps Barrett Brownings and Sands as well, but the publisher has not yet been born who is willing to print them.

This is a consoling account of Stoddard's own relatively unsuccessful career as a novelist, but the story's intertexts provide a more poignant one. The diary entries printed in the story are partly invented, but they are also partly drawn from Stoddard's own diaries. More specifically, they are drawn from the diary she kept a few years earlier while trying and failing to write her third novel, which she would ultimately publish as *Temple House* (1867). In this real-life diary, it is not impending death or "unborn publishers" that prevent a novel from being written but rather Stoddard's own creative exhaustion. An entry that begins, "Splendid spot to read & write in" (348) is followed by one that reads, "Seven days gone. & no writing" (354) and another, "My novel lags, and so do I" (355). By intermingling real and invented entries, and by attributing both to the unpublished Brontë of the United States, Stoddard's story—the last important work she would write—mourns the end and the failure of her own literary career. In this way, Stoddard neither competes with nor feels oppressed by the achievements of Charlotte Brontë. On the contrary, she identifies her own ambitions with those achievements ("to tell the truth about men and women"), and this identification becomes all the more precious once it becomes clear that her ambitions will not themselves be achieved.

But if Stoddard was connected to Charlotte Brontë through literary ambitions only partly achieved, she was connected to Anne Brontë through their shared engagement with the Anglo-American movement for temperance reform. This movement had given rise, as I showed in the previous chapter, to the experience meeting and the narratives that were typically recounted there: the temperance conversion narrative and the cautionary temperance tale. But it would also give rise, as I will show in this chapter, to the temperance pledge and, with the pledge, a revision of the conventional marriage plot. This revision took place in women's temperance fiction. Women had begun writing temperance fiction only a few years after men, and they soon came to dominate the field. And yet temperance reformers kept issuing calls for a specifically female temperance fiction, a fact that suggests that the genre was defined less by the gender of its authors than by its attention

5. Stoddard, "Collected by a Valetudinarian" (1870), reprinted in *Morgesons and Other Writings*, 298.

to female forms of suffering.[6] Where the early temperance fiction written by men had focused on the male drunkard, temperance fiction written by women focused instead on the harm done by male drunkards to women—to their mothers, sisters, daughters, and most of all to their wives. Only rarely in women's temperance fiction is the wife herself a drunkard. This focus on male drunkenness is in accord with the genre's fundamental concern, namely, female vulnerability within the family and within the domestic sphere. The causes and consequences of drinking are of interest only insofar as they throw this vulnerability into relief. That the domestic sphere is not the defense many women imagine it to be is made literal in one of the genre's most prevalent tropes. In story after story, the protagonist first recognizes the gravity of her husband's drinking or decides that she must flee only after he has in his drunkenness locked her out of their home.

The writers of women's temperance fiction created tropes and plots that would then be taken up by novelists who seem to have nothing at all to do with reform. From the short stories found in temperance newspapers, through the didactic fiction of Sarah Stickney Ellis, to the novels of Anne Brontë and Elizabeth Stoddard, drunkenness provided a way of describing the more general sufferings of marriage and sobriety, a way of emplotting their resolution. Indeed, so common was this usage of temperance tropes and plots that even so seemingly hermetic an author as Emily Dickinson remarked on it. "Do we 'get drunk'?" she asks in one of her poems. "Do we 'beat' our 'wife'?" The quotation marks slyly signal that the connection between drunkenness and abuse had already become a cliché.[7]

Marriage Reform and Women's Temperance Fiction

In the middle of the nineteenth century, reformers in both the United States and Great Britain sought to alter the conditions of marriage. Some reformers were radical in their conviction that marriage should become something altogether new. These were most commonly found in the United States, where various utopian communities experimented with plural or complex

6. See, for instance, the 1854 call from the New York State Temperance Society, which announced ten-dollar prizes for the best temperance stories written by women. Temperance stories written by men "dwell on the surface of things," the announcement claims, while temperance stories written by women would go "down to the great foundational principles on which the cause rests" ("$10 Premiums," *The Lily*, 1 May 1854, 1).

7. Emily Dickinson, "We—Bee and I—" *Poems by Emily Dickinson*, ed. Martha Dickinson Bianchi and Alfred Leete Hampson (1890; Boston: Little, Brown, 1957), 307.

marriage and the Mormons instituted a divinely sanctioned polygamy. Far more common, in both nations, were liberal efforts to reform marriage, specifically by rectifying the injustices of marriage law. These liberal efforts too began in the United States, but they soon spread to Britain, in large part through the personal friendship of Barbara Bodichon, an Englishwoman who also campaigned for women's education, with Elizabeth Cady Stanton and Lucretia Mott, two leaders of the U.S. campaign for women's rights. In the short term, these efforts to reform marriage law would give rise to a host of new divorce, custody, and property laws passed by state legislatures in the United States and to the Matrimonial Causes Act of 1857 and the Married Woman's Property Act of 1870 in Britain. In the longer term, they would give rise to the subsequent campaign for women's suffrage.

These efforts to alter the conditions of marriage emerged out of two existing reform movements: the antislavery campaign and temperance reform. Historians and literary critics of the present day who are interested in the women's rights movement have tended to focus their attention on the antislavery campaign.[8] The historian Ellen Carol Du Bois argues that the women's rights movement emerged from within the Garrisonian abolitionist wing of the antislavery campaign and then separated itself from the civil rights efforts of the Reconstruction era.[9] And the literary critic Karen Sánchez-Eppler has shown that women's rights activists drew extensively on the tropes of the antislavery campaign in their own reformist writings. But nineteenth-century historians of the women's rights movement placed equal emphasis on temperance reform. *The History of Woman Suffrage* (1881–1922), a monumental encyclopedia and compendium of documents inaugurated by Stanton and Susan B. Anthony, devotes equal time to each, and its two authors reproduce in themselves this coequal history, with Stanton having been active in the antislavery campaign and Anthony in temperance reform.

---

8. In this way, feminist critics and historians reflect the more general twentieth-century preference for antislavery over temperance reform. Ronald G. Walters has argued that the two movements are respectively over- and underemphasized in large part because the politics of the antislavery movement are recognizably liberal, even radical, while the politics of temperance reform are far more mixed. Equally important, in Walters's view, is the fact that it was the antislavery campaign that dominated national politics during the 1850s, while temperance was far more local—and far more successful. While the debate over slavery was vehement but fruitless, more than ten states outlawed the sale of alcohol entirely during the 1850s. Most of these laws were repealed, as was the constitutional amendment passed in the 1920s, but an irrevocable change in drinking habits was nonetheless achieved. *American Reformers, 1815–1860* (New York: Hill and Wang, 1978).

9. Ellen Carol DuBois, *Feminism and Suffrage: The Emergence of an Independent Women's Movement in America, 1848–1869* (1978; Ithaca: Cornell University Press, 1999), 22.

I will follow the lead of these nineteenth-century historians by paying attention to the antislavery movement's neglected counterpart.[10]

Drawn to these causes by a properly feminine concern for the suffering of others, women reformers found in both movements a training for causes of their own. Some antislavery societies provided money for women's rights speakers, and some antislavery newspapers provided space for articles about women's rights. The first women's rights newspaper in the United States, edited by Amelia Bloomer, was a temperance newspaper as well. More generally, female reformers learned from their participation in both movements how to organize a movement of their own. And they were soon motivated to do so. Active in both movements, they were nonetheless relegated to auxiliary roles and even forbidden to speak. In 1840, the British organizers of the World Antislavery Conference refused to seat female delegates from the United States, and the outrage of these delegates was the impetus behind the Seneca Falls Convention of 1848, the world's first convention for women's rights. In much the same way, female auxiliaries were not permitted to speak at the Sons of Temperance Convention in 1852 or at the World Temperance Convention of 1853. In response, Susan B. Anthony formed, and Stanton joined, the New York Temperance Woman's Society.

When these female reformers joined the campaign for women's rights, they brought with them the rhetorical resources of both temperance and antislavery reform. The two movements provided a powerful rhetoric for articulating the suffering that took place within the home. In describing the effects of drunkenness, temperance reformers depicted husbands who impoverished their families, husbands who beat their wives, and fathers who failed even to grieve for their children's deaths. In describing the effects of slavery, antislavery activists depicted sexual infidelity, illegitimacy, and domestic rape. But the two movements also provided a heuristic for analyzing the causes of this suffering, and it is here that they importantly diverged. They differed in their sense of what caused the problems in marriage and how these problems could be rectified.

From the antislavery campaign came a critique of marriage as unjust in its very structure. The slave served as a trope, as Sánchez-Eppler has shown, through which female reformers could articulate other ways in which persons are "owned, absorbed, and un-named."[11] This gave rise,

---

10. After all, temperance was a mass social movement, while antislavery activism, particularly of the abolitionist variety advocated by Stanton and Stone, was never more than a fringe cause.

11. Karen Sánchez-Eppler, "Bodily Bonds: The Intersecting Rhetorics of Feminism and Abolition," *Representations* 24 (Autumn 1988): 31.

most obviously, to a pointed critique of marital coverture. The legal convention that the wife was "absorbed" into the person of the husband was echoed by the cultural practice of having her adopt his name. Stanton protested this "unnaming" at the Woman's Rights Convention of 1856: "A woman has no name! She is Mrs. John or James, Peter or Paul, just as she changes master; like the Southern slave, she takes the name of her owner."[12] Lucy Stone went further, simply refusing to change hers. More generally, antislavery reform created a framework for thinking about the legal conferral and denial of personhood that put the person of the wife under the husband's control.

Like the antislavery critique of marriage, the temperance critique also focused on the unjust provisions of marriage law. But it presented itself not as challenging but rather as upholding the domestic ideal. The official account of temperance reformers' views on marriage is exemplified by Amelia Bloomer's speech "Women's Rights and Wrongs" (1853), the title of which was a familiar part of temperance rhetoric. Temperance reformers often suggested that women were merely seeking to defend themselves against "wrongs," not making a more threatening claim for "rights." In this speech, Bloomer argues that women are defended from the cruelty of male laws by the goodness of male hearts.[13] The distinction she draws between laws and hearts makes it easier for her to argue that the laws should be reformed, but it also requires an account of why, at times, male hearts are not defense enough. And here the difference between antislavery and temperance reform becomes clear. Antislavery activists increasingly insisted that the evil was in the system, not the slave owner, who might himself be kind or cruel. Temperance reformers, on the other hand, were able to say that the problem was not marriage itself but rather the bad husbands, their hearts perverted by drink, who abused its provisions.

Or this, at least, is the official temperance claim. What I want to argue, however, is that women's temperance writings, as opposed to the more politic temperance speeches, also criticize the institution of marriage itself, specifically, the ways in which it constrains female autonomy. Here, the problem is not, as it is in antislavery writings, the fact that women are owned by men, but rather the fact that they cannot own the property that grounds the autonomous self. Whereas antislavery writing is a kind of critique of possessive individualism, the claim that the person who does not own

12. Elizabeth Cady Stanton to the National Woman's Rights Convention at Seneca Falls, New York (24 November 1856), reprinted in *The History of Woman Suffrage*, ed. Elizabeth Cady Stanton, Susan B. Anthony, and Matilda Joslyn Gage (New York, 1881), 1:860.

13. The speech itself has been lost but was described in "Woman's Rights and Woman's Wrongs," *Milwaukee Daily Free Democrat*, 22 October 1853, 3.

him- or herself is not a person at all, temperance writing seeks instead to secure property for women as well as men. Alcohol is a useful figure in this context, not only because it displaces responsibility for "men's cruelty," but also because it conjures up the draining away of a family's resources, resources that the wife is seeking covertly to control.

Female temperance fiction is characterized by its attention to the sufferings that take place within marriage. Some of these stories simply lament these sufferings, while others use them to argue for divorce; all of them, however, focus their depiction of marriage specifically on the marriage vow. We can see this most vividly in Rose Terry Cooke's "The Ring Fetter" (1859). The story describes a woman who devoted her youth to the solitary care of an aged father and entered middle age worn and alone. She is vulnerable, therefore, to the appeal of an intemperate ne'er-do-well, the son of a tavern owner, and she marries him despite her neighbors' warnings. At this point in the story, the narrator pauses to addresses us. Convention requires, the narrator reminds us, that the story end at that point: just as the law brings a woman's legal existence to an end when she marries, so too the novel ends her existence as a character. But these conventions, legal and fictional, do not alter the fact that a woman continues to live, to either suffer or feel happiness, even after marriage. In the case of the protagonist, the narrator tells us, happiness could have come only if her literal death had coincided with the legal one. The story dramatizes this point by making the protagonist exist in a grim death-in-life, kept alive by her husband despite her wishes to die only so that he can have continued access to the money she holds in trust. "The Ring Fetter" culminates, as its title suggests, in a horrifying literalization of inviolable marriage: the husband welds his wife's wedding ring to a chain he padlocks around her hand, so that the ring "is as tight as the promise" it symbolizes.[14] Only then, after the truth of marriage as it is has been graphically displayed, is the wife granted the refuge of suicide.

Other stories straightforwardly advocate divorce. One is Frances Dana Gage's "Tales of Truth, Number One" (1852), which argues that the drunkenness of the husband should be understood as a unilateral revocation of the marriage vow: "Edward Harris had broken, in the sight of God and man, *his* marriage vow. The compact entered into, he had made null and void. He did neither *love, cherish,* nor *protect,* nor did he, *'leaving all others, cleave only unto her.'*"[15] Mary Chellis, in *Our Homes* (1881), secures a wife's freedom from a drunkard by allowing her to discover that her marriage is bigamous. "I am glad to know," the woman declares upon meeting her husband's other wife,

14. Rose Terry Cooke, "The Ring Fetter," *Atlantic Monthly,* August 1859, 170.
15. Frances Dana Gage, "Tales of Truth, Number One." *The Lily,* 1 January 1852, 2–3.

"that this man is not my husband."[16] In another novel, *Wealth and Wine* (1874), Chellis goes farther, pleading directly for divorce.

Another set of stories also depict the sufferings of marriage, but they imagine an alternative to death or divorce. They imagine that the failed marriage vow can be somehow rectified by a temperance pledge. Temperance was uniquely suited, among reform movements, to rethink marriage because one of its central structures, along with the conversions discussed in the last chapter, was the promise. There had been scattered writings against drinking in the seventeenth and eighteenth centuries, such as Increase Mather's *Wo to Drunkards* (1673) and Benjamin Rush's *An Inquiry into the Effects of Spirituous Liquors on the Human Body* (1790). But the temperance movement proper did not begin until the 1820s, when groups of elite men, first in the United States and then in Britain, began to form societies that were constituted by the signing of the temperance pledge. At first these pledges were understood as confirmations, the proof of a preexisting status; the already temperate signed the pledge to demonstrate that they drank wine only in moderation and drank liquor not at all. But as temperance gave way to teetotalism, to the thoroughgoing rejection of alcohol in all its forms, the pledge came to be seen as a way of transforming the self. It made the drunk into the sober by setting the will against the body, using the single act of signing a pledge to bring a lifetime of repetitive drinking to an end. By 1834, the American Temperance Society was able to announce that nearly one million men and women had taken the temperance pledge. As teetotalism became more and more radical, debates within the movement continued to center on the pledge, in particular on the differences between the so-called short and long pledges, the latter of which rejected medicinal alcohol and even communion wine. Only at mid-century did an emphasis on pledges turn to an emphasis on laws, with the rise, particularly in the United States, of prohibitionism.

Temperance reformers were highly conscious of the power of the pledge, aware of the ritual significance of its signing. In the *Preston Temperance Advocate*, an early and influential publication of British teetotalism, there is a warning to the organizers of temperance meetings that the pledge should be made as central as possible:

USEFUL ADVICE TO TEMPERANCE SOCIETIES

In attending many Temperance meetings of late, I have been struck with the careless manner in which signatures are received. For want of more formality

---

16. Excerpt from Mary Dwinnell Chellis, *Our Homes*, in *Water Drops from Women Writers: A Temperance Reader*, ed. Carol Mattingly (Carbondale: Southern Illinois University Press, 2001), 88.

> in this, the entrance is not made so impressive as it might be. . . . I would recommend that the Registrar should be fixed in a prominent part of the meeting place, and where he would be easy of access; that he should have a book regularly ruled with columns for date, name, trade, residence, and mark, and at the head of each page should be written or printed the pledge; that this pledge should be frequently read at the conclusion of the meeting; that every person wishing to join should either write his own name, or make his mark opposite, in a column for that purpose; and that every person should receive, upon entrance, a bill or tract containing his pledge.[17]

Certain temperance rituals, such as the signing of the pledge on the Fourth of July, implied that the pledge could ratify and secure other sorts of public promises. Women's temperance fiction suggests that it might do the same for the marriage vow as well.

These stories follow what I will call the "plot of doubled promising," in which the marriage vow is supplemented by the temperance pledge. Sometimes the pledge is made into a precondition for the vow, as when the heroine insists that, in the words of the famous temperance poem, "Lips That Touch Liquor Shall Never Touch Mine."[18] More interesting, however, are those narratives in which the vow is followed by the pledge and thus rectified by it. These stories often open with a marriage vow, that traditional structure of narrative closure, and go on to describe sufferings that are brought to an end only by a temperance pledge that serves the function of a second marriage vow. In *Teetotalism Triumphant: A Tragic-Comic Dramatic Tale* (1839), for instance, the main courtship plot is paralleled by three subplots, each of which pairs the two promises. The marriage of the protagonists, made possible by the man's newfound sobriety, is preceded by a triptych of scenes in which three already-married couples celebrate the rescue of their marriages from poverty by the husband's conversion to temperance. And *The Gin Shop*, a series of illustrations by George Cruikshank, concludes with what would become the emblematic image for this genre: the husband and wife standing a second time at the church altar, this time so that the husband can take the temperance pledge.[19]

---

17. "Useful Advice to Temperance Societies," *Preston Temperance Advocate*, May 1836, 34.

18. Harriet Glazebrook, "Lips That Touch Liquor Shall Never Touch Mine," in *Temperance Selections: Comprising Choice Readings and Recitations in Prose and Verse* (1893; Freeport: Books for Libraries Press, 1970), 139–43. For a narrative version, see Louisa May Alcott's *Silver Pitchers: and Independence, a Centennial Love Story* (Boston: Roberts Brothers, 1876).

19. See also Elizabeth Fries Lummis Ellet, "A Country Recollection; or, The Reformed Inebriate," in *The Adopted Daughter and Other Tales*, ed. Alice Cary (Philadelphia, 1859).

One of the earliest instances of the plot of doubled promising is Lucius Manlius Sargent's "My Mother's Golden Ring" (1833). Written by a man, the story is narrated by a woman. It opens with a rather cursory reference to the narrator's marriage ("Our wedding day—and it was a happy one"), before moving on to describe the ways in which that happiness is undone by her husband's increasing drunkenness. The central opposition in this story is between the good neighbor, who bails the narrator's husband out of jail and ultimately persuades him to stop drinking, and the bad minister, to whom the narrator earlier appealed and by whom she has been rebuffed. "My Mother's Golden Ring" in this way differs from later works of women's temperance fiction by making the negotiations of drunkenness and sobriety entirely a matter for men: the narrator-wife weeps and cajoles but has no power to make a difference. The story also differs from later fiction by understanding the temperance pledge to be a confirmation rather than a transformation; the husband and his good neighbor agree that he should wait through six months of sobriety before publicly signing the temperance pledge, for fear that an early lapse would discredit the clause. Where the story does importantly point to later versions of the plot is in its figuring of becoming sober as a new kind of marrying. In the six months before he signs the pledge, the husband wears a "golden ring" to remind him of his commitments.

By focusing on the temperance pledge, these stories subjected the marriage vow to critique—and even revision. This critique was both ideological and formal. Temperance fiction showed, on the one hand, that the marriage vow was not an adequate protection of a woman's rights, while it also showed that it was not an adequate form of closure for a narrative. These authors therefore opened up a possibility that the Anglo-American novel worked hard to deny, the possibility of a desire that transcends the limits of marriage. Written in this genre, the novels of Anne Brontë and Elizabeth Stoddard are haunted by adultery, even as they are fascinated by property.

Sarah Stickney Ellis and the Ends of Marriage

In *The Wives of England* (1844), the conduct writer Sarah Stickney Ellis offers an account of what is wrong with the conventional courtship plot. The novels young women read, organized as they are around courtship, are dangerous because they imply that marrying is "the end of woman's existence."[20] The courtship plot permits the single act of marrying to eclipse the ongoing

20. Sarah Stickney Ellis, *The Wives of England: Their Relative Duties, Domestic Influence, and Social Obligations* in *The Prose Works of Mrs. Ellis*, vol. 1 (New York: Appleton, 1843), 6.

state of marriage, the project of becoming a bride to obscure the work of living as a wife, and in doing so it prevents young women from seeing "marriage as it is."[21] For Ellis, the phrase "marriage as it is" does not name a verisimilar impulse to represent the actual experiences of marriage but rather an ideological impulse to inculcate the values of marriage as it should be. It is these values that shape the short stories she published two years earlier in a collection entitled *Family Secrets: Hints to Those Who Would Make Home Happy* (1841). Despite the collection's general title, there is only one secret to tell: all of these homes are threatened by drunkenness. And two of these stories resolve this threat through the plot of doubled promising.

"The Dangers of Dining Out" begins with the marriage of a promising young doctor and his beautiful young wife, and it traces the process by which the doctor's love of drink destroys first his social standing and his good looks, then his medical practice and his health, and finally almost his sanity. "The Favorite Child" begins with the marriage of a spoiled young woman who imagines herself to be an invalid and a narrow-minded and miserly old man, and it traces the process by which the young woman's growing reliance on patent medicines, stimulants, and even straight spirits leads her to humble herself before her maid and then her seamstress, and finally to steal from her husband, in order to get the alcohol she needs. Both of these stories begin with the marriage vow, and both are brought to an end by a temperance pledge.

In "The Dangers of Dining Out," the wife is called away for a few days, leaving the drunken husband at home with their children. He discovers his family has been eating coarse bread and milk, while he has been feasting on dainties; that his wife and daughters have been waking at dawn and taking in sewing, while he has been lying every morning in a stupor; and that his oldest son was taken from school so that his wine merchant's bill could be paid. The husband is anguished by these discoveries, but anguish alone cannot make him temperate. It is only the sight of his youngest son kneeling in prayer that moves the husband to utter a prayer of his own. In "The Favorite Child," the drunken wife is also saved by a child. After her drinking is discovered, she becomes an outcast within her own family; she is kept by their vigilance from further drinking, but no efforts are made to encourage true repentance. In the depths of her lonely rebelliousness, she becomes transfixed by a bottle of laudanum she finds, but her disordered thoughts are interrupted when her crippled young stepdaughter calls out in a dream,

---

21. Ellis, *Wives of England*, 5.

"mother, mother."[22] The wife asks what she might do to become in truth such a "mother" to the girl, and the girl replies with a request whispered in her ear, a request that makes her feel the shame of her drinking for the first time. The climax of both scenes comes when the drunkard, full of shame and repentance, falls on the floor in front of a child and starts to pray.

Made by a drunkard praying at the feet of a child, the temperance pledge reconfigures the marriage vow in two ways: by expanding a promise between husband and wife to include the entire family, and by altering that promise to require submission. Submission is something that Ellis's conduct books insisted on for wives, but her stories insist on the parallel submission of husbands. For it is to God, made present through the child's innocence and injury, that these second vows are made. The hierarchical relations between women and men are flattened, or even inverted, under the superior superintendence of God.

In this way, the plot of doubled promising enforces Ellis's evangelicalism. But the plot also enables critique. By extending narrative beyond the end set by the courtship plot, the plot of doubled promising requires that marriage itself be described, and this raises the possibility that marriage will be described, in a verisimilar sense, "as it is." As a consequence, Ellis's stories end up saying more than she perhaps intends. Specifically, they critique the very domestic ideal that she celebrates in her conduct books. They do so, in part, by underscoring the loneliness of a woman confined to the home. In "The Dangers of Dining Out," it is the husband who becomes the drunkard, and in "The Favorite Child," it is the wife, and the causes of their drinking are complementary. For men drink, according to Ellis, in the company of other men. They drink because they thrive on conviviality, because they are nostalgic for their bachelor days, because they fear seeming to be inhospitable or overly subject to the wishes of their wives. And women drink in order to alleviate the ailments they suffer, or imagine they suffer, when they are left at home alone. What drunkenness reflects, then, is men's departure from the home and women's confinement within it; it is a dangerous response to the emergence of separate spheres.

More extensively, however, these stories also criticize the workings of domestic economy. This is most clear in "The Favourite Child." After her wedding tour, the new wife moves into the house her husband shares with his daughters. Pleased by her reception and by the elegance of his rooms, she falls asleep dreaming of both the furniture she has already seen and the

---

22. Sarah Stickney Ellis, "The Favorite Child," in *Family Secrets; or, Hints to Those Who Would Keep Home Happy*, vol. 1 (1841; Philadelphia: Lea and Blanchard, 1842), 228. All further references will be marked in the text.

"treasures undisplayed" that she imagines must be hidden somewhere, "behind the scenes" (197). But when she awakens from her dreams, it is to discover that what lies "behind the scenes" of the Victorian house is not "treasure" but rather labor. For she returns to the drawing room in which she was received the day before, only to find that the chairs and sofas have been covered by damask cloths, that the curtains and rugs have been protected by calico sheets, and that all the movable ornaments have been put away. Her stepdaughters bustle around, erasing through the very act of housekeeping the rooms the wife first saw. The reality that returned to her as a memory in a dream is now shown to have been an illusion after all.

The obvious objects of criticism here are the stepdaughters who value efficiency over true comfort and the husband who values economy above all. But what begins as a criticism of a particular family modulates into a critique of domestic economy more generally. While the husband is unusual in bragging that his daughters save him the cost of a servant and his daughters unusual for delighting in their cheap methods for doing everything, the economic arrangements of their household turn out to be not so unusual after all. The daughters pride themselves, as Ellis's conduct books would have them do, on their domestic skills, on their ability to make by hand what others must buy. But Ellis here describes women's work in an economic language that strips away all presumption of love or generosity and lays bare the uncompensated labor on which all households depend: the husband need pay, Ellis points out, "for the raw material only," since he gets "the advantage of [his daughters'] labor gratis" (203).

If "The Favourite Child" lays bare women's responsibility for the workings of domestic economy, "The Dangers of Dining Out" shows the more troubling consequences of the fact that even this domestic economy is not under their control. A few months after their marriage, the husband announces that he has invited some friends over for dinner. The wife happily superintends an elaborate meal, complete with candles and flowers, but she is surprised to find, once she has left the gentlemen to their port, that they are very slow to rejoin her. She hears peals of laughter coming from the dining room, then snatches of song, then sounds that belie, Ellis tells us, the very humanness of their makers. Finally, the guests burst into the drawing room. One attacks the wife's young sister, tearing her dress from neck to hem, upending tables, breaking ornaments, and scattering the servants to every corner of the house. The wife is alarmed but unwilling to call for outside help and thus expose "the disorder of her household."[23] And it is precisely such "disorder" that her husband's debauches make literal, as he

23. Sarah Stickney Ellis, "The Dangers of Dining Out," in *Family Secrets*, 1:17.

and his friends undo the domestic labor that the wife has performed: she awakens the next morning to find glasses shattered, carpets torn, and the furniture grouped in ominous configurations. What this undoing of the housekeeping foreshadows, of course, is the coming loss of the house itself, the necessary sale of its furniture, as the husband's drinking drives the family into poverty. And once again, as during the drunken dinner party, there is nothing that the wife can do.

In the process of describing the pressures that drive wives to drink and the injuries they suffer when their husbands do, Ellis has stumbled upon other problems hidden within the home. That drunkenness might be a convenient figure for domestic problems more generally is further suggested by the collection's title. What this title suggests is not simply that drunkenness stands in for a range of problems, for all kinds of "family secrets," but also that temperance reform offers "hints" for solving them or, more precisely, a narrative structure through which their remedy can be imagined. For Ellis, the remedy is straightforward: she believes in temperance and she believes in the God before whom the temperance pledges are made. As a consequence, the critiques in her stories remain latent, and we are meant to believe that the temperance pledge has brought them to a true and happy end.

But while the plot of doubled promising reflects Ellis's commitment to temperance reform, the plot structure was subsequently taken up by novelists who were either skeptical of or ultimately indifferent to temperance. These authors, Brontë and Stoddard among them, drained the plot of reformist content and used it instead as an empty structure of closure. For them, the plot of doubled promising served purposes unrelated to temperance reform; indeed, purposes so unrelated that the doubled promise in both novels is not a temperance pledge but rather a second engagement promise or a second marriage vow. For Brontë and Stoddard, the plot served, as it had inadvertently done for Ellis, to throw into relief the property relations of marriage. They not only used a drunken husband to figure the threats to a woman's property but both also used the narrative space opened up between one promise and the next to renegotiate the property arrangements of marriage. The plot of doubled promising also served, as the cautionary temperance tale had done for Dickens, to license and organize the depiction of experiences that had so far been excluded from the novel: the repetitive sequence of days that makes up a marriage in Brontë; the desires that occur outside of marriage in Stoddard. In this way, the plot contributed to the development of realism. But in extending narrative beyond the marriage vow, the plot of doubled promising also raised the specter of adultery—a specter that Brontë suppressed and Stoddard embraced.

Marriage and Repetition in *The Tenant of Wildfell Hall*

Although little is known about the life of Anne Brontë, we have every reason to believe that she, along with her sisters, disapproved of drunkenness.
When they were young, their father founded a temperance society in his
parish; when they were older, they watched their brother Branwell slide into
drunkenness and dissipation. And so it is hardly surprising that nearly all of
the Brontës' novels contain some criticism of drinking. Hindley Earnshaw
drinks himself to death in *Wuthering Heights*, as does John Reed in *Jane Eyre*.
In *Villette* (1853), Lucy Snowe is hired to replace an Irishwoman discovered
with gin on her breath, while Jane Eyre attributes the strange noises coming
from the attic to the bottle of porter in Grace Poole's hand. In all of these
novels, however, drunkenness is confined to the margins of the text. Only
in *The Tenant of Wildfell Hall* does it become central, with much of the novel
devoted to tracing a drunkard's moral and physical decline.

When *The Tenant of Wildfell Hall* was first published, it shocked contemporary readers, who were accustomed to reading about drunkenness only
in temperance tracts, if at all, and it prompted a lively critical debate. The
reviewers agreed that *Tenant* was a powerful condemnation of drunkenness,
and they agreed that it was a triumph of verisimilitude, particularly in its
depiction of the drunkard's profanity, adultery, and threats of violence. What
they disagreed about was whether such verisimilitude belonged in the novel.
A reviewer for the *North American Review* praised its characters for being
"drawn with great power and precision" and its scenes for being "as vivid as
life itself," while a reviewer for the *Spectator* said that its subject matter was
too "coarse and disagreeable" for the novel itself ever to be "attractive."[24]
Brontë responded to her critics, in the preface to the novel's second edition,
by shifting the terms of the debate. Where her critics had focused on the
things she described, she drew attention to her motives for describing them:

> I find myself censured for depicting con amore, with "a morbid love of the
> coarse, if not of the brutal," those scenes which, I will venture to say, have not
> been more painful for the most fastidious of my critics to read, than they were
> for me to describe. I may have gone too far, in which case I shall be careful
> not to trouble myself or my readers in the same way again; but when we have
> to do with vice and vicious characters, I maintain it is better to depict them
> as they really are than as they would wish to appear . . . and if I have warned
> one rash youth from following in their steps, or prevented one thoughtless girl

24. E. P. Whipple, "Novels of the Season," *North American Review*, October 1848, 354–69;
rev. of *The Tenant of Wildfell Hall*, *Spectator*, 18 December 1847, 1217.

from falling into the very natural error of my heroine, the book has not been written in vain.[25]

This is an early defense of what would become purposeful realism, with Brontë justifying her depiction of the "coarse" and the "brutal" by the intentions that went into writing the novel and the effects she hopes it will achieve. In offering this defense, Brontë claims that the novel's verisimilitude is in the service of its reformist agenda: it is only in order to save a "rash youth" or a "thoughtless girl" that the novel has depicted drunkards "as they really are." But the novel is better understood when we see that its reformist agenda is also in the service of its verisimilitude. Moreover, the novel's verisimilitude is most innovative not when it uses a reformist agenda to justify the depiction of subjects that have hitherto been forbidden (brutality and drunkenness) but rather when it uses a reformist narrative to organize the depiction of more ordinary experiences that would otherwise be unrepresentable because of their repetitiveness.

Wildfell Hall is constructed as a narrative embedded within a narrative, much like its contemporary, *Wuthering Heights*. The embedded narrative is a diary, and it begins with a courtship plot. The diary's author, a young woman named Helen, has just returned from her first season in London, and she describes the various men whom she met there. She has rejected the proposal of one of these men, on the grounds that he is too old and too serious, but she clearly hopes to be proposed to by another, who is distinguished by dashing good looks and somewhat rakish ways. In due time, the rake proposes, and Helen accepts, despite the strenuous warnings of her guardian. The two marry, but the diary does not stop here. Instead it goes on, as Sarah Stickney Ellis's stories did, to tell the story of married life. But the author of this story, the diary-keeping Helen, finds her ability to tell it constrained by cultural as well as novelistic expectations.

The cultural expectations concern the woman's role in marriage. Helen's husband articulates these expectations, sounding as if he is reading from one of Ellis's conduct books. A wife, he believes, "is a thing to love one devotedly and to stay at home—to wait upon her husband, and amuse him and minister to his comfort in every possible way, while he chooses to stay with her, and, when he is absent, to attend to his interests, domestic and otherwise, and patiently wait his return" (233). Helen has no language in which to articulate an alternative. All she can say is that her husband's "notions of matrimonial

---

25. Anne Brontë, *The Tenant of Wildfell Hall* (1848; Oxford: Oxford University Press, 1993), 3–4. All further references will be marked in the text. Brontë is quoting from the *Spectator* review of 8 July 1848.

duties and comforts are not my notions" (232). Nor can Helen articulate a critique of her husband's actions. He seduces one of their houseguests while Helen is watching and dismisses their son as a "senseless, thankless oyster" and a "little worthless idiot" (230, 231), but all Helen can say in response, even in the privacy of her own diary, is that he is "not 'a *bad* man'" (232), merely a man whose notions of marriage are not Helen's own.

The representation of married life is also constrained by the formal expectation that novels should progress through a series of different events from beginning to end. Marriage, as Helen experiences it, is nothing but repetition. Every spring, her husband abandons her to spend four or five months in London; every fall, he returns to chafe against their quiet country life. During the day, when he is unable to ride and unwilling to read, he peevishly tries to distract her from the book or the child that absorbs her. In the evening, after dinner, it is the same all over again. Together, Helen and her husband endure the crushing boredom of country house life when it rains, when hunting season is over, when the guests have stayed too long. The difficulty of representing such repetition is registered in Helen's inconsistent entries in her diary. She writes only when something new has happened, allowing weeks or even months—once, a full year—to elapse between one entry and the next. But even though she writes only occasionally, her entries nonetheless resemble one another to a remarkable degree.

Brontë resolves the problem of repetition by taking up an alternate plot, namely, the cautionary temperance tale. The cautionary temperance tale enables the novel to articulate Helen's complaints about marriage. After her husband returns from a four-month sojourn in London entirely enervated by drink, Helen can for the first time openly criticize his behavior, first to herself and later to him. The fact that he has drunk to excess in London licenses her to admit that she would prefer that he stay with her at home; the fact that it is drink that has destroyed his health licenses her to question his insistence that she care for him, "wait upon" him, "amuse" him, "minister to his comfort," as he would like. In this way, his intemperance enables a range of criticisms that goes much further than drinking. Indeed, Helen first chooses to discuss her husband's drinking with him on the night that she witnesses his flirting with one of their guests. Even she admits that the flirtation is "not referrable to wine" (223), and yet it is the wine that somehow justifies her in her complaint.

The drunkenness of Helen's husband not only provides a language for articulating the novel's analysis of marriage but also provides a plot capable of structuring its depiction. The cycles of her husband's hunting, his going to London, and his boredom when he can do neither threaten to go on forever, but his drinking is a repetitive act that takes place in relation to a foreseeable end. Each drink leads to another just like it, but every bad consequence of drinking, every bout of illness or temper, prefigures the worse consequences yet to come. These consequences are visible to us almost from the beginning, made so, significantly enough, when Helen's husband callously refers to Helen's own father as having "dr[u]nk himself to death" (256). In this way, the downward trajectory of the cautionary temperance tale confers meaning on otherwise repetitive events. Everything that happens is now significant because it either hastens or slows the inevitable decline of Helen's husband, and our sense of relief, our patience with seemingly trivial details, comes from the fact that we can now project the narrative's end.

What I am arguing, then, is that Brontë took up the subject of drunkenness because it helped to resolve certain representational problems that had emerged in the middle of the novel. Certainly, there is little reason to believe that she took up the subject in the hopes of acting on her readers. In the world of the novel, after all, temperance writings have remarkably little power. This becomes clear when we see how little effect Helen's diary, a cautionary temperance tale, has on the characters who read it. Helen's diary becomes a text that can be read by other characters when we move from the embedded narrative to the frame story. The frame story begins in a small farming village with the arrival of a mysterious widow and child, who will prove to be Helen and her son. Helen's difference from the villagers is highlighted during the first visit that she pays, when they offer her young son a glass of wine. He shrinks from it, and Helen explains that she has trained him to be disgusted by wine. The villagers are shocked by this, none more so than a young gentleman farmer, who fancies himself the beau of the village. He argues that Helen's policy will deprive her son of the manliness that comes from meeting and triumphing over temptation. Helen is not persuaded, and the two part on bad terms. Over time, however, the "beau" falls in love with Helen and tries to court her. She demurs, he persists, and finally she rejects his proposals, giving him her diary in order to explain her reasons. Reading this diary, which makes up the middle section of the novel, the suitor learns that she is not a widow but a still-married woman who has fled her husband because of his adultery, his brutality, and his mistreatment of their child.

Reading this diary, Helen's new suitor might have learned something else as well, namely, the danger that convivial drinking can lead to dissipation and the destruction of a home. But he does not. At no point does he imagine that the consequences of Helen's husband's drinking might constitute any warning about his own. He reads the diary and is not reformed. The suitor is, of course, notoriously fatuous and obtuse, and yet he is not entirely wrong in his reading. For the suitor's drinking is, like Helen's own advocacy of temperance, a topic that the novel suddenly and entirely abandons toward its end. We see this after Helen's husband dies and she and the suitor are finally free to marry. Helen, who has lived through and fled from the drunkenness of one husband, marries another without insisting that he stop drinking or even discussing whether he should. Moreover, she and the suitor never resolve the question over which they first argued, about whether or not she is right in refusing to allow her young son to drink. Whatever Brontë's own commitment to temperance might have been, Helen's commitment to it has been entirely forgotten. And in this we see that the cautionary temperance tale is employed for formal, rather than reformist, reasons.

Brontë borrows another plot from temperance fiction as well, the plot of doubled promises. Helen's first marriage is reiterated and seemingly rectified by her second. But this rectification is at best incomplete, as a comparison of the novel's two proposal scenes suggests. In the first proposal scene, it is the husband-to-be who answers, as well as asks, all of the questions, while Helen oscillates between ineffectual protests and telling silences: "Silence again?" he asks. "That means yes.—Will you bestow yourself upon me?—you will!" (159). In the absence of verbal exchange, there is a bodily progression. Helen's shoulder is "gently touched," her hand is "forcibly possessed" and then "taken" once more, she is "half embraced," she is fully embraced, she is "nearly squeezed to death" in her future husband's arms, and finally she is again "caught . . . in his arms" and "smothered with kisses" (158–59). It is at this point that the two are discovered by Helen's aunt, who sternly reminds them that marriage requires more rational deliberation than they have so far shown. It is the passion of the proposal scene that distresses Helen's aunt, but it is the economics of the marriage that will disturb her uncle, economics that have already been figured in both Helen's silence and her intended husband's embrace.

Helen and her intended husband approach one another on terms of economic equality, she with her small inheritance and he with his greater holdings and greater indebtedness. But this equality is quickly undone by Helen's insistence that the two be, as she phrases it, "united." She forbids her uncle to negotiate marriage settlements on her behalf, proclaiming that "all I have will be his, and all he has will be mine" (168–69). But this is a fond hope under Victorian marriage law. The "uniting" that Helen insists on erases the distinctions that settlements would have secured: her property and her legal identity are subsumed into her husband's, just as she has been enclosed within his embrace and spoken for by his words.[26] It is, quite simply, on

---

26. The right of married women to retain control of the property they had brought into the marriage was not secured until 1882. See Lawrence Stone for the most important account of changes in England's marriage laws (*The Road to Divorce: England, 1530–1987* [Oxford: Oxford University Press, 1990]).

the difference between "his" and "mine" that the difference between "he" and "I" depends. Having given up her property, then, Helen gives up her freedom, subjecting herself instead to her husband's domestic tyranny; the money she will secretly earn as she plans her escape figures the grounding of freedom in property.

The novel's second proposal scene attempts to rectify the failures of the first. The suitor is diffident where the husband was overbearing, Helen is articulate where earlier she was silent, and the passionate embraces are replaced by a rose that is extended, snatched away, and fervently kissed. And yet, despite these surface differences, the two scenes lead to the same end. The suitor has come to court Helen as soon as he learns that her husband has died, but he is held back from proposing to her by the discovery that she is now a wealthy woman, having inherited her uncle's large estates. Helen breaks this impasse in a surprising way: by ceding to her suitor control over her property. As soon as she has done so, she then tries to exact in return a set of promises about its disposition and about the treatment of her relatives. In this way, Helen attempts to remedy the failures of the first marriage vow by negotiating her own marriage settlements before the second. But this is an unsatisfactory solution. Helen is ceding the very property that secures her autonomy as a contractual agent, and the promises she exacts from her suitor inevitably lack the force of a contract.

In this way, Brontë makes use of what Ellis somewhat inadvertently achieved. She uses one temperance narrative (the cautionary temperance tale) to represent "marriage as it is," and she uses another such narrative (the plot of doubled promising) to throw into relief the property relations of marriage—and even to attempt to remedy them. But Brontë departs from Ellis in exploring what it would mean for the marriage vow to be no longer closural, whether formally or ideologically. The Anglo-American novel has traditionally understood this problem in terms of adultery. But *Tenant* suggests, by contrast, that the displacing of the marriage vow will lead to something altogether more alarming than adultery: a series of courtships that become meaningless through repetition.

The novel's most characteristic grouping is Helen alone among people who are at best unsympathetic and at worst actively hostile. Helen surrounded by a crowd of London beaux and debutantes gives way to Helen surrounded by her husband's drunken guests, which gives way in turn to Helen surrounded by the suspicious and gossiping villagers. Within each of these groupings, there is one man who actively, aggressively, even violently pursues her—her husband in London, his friend at their estate, and finally the suitor in the village Helen hopes will be a refuge. Having succumbed to her husband's pursuit, having believed his false promises, and having suffered the consequences, Helen is wary of other pursuers, even when they pose as rescuers. She attempts to fend them off by securing from each the promise to pursue her no more, but this is a promise that each breaks, easily and soon. In thematic terms, the failures of their promises, particularly the failure of the promises made by the suitor whom she will take as her second husband, undermine our confidence in the novel's conclusion; in formal terms, the courtship plot is reduced to incoherence by the almost meaningless repetitions of pursuit and promising. In Ellis's marriage stories, the temperance pledge was structurally as well as ideologically conclusive because it was endowed with religious authority; in *The Tenant of Wildfell Hall*, however, the second promise is finally no different from the first.

One sign of this is interchangeability. Helen's suitor resembles her husband to a striking extent. Not only does the suitor believe, as the husband did, that drinking is the prerogative of manliness, but he too is the cosseted son of an indulgent mother, he too behaves irreverently in church, and he, even more than the husband, responds to provocation with violence. His violence is all the more troubling because it comes as a surprise. The husband's drunkenness offered Brontë a conventional occasion for depicting male violence, but it is an occasion she seldom makes use of. She chooses to channel the novel's violence through the suitor instead. To be sure, the suitor refuses this characterization of his behavior, and when his actions are called "brutality" by another character, the word enters his own narration in the quotation marks of denial (397). But "brutal" the suitor certainly is, responding to all provocations with violence. What begins as a metaphorical violence—slamming doors, stalking through fields—gradually becomes more real and more dangerous. He grabs the reins of the horse another man is riding, and he later attacks this man, beating him in the head with a metal-handled whip, leaving him dazed and bleeding on the side of a rarely traveled road. The man he has attacked turns out to be Helen's brother, but even this knowledge when it comes cannot transform the suitor's hatred into anything more benign than rivalry and suspicion.

The suitor's acts of violence thus stand as the physical correlate for passions that are not simply socially transgressive, as is his love for Helen, but more deeply unsettling in their lack of reason and lack of motivation. The irrationality of his behavior prompts us to ask whether he is in fact an improvement over her husband. But to articulate the question in terms of choice, to argue that Helen may have chosen unwisely again, is to miss the ways in which her marriage to the suitor empties out the very possibility of choosing. That the suitor is not simply flawed but flawed in precisely the same ways as Helen's first husband demonstrates the essential interchangeability of husbands. Helen may feel that the suitor is different, Brontë may intend the second marriage vows to confirm his reformation, but the novel is structured by the interchangeability of men—and the repetitions of their promises.

Marriage and Possession in *The Morgesons*

In her columns for the *Daily Alta California*, Elizabeth Stoddard commented on many of the reform movements of the day. She tended to take a dim view. She was especially critical of reformers' attempts to alter marriage law. Her earliest articulation of this critique was prompted by the 1855 marriage of the British antislavery activist Henry Blackwell and the U.S. antislavery activist Lucy Stone. Together, the two had written a "Marriage Protest," which was read aloud at the ceremony and then published in a number of newspapers, including William Lloyd Garrison's abolitionist *Liberator*. The "Protest" begins by announcing that their wedding is intended to acknowledge Stone and Blackwell's affection for one another, without conferring any sanction on or suggesting any agreement with "the present laws of marriage," laws that, in their view, confer on husbands rights that "no honorable man would exercise" and that "no man should possess." The "Protest" then goes on to catalogue the particular laws that Blackwell and Stone find most objectionable, including the ones that deny mothers any control over their children, wives any control over their property or earnings, and widows any significant share of their husbands' estates. But above all else, Stone and Blackwell protest the fact that the law gives to the husband "custody of the wife's person."[27] A few years later, John Stuart Mill and Harriet Taylor would marry in a similar gesture of protest, with Mill explicitly renouncing all unjust rights that marriage would confer on him.

In attacking Blackwell and Stone's marriage, Stoddard takes a position that is conservative and radical at the same time. From a conservative perspective, Stoddard criticizes Stone for failing to meet conventional standards of womanliness. She begins by noting that Stone was attended to the altar by Blackwell's two sisters, one the first woman doctor in Britain and the other a translator of George Sand. Of these women, Stoddard says only, in an irony no doubt clear to her audience, that they are "homely and honorable women all." And she concludes her column in much the same vein, ridiculing Stone for the dirtiness of her stockings, the shabbiness of her bonnet, and her "damp, mouldy smell." But Stoddard is quite radical when she criticizes

27. Quoted in Andrea Moore Kerr, *Lucy Stone: Speaking Out for Equality* (New Brunswick: Rutgers University Press, 1992), 72. Chris Dixon has discussed the self-consciously exemplary nature of the Blackwell-Stone marriage in *Perfecting the Family: Antislavery Marriages in Nineteenth-Century America* (Amherst: University of Massachusetts Press, 1997).

both Stone and Blackwell for allowing prudential concerns rather than passion to govern their behavior. Here, she compares them unfavorably with the very George Sand whom she disparaged just one paragraph before. Sand may have erred morally in her liaison with Chopin, Stoddard notes, but she did so in accordance with her deepest convictions. And she was large-souled in her love for him and generous in her care once love had gone and illness had set in. Quite different, in Stoddard's view, is the process by which Stone and Blackwell "took sundry precautions, one against the other, by contract beforehand."[28] For Stoddard, passion is opposed to interest, and prudence to love. In this way, Stoddard comes closer to those radicals seeking to redefine marriage entirely than to liberal reformers like Blackwell and Stone.

Two years later, however, Stoddard would come to a different view of liberal reforms, in particular of Stone and marriage and woman's property more generally. In a *Daily Alta* column from 1857, Stoddard describes the Seventh Annual Woman's Rights Convention, at which Stone was one of the speakers. Stoddard's tone is equivocal throughout the piece. "These Conventions make people think," she admits, before going on to add, "after they have done laughing." Once Stoddard herself has done laughing, however, she finds herself persuaded by much of what the speakers have to say. She agrees that women should have access to employment and should enjoy full property rights, and she is at least partly persuaded by one speaker, Mary Davis, who observes that wives are the property of their husbands and insists that they should not be. "Here she became worth the listening," Stoddard recalls. "Taking for a text an opinion of Judge Reeves, 'That a woman should have no individual rights, because her husband has the right of possession of the person of his wife'—she came down on the audience with Thor's hammer." Stoddard watches, with some amusement, as the other speakers seek to distance themselves from this last speech, and she then concludes, "Mrs. Davis is right for all that; I am glad to get the truth anywhere." And the "truth" is, Stoddard tells us, that women have a "right to self-possession."[29]

Stoddard offers her own liberal critique of marriage law in the short story entitled "Lemorne versus Huell" (1863), and she relies on antislavery tropes to do so. She uses them to show that the self-possession Davis and other activists are seeking is the very foundation of personhood. The protagonist of the story, a dependent young woman, is forced to work as companion to her invalid aunt, who has long been embroiled in the lawsuit named in the title.

28. Stoddard, "Our Lady Correspondent," *Daily Alta California*, 19 May 1855, reprinted in *Morgesons and Other Writings*, 317, 318.
29. Stoddard, "Our Lady Correspondent," *Daily Alta California*, 11 January 1857, reprinted in *Morgesons and Other Writings*, 327.

She is sent riding every afternoon by her aunt, and she one day encounters the saturnine lawyer who is representing her aunt's opponent. Upon meeting him, the niece abruptly announces, "I am a runaway," and then asks him, "What do you think of the Fugitive Slave Bill?" To this, the lawyer replies that he approves of "returning property to its owners."[30] In this way, the protagonist identifies herself as property, and the story then explores the psychic consequences of living in this state.

The protagonist is unable to make sense of what is happening around and to her until after she ceases to be property. When the aunt and the lawyer finally meet, a conversation takes place in front of the protagonist that the protagonist does not seem to understand: the aunt informs the lawyer, in front of her niece, that she would leave all of her money to the niece if she were to prevail in the suit against the lawyer's client. The offer is clear, the lawyer soon proposes, and the niece accepts. The niece has heard the aunt's offer, but she does not seem to take in its meaning. The aunt does, indeed, win the case, and the niece becomes her acknowledged heir. The story ends with the niece suddenly awaking in the middle of the night, recalling the conversation, and realizing, in what serves as the story's closing line, "*My husband is a scoundrel*" (283). This is the most anticlimactic of revelations; it is something that we have known ever since the proposal scene. But it is something that the niece did not know—could not know—until she was no longer the "property" of another but rather, because of her inheritance, self-possessed.

Where "Lemorne versus Huell" uses antislavery tropes to reveal the consequences of failing to possess oneself, *The Morgesons* uses temperance narratives to emplot its protagonist's efforts to secure the property on which the autonomous self depends. The reclamation of a drunken man serves, as it did in Sarah Stickney Ellis, to secure a woman's control over the household economy. At the same time, however, drinking serves as a powerful figure for desire of all kinds. Stoddard took this view of drinking in one of her early columns on temperance reform. When the so-called Maine Law was passed in New York City, prohibiting alcohol as of July 1855, Stoddard wrote a column first satirizing, then attacking, its utopian presumptions. She begins by listing all the benefits that are certain to follow prohibition: happy wives, virtuous children, and no more orphans, which is to say, no more death. And she then goes on to make the same sort of objection more seriously. The problem with prohibition, she argues, is that it imagines human nature can be changed. Men cannot be made chaste by imprisoning prostitutes, nor

---

30. Stoddard, "Lemorne versus Huell," *Harper's New Monthly Magazine* 26 (1863), reprinted in *Morgesons and Other Writings*, 275.

can they be made sober by outlawing alcohol. "The tendency of all life," Stoddard concludes, "is to excess."[31] Excess, in this account, is what dooms reforms to failure, and it is also aligned with the actions of large-souled women like Sand. The tension between drinking and temperance, between desire and self-possession, structures *The Morgesons*.

The Morgesons was perhaps best captured in the letter Thomas Wentworth Higginson wrote to his wife upon first meeting Emily Dickinson. Trying and failing to describe the reclusive and eccentric Dickinson, Higginson concluded by saying that she could have been a character in *The Morgesons*. With this remark, Higginson pointed to the strangeness of the characters, particularly the protagonist's sister, who pins living butterflies under her apron when she is a child, lives exclusively on milk and toast through her adolescence, and spends much of her life in a house on the shore, refusing ever to look at the sea. But Higginson's remark is also suggestive because it points to the thematic and formal similarities between Stoddard's fiction and Dickinson's poetry. Both emerge out of, and struggle with, an old New England Puritanism, and both figure the erotic in remarkably violent terms. Moreover, Stoddard's narration is nearly as elliptical and elusive as Dickinson's poetic voice.

A bildungsroman modeled on *Jane Eyre*, *The Morgesons* follows its protagonist, Cassandra Morgeson, as she is formed by three extended visits in three representative milieux. First sent to Barmouth to be educated in the home in which her mother was reared, Cassandra is confronted by the narrow Puritanism of the artisanal class, and she learns to rebel against the model of dutiful daughterhood exemplified by her aunt. Then sent to Rosville to be finished in the home of a distant cousin, she finds herself in the extravagant world of the rising industrial class; in her cousin's house, she learns to reject the model of passionless wifehood exemplified by her cousin's wife. Finally, Cassandra is invited to the home of a prominent old New England family in Belem, where she discovers an elite world of cultured and snobbish women and frustrated and resentful men; here, she sets herself against the powerful mother, who does everything she can to destroy the growing attraction between Cassandra and her son. Upon returning home from this last visit, however, Cassandra finds her own mother dead. It now falls to her to manage the household, tend to the family, and in all ways take on her mother's role.

In this way, Cassandra's own *Bildung* comes to an end. To be sure, she continues to grow and develop—both in evident ways and more covertly. But the plot is now propelled not by her development but rather by the

31. Stoddard, "Our Lady Correspondent," *Daily Alta California*, 19 May 1855, reprinted in *Morgesons and Other Writings*, 316.

development of the two brothers who come to court Cassandra and her sister. Suddenly balked of the inheritance they expected, the brothers are suited to do no productive work, and the mark of their unsuitedness is drunkenness and dissipation. This is a surprising turn for the novel to take, given Stoddard's own suspicion of temperance reform, a suspicion that is fully expressed within the novel. *The Morgesons* takes place in a world in which drinking is still a matter of course: wine comes with dinner; sherry with afternoon tea; port with traveling. But temperance reform is encroaching on the periphery. Cassandra returns from a year away to find that a temperance hall has been erected in her hometown. And this emergent temperance is capable of recoding all that surrounds it. The name of the Morgesons' family retainer—Temperance—seems Puritan at the beginning of the novel but more and more teetotal as the novel progresses, and the lines that one character quotes from a poem by Ben Jonson at first sound as if they were taken from a temperance publication: "Drink to me only with thine eyes, / And I will pledge with mine, / The thirst that from the soul doth rise, / Doth ask a drink divine" (174). In the face of all this, Cassandra is as skeptical and satirical as Stoddard herself would be. Riding in a stagecoach, Cassandra finds herself seated with passengers traveling to a temperance hotel and silently offers them a swig from her flask.

Even more than in *The Tenant of Wildfell Hall*, drunkenness is made a subject of the novel in order to make available two temperance plots. Stoddard uses these plots to carry the novel forward once Cassandra's *Bildung* has been brought to an end. The cautionary temperance tale is enacted by Cassandra's sister and the Somers brother who courts her. Once the two marry, the brother, who has briefly become more temperate, quickly returns to his earlier habits of drink. As his bouts of drunkenness become more severe and more frequent, Cassandra's sister remains remarkably disengaged. "Why do you drink brandy?" (244), she whimsically asks, before wandering out of the room. This is far different from the tears and pleadings of Ellis's heroines or Brontë's. In the end, not only does the brother die, but he also leaves behind him a baby that neither cries, nor moves, nor sees.

The plot of doubled promising is present as well. Stoddard uses it, as Ellis and Brontë did, to renegotiate the property relations of marriage, but she also uses it to depict what Ellis could not conceive of and Brontë worked to deny: that desire exists outside of the courtship plot and after the wedding vow. In this way, Stoddard shares Stone's and Davis's intense concern with the property rights of women and the necessity of female self-possession. On the other hand, she is attentive to all that Sand represents, namely, the unruly passions that exist before and outside and after the courtship plot. The doubled promises, like so much else in *The Morgesons*, are quite oblique, constituted not by explicit utterances but rather by the exchange of two watches that are scratched with hidden inscriptions taken from Latin verse. The brother who is courting Cassandra, Desmond Somers, sends one of these watches to her after she confesses that she has loved another man, her cousin, before him. The sending of the watch thus marks Desmond's acceptance of the fact that Cassandra's passions precede his courtship of her. That he sends her not a ring but rather another piece of jewelry, underscores the fact that his passions precede the courtship as well as hers. Both he and Cassandra wear rings already—Cassandra the diamond ring that her cousin has given her, and Desmond the golden ring he once gave to a nameless young woman he loved and abandoned.

In this way, their courtship encodes the extramarital desires that everywhere surround them. The novel is full of vaguely adulterous mothers, mothers whose late-life babies cannot be entirely explained: Cassandra's sister reports to her that the family minister "likes" their mother and "watches her so" when she is holding her newly born son (42–43), and it remains an open question how Desmond's mother, the wife of an invalid, was able to become pregnant again. The secret of adultery is something that Cassandra approaches more and more closely in each of the visits she pays. In Barmouth, she learns of her mother's previous love affairs; in Rosville, she becomes adulterous herself, desiring her married cousin; and in Belem, the doubling of two brothers courting two sisters leads to persistent confusion about who is being courted by whom. But she is able to come to terms with adultery once watches take the place of rings, thus bringing a series of erotic possibilities to an end.

That the piece of jewelry Desmond sends is a watch has another significance as well: it points forward to a future moment, thus signaling a promise whose performative effect is oddly delayed. "I was to wear [the watch] from the second of July," Cassandra tells us. "It was small and plain, but there were a few words scratched inside the case with the point of a knife, which I read every day" (227–28). What these words might have been goes unsaid. And indeed it is not until Desmond arrives two years later, on the second of July, that we begin to understand what the watch is intended to symbolize: Cassandra shows him the watch she has been wearing for the past two years, and he takes "one exactly like it from his pocket, and showed me the inscription inside" (250). We then understand that the watches have been functioning as a pair of preliminary promises used to create a period of time in which the two can prepare themselves for the real engagement promises to be made—or rather, in which Desmond can prepare himself. When he returns, he tells Cassandra what she seems to have already known, that he had "to break [his] cursed habits" in order to prove himself "worthy of you"

(250). It is only when he succeeds in doing so that his prior promise to marry Cassandra can be brought into existence, or at least to readerly awareness. In an important way, the first promise does not even exist until it has been rectified and made real by the second.

But Cassandra, too, has had her work to do during the intervening years, although that work is less clearly named. She has consolidated her possession of the Morgeson family house, and in doing so she has consolidated her possession of herself. The novel's opening words, spoken about Cassandra by her aunt, are "That child . . . is possessed" (5). In suggesting that Cassandra might be "possessed" by demons, her aunt is seeking to make sense of the more troubling fact that Cassandra is in fact possessed by no one at all. It is clear that Cassandra's coming into full personhood will require her to be possessed. But it remains an open question whether she will be possessed by another through marriage, a state that has left her sister with "a dispossessed air" (159), or whether she will possess herself by owning property. Cassandra does the latter and thus makes possible a marriage on more equal terms. The novel's final chapters do show, to be sure, Cassandra taking up the familiar tasks of domesticity, but they also show her sending away old servants, exiling her sister, and refusing to allow her father to return to the family house with his new wife. She is left entirely alone by the time of Desmond's return, and she feels what she calls "an absolute self-possession" (248).

But Stoddard does not celebrate this self-possession without ambivalence. For the property that Cassandra seizes control of, the property that grounds her autonomous self, comes from a questionable source. When Cassandra first attends school, at Barmouth, she finds herself among the daughters of wealthy merchants. These other girls do not know that Cassandra is also a merchant's daughter, and they look down on her and exclude her from their games. Cassandra consoles herself with the thought that the family money they pride themselves on comes from tainted sources. One student hides the fact that her grandfather—"'Black Peter,' as he was called"—made his money from excursions on the River Congo, and another hides that her grandfather made his money from "West India Rum" (34). There is a double resonance in these two repressed trades, the trade in slaves and the trade in rum, for both have their correlate in the newer mode of transatlantic exchange, the antislavery campaign and temperance reform. The triangle trade from which the Massachusetts merchants made their money thus foreshadows the two reform movements that would give rise to Stoddard's own novel. And this past history of exploitation calls into question whatever autonomy Cassandra may achieve. Cassandra mocks "Black Peter," the former slave trader, for never being able, no matter how respectable he later became, to approve of plans to resettle the slaves in Liberia. And yet she never tells us where her own family's money comes from—and how her own choices and commitments might be similarly constrained.

In this way, Stoddard casts a critical light on the genre that *The Morgesons* borrows from. While temperance reformers tended to argue that the wrongs of marriage would be righted when husbands were reclaimed from drunkenness, the authors of women's temperance fiction suggested, by contrast, that marriage cannot be reformed until its property arrangements are rectified. This rectification is what Sarah Stickney Ellis and Anne Brontë struggle to imagine. But Stoddard reminds us that property has its own history, a history that threatens to compromise whatever autonomy women might seek to achieve.

Chapter 5

George Eliot and Henry James

Exemplary Women and Typical Americans

In the autobiographical writings he composed at the end of his life, Henry James describes the last of his ill-fated encounters with George Eliot. In the fall of 1878, he had gone to the country to visit a friend and learned that Eliot was renting a nearby cottage with her companion, George Henry Lewes. When James called on Eliot and Lewes, he found them both in low spirits, and it quickly became clear that nothing would please them so much as his departure. He accordingly left after the briefest of visits, only to be recalled, at the door of his carriage, by Lewes. Lewes was holding a pair of volumes that James's friend had urged on Eliot a few weeks earlier, and he now asked James to return them. The request was made with considerable impatience and more than a little disgust: "Ah those books," Lewes exclaimed, "take them away, please, away, away!"[1] James did so, only to find that "those books" were the two volumes of his own most recently published novel, *The American* (1876–77).[2] What made the episode so humiliating, James recalls, was the fact that no insult had been intended. It was clear to him that Eliot and Lewes had simply forgotten either that the author of the

1. Quoted from Henry James, *The Middle Years* (New York: Scribner's, 1917), 83.
2. Fred Kaplan discusses this episode in *Henry James: The Imagination of Genius* (New York: William Morrow, 1992), 194, as does Leon Edel in *The Life of Henry James: The Conquest of London, 1870–1881* (Philadelphia: J. B. Lippincott, 1962), 369–70. Edel claims that Lewes was returning not *The American* but rather *The Europeans*, but in either case the specifically transatlantic nature of the rebuke remains.

unwanted volumes was Henry James or that Henry James was the name of their unwanted guest. But the "wrong" done to him by their forgetting was, James suavely argues decades later, the "only rightness" of the visit. Eliot's indifference to him and her ignorance of his works confirmed her magnificent preeminence among living novelists—a preeminence that lifted her far above a young man from the United States who took as his subject the misadventures of his compatriots abroad.

This was a view that James could take, however, only after he had achieved a preeminence of his own. In the early decades of his career, from the 1860s into the 1880s, he was much less resigned to Eliot's status. We can see this most clearly in the reviews he wrote of her works, eight of them in all. These reviews are filled with criticisms that are almost laughably inapposite. Rather than acknowledging that Eliot adheres to formal principles different from his own (omniscient rather than focalized narration, multiple rather than single plots), James instead implies that Eliot's novels have no form at all. He describes her as the master of the local, not the general; of the detail, not the structure. *Adam Bede* (1859), he says, is less strong in its "composition" than in its "*touches*," *Felix Holt* (1866) is "vigorous" at moments but "meagre" overall, and *Middlemarch* (1871–72) is a "treasure-house of details" but "an indifferent whole." In making these claims, James is also asserting a preeminence of a different kind.[3] What he tendentiously identifies as Eliot's focus on the detail is, he emphasizes, "feminine . . . delightfully feminine."[4] In this way, James counters Eliot's preeminence of age and nation with his own masculine superiority.

At this early point in his career, then, James saw Eliot as representing both a literary status that he envied and a set of formal practices that he rejected. She also represented a conception of realism that he would struggle against throughout the 1880s. James was among the first to recognize that Anglo-American realism differed in crucial ways from the realism of the continent, and he rightly recognized Eliot as its chief practitioner. He makes this point in the last of his reviews of Eliot, which used the publication of *George Eliot's Life* (1885) as an occasion for reflecting on her entire career. The *Life* reprints passages from Eliot's journals, and James seizes on one of them in order to distinguish between the two schools of realism: "We have just

3. Valerie Traub makes this argument in "Beyond the Americana: Henry James Reads George Eliot," in *Special Relationships: Anglo-American Affinities and Antagonisms, 1854–1936*, ed. Janet Beer and Bridget Bennett (New York: Palgrave, 2002), 164.
4. Henry James, "The Novels of George Eliot," *Atlantic Monthly* 58 (October 1866); review of *Felix Holt, the Radical*, by George Eliot, *Nation*, 16 August 1866; review of *Middlemarch*, by George Eliot, *Galaxy* 15 (March 1873), all reprinted in *George Eliot: Critical Assessments*, ed. Stuart Hutchinson, 4 vols. (The Banks, Mountfield: Helm Information, 1996), 1:472, 461, 485, 464.

finished reading aloud *Père Goriot*," Eliot wrote, "a hateful book." For James, Eliot's dismissal of *Père Goriot* as "hateful" highlights all of the differences between her and Honoré de Balzac: where Balzac conceived of the novel as "a picture of life, capable of deriving a high value from its form," Eliot conceived of it instead as a "moralized fable, the last word of a philosophy endeavouring to teach by example."[5] Balzac's commitment to "pictures" and "form" and Eliot's to "moralized fables" shaped their respective conceptions of realism. Balzac, and the continental realists more generally, took realism to be an end in itself, while Eliot and the Anglo-American realists believed that realism should serve some purpose. During his own realist phase, James would reject the purposeful realism that Eliot championed and align himself instead with Balzac, Gustave Flaubert, and above all Ivan Turgenev.

And yet, despite this rivalry and rebellion, James had a great deal in common with Eliot, particularly their respective responses to the entanglement of Anglo-American realism with reform. Eliot sought to rid the realist novel of its too-reformist purposes, while James sought to rid it of any purpose at all. And yet both were nonetheless drawn to the subject of reform. Both recognized in reformist fiction a starker version of the formal problem posed by all forms of realism—and at the center of their own careers. This is the problem of representativeness. Realist representation depends, as Georg Lukács has famously argued, on the interdependence of individual and type. The type is foregrounded in that variant of realism that would call itself naturalism, but it is implicit in realism more generally. Indeed, as Catherine Gallagher has recently argued the type secures the reality claim of realism. Realist novels are fictional insofar as they invent individual characters, she observes, but they seem real insofar as these characters refer to actually existing types.[6] Dorothea Brooke is a fictional creation, but she stands in for the many young women whose aspirations are limited by their gender, while Daisy Miller even more obviously stands in for all "American girls."

Realist representations need not be entirely constrained by type. Gallagher acknowledges as much when she argues that the most compelling realist characters are those who somehow exceed the type they represent: Dorothea and Daisy are especially memorable because they refer to, and yet go beyond, the type of the young woman. But in reformist writings such representational extravagance is more troublesome. Their characters are burdened with the necessity of standing in for a type that has been poorly

---

5. Henry James, review of *Life As Related in Her Letters and Journals*, by George Eliot, *Atlantic Monthly* 55 (May 1885), reprinted in Hutchinson, *George Eliot*, 1:528.

6. Catherine Gallagher, "George Eliot: Immanent Victorian." *Proceedings of the British Academy* 94 (1997): 158.

represented, if it has been represented at all, a type such as the worker or the slave. Eschewing the idiosyncrasies that make ordinary realist characters seem so real, the characters in reformist writings often aim to be one of two things: either typical or exemplary. A group can be represented by a typical member, chosen as if at random, or a group can be recognized by an exemplary figure, who embodies some truth about what the group is—or could become—that is not already present in each of its members. Lukács alludes to both possibilities when he argues that "what makes a type a type is not its average quality" (what I will call its typicality) but rather its capacity to distill all "the humanly and socially essential determinants" in their "highest level of development" (what I will call its exemplarity).[7]

If characters are often expected to be either exemplary or typical, so too are authors, as Eliot and James would discover to their chagrin. As she became more famous, Eliot found that she was expected to create exemplary women in her novels and to be an exemplary woman in her own life. And James found that he was expected not only to describe but also to be the typical American. Both rebelled against these expectations in their public lives, but, more important, both explored these expectations and what they required in their novels. They did so by taking as their subject those reform movements that were looking for typical figures and seeking to create exemplary ones.

Realism and Reform in George Eliot

In the late 1840s and 1850s, George Eliot was immersed in the world of social reform. Her translations of Ludwig Feuerbach and David Friedrich Strauss had introduced her to a handful of freethinking reformers, and she would meet many more through her work for the *Westminster Review*. The *Review*, which had been founded by Jeremy Bentham and James Mill in 1824, had since fallen into decline; in 1851, it was purchased by the publisher John Chapman, who sought to revive it as an organ for radical views. At Chapman's request, Eliot wrote a new prospectus for the *Review*, and this prospectus demonstrates how significant reform was to Eliot and her circle. Its opening sentence names the wide array of topics that the *Review* will consider, among them "Politics, Social Philosophy, Religion, and General Literature," but by the second paragraph the prospectus has narrowed its attention to the question of reform. It articulates the principles by which the *Review* will judge

---

7. Georg Lukács, *Studies in European Realism: A Sociological Survey of the Writings of Balzac, Stendhal, Zola, Gorky, and Others*, trans. Edith Bone (1948; London: Merlin Press, 1984), 6.

reforms—a "recognition of the Law of Progress" coupled with an attention to the wisdom of the past—and it then goes on to identify the specific reforms that the *Review* will support.[8] Nearly one-fourth of the prospectus is devoted to cataloguing these, among them expansion of the suffrage, extension of local government to the colonies, reform of Chancery courts and the tithe system, and the establishment of national schools.

After writing the prospectus for the *Review*, Eliot served as its anonymous editor from January 1852 to January 1854. In the issues she edited, there are essays on suffrage reform and legislative reform, reform of factories and reform of secondary schools, vegetarianism and teetotalism, and the Irish question. These essays focus on Britain, of course, but they are Anglo-American in their frame of reference. In part, this was because the owner of the *Review* was a bookseller with an extensive transatlantic trade, but more important it was because the United States was part of the imaginative horizon of British reform.[9] In an essay about poverty, for instance, the United States serves as a test case; the essayist argues that poverty must have moral rather than economic causes since it also exists in the United States despite the cheap land and high wages.[10] In an essay about suffrage reform, the United States represents both the past and the future of Britain. The future citizens of the United States carried the ballot box with them on the *Mayflower*, the essayist observes, and they have since taken democracy further than any other nation has done.[11] And, in an essay on slavery, the United States stands in need of British intervention; the essayist asks who will speak on behalf of the slaves in the United States if the people of Britain do not.[12]

After stepping down as editor of the *Review*, Eliot began writing articles of her own, on subjects that ranged from French women's writing of the seventeenth and eighteenth centuries to current theological debates. She also began to write literary reviews. She published a number of these in various newspapers and periodicals through the mid-1850s. And she was the sole author, from July 1855 to January 1857, of the *Westminster Review*'s "Belles Lettres" column, in which she reviewed scores of new books every quarter. It was in one of these columns that she brought the term "realism" into Anglo-American critical discourse. Reviewing the most recent volume

---

8. "Prospectus of the *Westminster and Foreign Quarterly Review*," *Westminster Review* 57, no. 1 (January 1852): 1.
9. Gordon S. Haight makes this argument about Chapman's motives in his *George Eliot: A Biography* (Oxford: Oxford University Press, 1968), 97.
10. "The Tendencies of England," *Westminster Review* 58, no. 1 (July 1852): 111.
11. "Representative Reform," *Westminster Review* 57, no. 1 (January 1852): 6.
12. "American Slavery, and Emancipation by the Free States," *Westminster Review* 59, no. 1 (January 1853): 142.

of John Ruskin's *Modern Painters* (1856), she argues that Ruskin teaches "a truth of infinite value," namely, "*realism.*" She then goes on to define this still-foreign term: "the doctrine that all truth and beauty are to be attained by a humble and faithful study of nature."[13]

Emerging out of the world of social reform, Eliot would become the great champion of literary realism. And yet Eliot was far from imagining, as contemporary critics like David Masson did, that realism and reform could easily work in tandem; on the contrary, she was quite attentive to the possible conflicts between them. She recognized that a number of reformist novelists felt free to eschew realism and write instead in abstract or idealizing ways. One of these was Frederika Bremer, whose *Hertha* (1856) argues for female emancipation. Bremer's novel raises questions that can be answered, Eliot claims, only by "the application of very definite ideas to specific facts," but it is instead filled with "a cloudy kind of eloquence" and romance.[14] In this way, Bremer was a chief example of what Eliot called, in another review essay, the "*oracular*" novelist. The oracular novelists seek to "expound" their "religious, philosophical, or moral theories," without submitting to the hard but necessary task of depicting "men and things as they are."[15]

Eliot also recognized that a number of reformist novelists sought to be realist and failed. She makes this criticism in her review of Charles Reade's *It Is Never Too Late to Mend* (1856), a novel that describes the sufferings caused by solitary confinement. The prison scenes, Eliot notes, "err by excess," and Reade's realism verges on the grotesque.[16] Charles Kingsley's *Westward, Ho!* (1855), a sectarian novel, fails in much the same way. Eliot compares Kingsley to an artist who lacks confidence in the power of his own images and therefore feels compelled to add captions to each, an "Oh, you villain!" underneath a murderer or a Jesuit, an "Imitate me, my man!" coming out of the hero's mouth.[17] Only once does Eliot praise the realism of a reformist novel, Harriet Beecher Stowe's *Dred* (1856), and she does so only after setting aside the novel's reformist agenda. Eliot's review begins by claiming that the novel must be judged without any reference to the "terribly difficult problems of Slavery and Abolition." Only after dismissing these

13. George Eliot, "Art and Belles Lettres," *Westminster Review* 65, no. 2 (April 1856): 626.

14. George Eliot, "Belles Lettres," *Westminster Review* 66 (October 1856): 571–78, reprinted in *Essays of George Eliot*, ed. Thomas Pinney (New York: Columbia University Press, 1963), 334.

15. George Eliot, "Silly Novels by Lady Novelists," *Westminster Review* 66 (October 1856): 442–61, reprinted in *Essays of George Eliot*, 310.

16. Eliot, "Belles Lettres," *Essays of George Eliot*, 330.

17. George Eliot, review of *Westward, Ho!* by Charles Kingsley, *Leader*, 19 May 1855, quoted in *Essays of George Eliot*, 123.

problems as having nothing to do with "polite literature" does Eliot go on to praise the realism of Stowe's representations of slave life.[18]

In these reviews, then, Eliot is seeking to distinguish the realist novel from reformist writings, but she does not abandon the idea of purposefulness in the course of doing so. On the contrary, she redefines purposefulness as an attribute of realism itself. This is most clear in the metafictional passages from her early novels. The most famous of these comes from *Adam Bede*, when Eliot pauses to defend her decision to describe a clergyman who is neither very wise nor very good. The defense goes on for several pages, and it takes several forms. Eliot briefly defends her realism on the grounds that it is simply more truthful than the alternatives, such as fantastic depictions of long-clawed griffins or idealizing depictions of perfectly virtuous clergymen. But Eliot's most extensive defense of realism concerns the effects it has on its readers. Idealizing descriptions make us impatient with real flaws, encouraging us to turn "a harder, colder eye" on the people around us. Realist descriptions, on the other hand, teach us to treat those people with "fellow-feeling" and "forbearance."[19]

This is the classic defense of a specifically Anglo-American realism, and it would be echoed, a few decades later, by Eliot's counterpart in the United States, William Dean Howells. Like Eliot, Howells sought to distinguish his own works from the too obviously didactic or reformist novels that he and Eliot both borrowed a German term to describe: "I despise the *Tendenz Roman* [thesis novel] as much as anybody," he confides in a letter. But he then goes on to articulate and defend his own novels' purpose: "I should be ashamed and sorry if my work did not unmistakably teach a lenient, generous, and liberal life."[20] In this way, both Eliot and Howells secured the literary status of the realist novel by distancing it from the reformist writings out of which it had emerged. At the same time, however, they made claims for its social power by redefining the purposefulness of realism as a kind of substitute for reform.

This is most clear in one of the last critical essays that Eliot wrote. The essay, "The Natural History of German Life" (1856), takes Wilhelm Riehl's study of the German peasantry as an occasion for defining what a purposeful realism can do. Riehl depicts the peasants as they actually are, and in doing so he counters the idealizing representations of pastoral paintings, opera stagings, and even contemporary social novels. For Eliot, Riehl's success draws

---

18. Eliot, "Belles Lettres," *Essays of George Eliot,* 326.
19. George Eliot, *Adam Bede* (1859; New York: Signet, 1981), 175, 176.
20. William Dean Howells to Thomas Higginson, 18 September 1879, quoted in Edwin Cady, *The Road to Realism: The Early Years of William Dean Howells, 1837–1885* (Syracuse: Syracuse University Press, 1956), 189.

attention to what is needed in English, a similarly comprehensive survey of the various social classes. Eliot calls for such a survey to be done:

> If any man of sufficient moral and intellectual breadth, whose observations would not be vitiated by a foregone conclusion, or by a professional point of view, would devote himself to studying the natural history of our social classes, especially of the small shopkeepers, artisans, and peasantry,—the degree in which they are influenced by local conditions, their maxims and habits, the points of view from which they regard their religious teachers, and the degree in which they are influenced by religious doctrines, the interaction of the various classes on each other, and what are the tendencies in their position towards disintegration or towards development—and if, after all this study, he would give us the result of his observations in a book well nourished with specific facts, his work would be a valuable aid to the social and political reformer.[21]

What Eliot is calling for here would not merely be an "aid" to reformers; it would be a reformist text, identical to the kinds of works that contemporary reformers were actually writing. But even as Eliot emphasizes the value of these reformist writings, she also emphasizes the superiority of the realist novel. Reformist writings, like sociological studies, present "generalizations and statistics" that are effective only where sympathy is "ready-made." But the novel, focusing as it does on individuals, creates a sympathy where none might otherwise exist. In this way, it does more to link "the higher classes with the lower" than "hundreds of sermons or philosophical dissertations" could do.[22] The necessity of linking the classes is made clear in the essay's final pages, when Eliot discusses the revolutions of 1848. Reform was the chief Anglo-American strategy for forestalling revolution, but here Eliot is imagining that the realist novel, rather than reformist writings, might assuage revolutionary impulses before they erupt.

In her critical writings, then, George Eliot sought to separate the realist novel from its origins in reformist writings and to suggest that the sympathy inculcated by the novel could do the work of reform. But the subject of reform would return in her fiction, when Eliot turned from her early autobiographical works to the social novels of her late period. This late period is framed by a pair of novels about the pre- and posthistory of reform. *Romola* (1862–63) is set in Florence, under the reign of Savonarola, and it thereby

---

21. George Eliot, "The Natural History of German Life," *Westminster Review*, July 1856, reprinted in *Essays of George Eliot*, 272–73.
22. Eliot, "Natural History of German Life," *Essays of George Eliot*, 270–71.

recalls the earliest meaning of reform, the rectification of church practice. And *Daniel Deronda* (1874–76) looks, through its Zionist plot, past the reform of existing states and toward the founding of new ones. The two novels that come in between, *Felix Holt* and *Middlemarch*, are set squarely in the era of reform. Indeed, they both take as their subject the inaugural event of British reform, the Reform Bill of 1832. It was the passage of this bill, which extended suffrage to middle-class men, that made observers like Edward Bulwer announce that an era of reform had begun.

Of these two novels, only one has actual reformist intentions. *Felix Holt*, which is set in the months preceding one reform bill, was published in the midst of the debate surrounding another: the Reform Bill of 1867, which sought to enfranchise most working-class men. Eliot, who had grown more conservative since her days at the *Westminster Review*, was opposed to this bill, and her novel's eponymous hero seeks to persuade his fellow workers that it would be best if they were educated before they were enfranchised. The nation must be governed by those who know how to govern, he argues, just as machines must be run by those who understand engines and crops planted by those who know the land. All of this is quite unconvincing as the speech of a self-described radical, but Eliot's intention, at these moments, is antireformist rather than realist. She is not seeking to describe workers as they actually are but rather to shape middle-class views about them. In the end, the 1867 bill was passed, and Eliot's publisher asked her to write an "address to the Working Men on their new responsibilities."[23] Eliot responded with the "Address to Working Men, Written by Felix Holt" (1868). Once again, as in the novel, Holt warns his fellow workers against trying to alter what they do not understand and urges them to improve themselves before attempting to improve the world. But whereas the novel is antireformist, the "Address" is something stranger, an attempt to console middle-class readers unsettled by recent reforms. Holt is a fiction, but so too is the audience Eliot is pretending to address. The "Address" was published in *Blackwood's Magazine*, which was as conservative in its politics as it was middle-class in its readership. It was therefore quite unlikely, as Eliot must have known, that the "Address" would be read by any working men at all. In this way, the real readers of the "Address," the members of the middle class, resemble no one so much as the credulous Amos Barton from the first of the stories in *Scenes of Clerical Life*. The Reverend Barton takes great comfort in reading a book, purporting "to be written by a working man," that confirms his own belief that workers should stay within the established church: he

---

23. Quoted in Rosemary Ashton, *George Eliot: A Life* (London: Penguin, 1996), 291.

"profoundly believed," the narrator dryly informs us, "in the existence of that working man."[24]

But while *Felix Holt* has a clear antireformist agenda, it is ultimately less interested in arguing for or against a particular cause than in exploring what it is to be a reformer—and to live in an era of reform. This is even more true of *Middlemarch*, which is not a reformist—or antireformist—novel at all, but rather the nineteenth century's great meditation on reform. In both novels, Eliot emphasizes what her prospectus for the *Westminster Review* showed, that reforms seldom come singly. Felix Holt not only combats what he takes to be an unwise extension of the suffrage but also attempts to set up schools for working-class children and tries to persuade working-class men and women not to drink. And in *Middlemarch*, some reformers are involved in a campaign to reform Parliament, while others seek to reform farming procedures and renovate the cottages of farm laborers, and still others, to reform medical practice and establish a fever hospital. Both novels also emphasize that reform is experienced as bound up with other forms of social change. In *Felix Holt*, the uneducated characters conceive of reform as "a confused combination of rick-burners, trades-unions, Nottingham riots, and in general whatever required the calling-out of the yeomanry."[25] And in *Middlemarch*, they confuse what they call the "Rinform" with the day when "them landlords as never done the right thing by their tenants ull be treated i' that way as they'll have to scuttle off."[26] The more educated characters also connect seemingly disparate things, conflating "cholera and the chances of the Reform Bill in the House of Lords, and the firm resolve of the Political Unions" (712).

Eliot is unusually acute in capturing how reform is experienced, and she is equally acute in reflecting on what reform entails. It entails representation. The novel's reformers do not conduct investigations, or pass laws, or administer institutions: they circulate representations in order to communicate to those around them both the truth of what is and the promise of what might be. Some of these representations are comic caricatures, such as the editorials and cartoons that attend the parliamentary campaign, and some are figurative, such as the metaphors through which the reforming doctor seeks to understand the structure of human tissue. Strikingly, only a very few of these representations are realist. The novel's signal example of a reformist realism comes in a conversation between Dorothea Brooke and her uncle about the

24. George Eliot, *Scenes of Clerical Life* (1857; Oxford: Oxford, 1985), 14.
25. George Eliot, *Felix Holt* (1866; London: Everyman, 1997), 7. All further references to this edition will be marked in the text.
26. George Eliot, *Middlemarch* (1871–72; London: Penguin, 1994), 396–97. All further references to this edition will be marked in the text.

conditions on his estate. Here, Dorothea describes some of her uncle's tenant farmers: "Think of Kit Downes, uncle, who lives with his wife and seven children in a house with one sitting-room and one bed-room hardly larger than this table!—and those poor Dagleys, in their tumble-down farmhouse, where they live in the back kitchen and leave the other rooms to rats!" (389). This is the realism that Eliot called for in her reviews of reformist novels. Dorothea presents "specific facts" (seven children, one bedroom, rats), and she restricts herself to them, neither exaggerating these facts into grotesqueness nor offering a too-obvious commentary on their meaning. And she uses these facts, as a novelist would do, to create a new sympathy ("Think of Kit Downes, uncle!"). Dorothea's speech throws into relief the reformist work that realist representations can do. They make visible a suffering that has been invisible or, in this case, defamiliarize a familiar suffering that has too long gone unseen. Because Dorothea's uncle is reluctant to assume the expense of improving the cottages on his estate, he has chosen to see their tumbledown state as picturesque rather than dilapidated. But he is unable to continue doing so once Dorothea shows him the cottages anew. He finally hires a land steward to improve them.

This is the one instance in *Middlemarch* of a realist representation leading to some kind of reform, and it bears almost no relation to reform's more ordinary workings. Because the estate is entirely under the control of Dorothea's uncle, she need do no more than persuade him—and the secretary who guides him—of what should be done. But in order to alter the world beyond the estate, a reformer must persuade large numbers of people, many of them ignorant, irrational, or self-interested. *Middlemarch* foregrounds this problem in its account of a parliamentary campaign. Campaigning requires that the candidates give speeches representing the world as it is and as it could be, and the hapless radical candidate, Dorothea's uncle, entirely fails at both tasks. His secretary has forced him to memorize a campaign speech, but the candidate forgets it as soon as he faces the town's voters and begins wandering among his own memories and reflections instead. In the process, he inadvertently stumbles upon the central political question of the era, the industrial revolution and the machine breaking it prompted. "I've always gone a good deal into public questions—," he begins, "machinery, now, and machine-breaking—you're many of you concerned with machinery, and I've been going into that lately. It won't do, you know, breaking machines: everything must go on—trade, manufactures, commerce, interchange of staples—that kind of thing—since Adam Smith, that must go on" (504). At this point, the voters begin to heckle him and then to throw vegetables and eggs, bringing his ill-fated campaign to an end.

The candidate fails at speechmaking because he is a vague and selfish man, but the novel does not value speechmaking very highly. *Middlemarch* evinces considerable skepticism about many of the reformist representations it describes. This skepticism is voiced most pungently by Will Ladislaw, who serves as the candidate's long-suffering secretary before going on to pursue reforms of his own. When the candidate asks him to gather some documents depicting the consequences of industrialization, he replies with considerable impatience: "As to documents . . . a two-inch card will hold plenty. A few rows of figures are enough to deduce misery from, and a few more will show the rate at which the political determination of the people is growing" (460). The candidate urges Ladislaw to make this claim in a newspaper article, thereby showing how thoroughly he has missed Ladislaw's point. The "two-inch card" that Ladislaw here conjures up stands in stark contrast to other genres of reformist writings and to the realist novel as well. Where reformist writings produce information and the realist novel sympathy, the "two-inch card" is a genre that Eliot associates with action. Of the many reformers in the novel, Ladislaw is the only one who succeeds.

Toward the beginning of *Felix Holt*, the narrator looks past the coming passage of the Reform Bill of 1832 and toward a moment when even this victory will feel like a defeat. Reform gives rise to a "time of hope," in which abuses are identified and remedies imagined, but there necessarily follows a "time of doubt and despondency," when "ardent Reformers" come to realize that they may rectify abuses without ushering in an era of "wisdom and happiness" (167–68). The ending of *Middlemarch* is even more elegiac because the abuses are not even rectified. The reform candidate is not elected to Parliament, and the Reform Bill is thrown out when the new Parliament meets. The reforming doctor abandons his medical researches, and his innovative fever hospital is enfolded into a more conventional infirmary. And Dorothea marries a second time and vanishes into obscurity, having improved a few cottages and done nothing more. But on the periphery of the novel, Ladislaw continues with his reforms. The narrator refers once to his attending meetings at a mechanic's institute and another time to his investigating the possibility of founding a utopian community in the west. Otherwise, however, we are told nothing about his reforms—except, in the epilogue, that he has been elected to Parliament and is now pursuing them there. By refusing to represent the one reformer who succeeds, *Middlemarch* emphasizes what Eliot knew and Ladislaw learned, that realist representations are at odds with reform.

Exemplary Women

As the anonymous editor of the *Westminster Review*, George Eliot was free to take a distanced view of reform. She recognized, as the prospectus makes

clear, that reform was the defining feature of the era, but she was less interested in advocating for or against specific reforms than in creating a context in which they could be evaluated and debated. Little changed when
she became the pseudonymous author of the early works, some of which
are set at the same moment of early-1830s reformist ferment that would
be the subject of *Felix Holt* and *Middlemarch*. But once the pseudonym was
revealed, once the beloved novelist and the prominent intellectual were
shown to be one and the same, Eliot was called on to take a public position
on various reformist questions—and to advocate those positions in her
works. Not only would her publisher ask her to write an essay opposing
suffrage reform, but her old friends from her freethinking days would ask
her to write a novel illustrating the social theories of Auguste Comte. She
was most often pressured, however, to speak or write on behalf of women's
rights. Even before her pseudonym was revealed, Eliot had confided in
a friend that she looked forward to heaven, where she would be "quite
delivered from any necessity of giving a judgment on the Woman Question."[27] And after her identity had been revealed, the expectation that she
would have and give a judgment on the Woman Question only intensified.
So, too, did the expectation that she would act to further the cause, in her
life as well as through her fiction. More specifically, Eliot was expected
to create exemplary women characters—and to be an exemplary woman
herself.

The latter expectation was articulated most urgently by persons active in
the campaign for women's rights. This campaign was led, in mid-century
Great Britain, by Eliot's two closest female friends, Barbara Bodichon and
Bessie Rayner Parkes, and nearly all of her female friends were involved in
it in some way. Bodichon and Parkes advocated female independence across
a number of domains: financial independence within marriage, through the
passage of a married woman's property act; financial independence outside
of marriage, through improved education and access to the professions; and
political independence, through the right to vote.[28] They advocated these
things in an array of reformist writings, among them Bodichon's *A Brief
Summary in Plain Language of the Most Important Laws of England concerning
Women* (1854) and *Women and Work* (1857), as well as the *Englishwoman's
Journal*, which Bodichon edited with Parkes. They also established a school

27. *The George Eliot Letters*, ed. Gordon S. Haight, 8 vols. (New Haven: Yale University
Press, 1954–1978), 2:383.
28. Gillian Beer emphasizes the significance of independence in her *George Eliot* (Bloomington: Indiana University Press, 1986), 169.

for girls, which offered education irrespective of religion or class, and they helped to found Girton College.[29]

Parkes and Bodichon were often referred to as the "Ladies of Langham Place." But while their campaign was importantly centered in the offices located there, it nonetheless included the United States in its imaginative horizon. The women's rights campaign in the United States had begun, as I showed in my last chapter, with a conflict between British and U.S. antislavery activists over the place of women in the movement, and slavery continued to be an important point of reference for Parkes and Bodichon as well. Bodichon compared marriage to slavery in her defense of a married woman's property act, and she would elaborate on the similarities between them when describing her tour of the southern United States in her *American Diary* (1857–58). Slavery is present in Eliot's description of marriage as well, one of the clearest signs that the Anglo-American women's movement influenced her work. In *Daniel Deronda*, Daniel's mother refers to the "slavery of being a girl."[30] And in *Felix Holt*, the metaphor is made real. A man returned from years in the east blandly acknowledges that his first wife was "a slave—was bought, in fact" (388).

The female independence that Bodichon and Parkes were campaigning for was something that Eliot had largely achieved. She pursued a successful career, managed her considerable income, and spoke out on various political questions. And so it is hardly surprising that Parkes and Bodichon pressed her to publicly support property rights for married women, as well as suffrage rights and education for all. More generally, they wanted her to serve as an example of what women, at their best, can do and be. But Eliot was often reluctant to do so. She signed and circulated Bodichon's 1855 petition in favor of the Married Woman's Property Act, but this was as much support as she would ever lend the cause. A decade later, she refused to sign John Stuart Mill's petition for suffrage to be extended to women as well as to working-class men. And she would even waver in her support of Girton College.[31]

Eliot's reluctance to serve as an exemplary woman in the campaign for women's rights can be partly explained by her lack of commitment to the

---

29. Nancy Pell offers a helpful account of Eliot's friendship with Bodichon in "George Eliot and Barbara Leigh Smith Bodichon," in *Nineteenth-Century Women Writers of the English-Speaking World*, ed. Rhoda B. Nathan (Westport, CT: Greenwood Press, 1985), 151–58. See also Muriel C. Bradbrook, "Barbara Bodichon, George Eliot and the Limits of Feminism," in *Women and Literature, 1779–1982: The Collected Papers of Muriel Bradbrook* (New York: Barnes and Noble Press, 1982).

30. George Eliot, *Daniel Deronda* (1876; London: Penguin, 1986), 694.

31. Pauline Nestor summarizes Eliot's vexed relation to the campaign for woman's rights in *George Eliot* (London: Palgrave, 2002), 21–22.

cause. Not only did she grow more conservative as she grew older, but even at her most radical, she was never a champion of women's rights. Her correspondence with various activists, Parkes and Bodichon among them, shows her to be quite equivocal: she claims that her sympathies lie equally with women and men; she suggests that female subordination has made women more noble in their suffering and men more tender toward them; and she confesses to a fear that university education will leave women lamentably "unsexed."[32] But if Eliot was ambivalent about the cause, she was also doubtful about her own ability to aid it, notorious as she was for living in an extramarital liaison. She shared with Bodichon and Parkes a sense that the women who exemplified the cause must be beyond reproach. Bodichon and Parkes masked their own support for Girton so that the cause of female education would not be compromised by the more controversial cause of female suffrage. And Eliot, when she gave money to Girton, did not do so in the name of Marian Evans Lewes, or in the name of George Eliot, but as "the author of *Romola*," her most learned and pious book.

Intersecting with Bodichon and Parkes's demands were the expectations of Eliot's female readers. These readers were hoping to find in Eliot's works characters who fully exemplified female possibility, but their hopes were disappointed by the many novels and narrative poems that described women forced to sacrifice love or ambition—or both. Fedalma, in *The Spanish Gypsy* (1868), must renounce her lover in order to lead her nation, while Dorothea Brooke, in *Middlemarch*, marries happily but lives in obscurity and dies unknown. Maggie Tulliver, in *The Mill on the Floss* (1860), is allowed neither learning nor love, and the eponymous heroine of *Armgart* (1871) first dismisses her lover to devote herself to her singing and then loses her extraordinary voice. Armgart rails against what she identifies as an old familiar story, "The Woman's Lot: a Tale of Everyday," and many female readers asked why Eliot would not write a new one.[33] One woman wrote to Eliot after reading *The Spanish Gypsy* to ask, "[M]ust noble women always fail? Is there no sumptuous flower of happiness for us?"[34] But of course "noble women" did not "always fail," as Florence Nightingale was quick to point out in her 1873 review of *Middlemarch*. It is strange, she notes, that Eliot permits Dorothea to do no more than renovate a few cottages when Eliot's own stepson married into a family of reformers, one of whom, Octavia Hill,

32. George Eliot to Emily Davies (1868), quoted in *George Eliot Letters*, 4: 467. Kate Flint helpfully parses Eliot's views on women in "George Eliot and Gender," in *The Cambridge Companion to George Eliot*, ed. George Levine (Cambridge: Cambridge University Press, 2001), 160–63.

33. George Eliot, *Armgart*, in *Complete Poems* (1870; New York: Doubleday, 1901), 350.

34. Harriet Pierce to George Eliot, quoted in Haight, *George Eliot Letters*, 8: 463.

renovated more than six thousand buildings in London's East End. "Could not the heroine . . . have been set," Nightingale asks, "to some such work as this?"[35] The same question would be asked a century later by the first generation of feminist critics. These critics too were searching in literature for exemplars of what women could do and be, and, like Eliot's contemporary readers, they were bitterly disappointed not to find such characters in her novels. Nightingale had asked why Eliot had not written about a woman like Hill; these critics asked why she had not written about a woman like Eliot.[36]

Eliot never responded directly to her contemporary readers, but her views about exemplarity can be inferred from her critical writings and her novels. From her critical writings, we can see that exemplarity would be objectionable to Eliot on formal grounds, as a subset of that idealism that her own realism was everywhere fighting against. But we can also see that Eliot objected to exemplarity on strategic grounds as well. In her view, reformist writers were too quick to create characters who rise above their circumstances. The "idealized proletaires" of a Eugene Sue suggest that "high morality and refined sentiment" exist even in "harsh social relations."[37] Such a suggestion is not only false, Eliot implies, but also pernicious. It makes it possible for people to believe that the "relations" are not so "harsh" after all. Indeed, if slaves are as perfectly virtuous as Harriet Beecher Stowe describes them as being, then "slavery has answered," Eliot sardonically jokes, "as moral discipline."[38] Far better, she believes, for reformist writers to follow Mary Wollstonecraft and Margaret Fuller, who acknowledged that women were not yet the equals of men and could not be, given the restrictions placed on their development. For them to have done otherwise, Eliot argues, would have suggested that virtue had arisen out of women's "slavery and ignorance," which would have been "an argument for the continuance of bondage."[39]

But Eliot's fullest account of exemplarity can be found in her novels. By this I do not simply mean that her novels contain exemplary characters, such as Dinah Morris and Daniel Deronda, but rather that they also contain

35. Quoted in Elaine Showalter, "The Greening of Sister George," *Nineteenth-Century Fiction* 35 (1980): 305–6.

36. This group of critics includes Showalter, "Greening," as well as Kate Millett, *Sexual Politics* (Garden City: Doubleday, 1970); Zelda Austen, "Why Feminist Critics Are Angry with George Eliot," *College English* 37 (1976): 549–61; Ellen Moers, *Literary Women* (Garden City: Doubleday, 1976); and Kathleen Blake "*Middlemarch* and the Woman Question," *Nineteenth-Century Fiction* 31 (1976): 285–312.

37. Eliot, "Natural History of German Life," *Essays of George Eliot*, 272.

38. Eliot, "Belles Lettres," *Essays of George Eliot*, 327.

39. George Eliot, "Margaret Fuller and Mary Wollstonecraft," *Leader* 6 (13 October 1855): 988–89, reprinted in *Essays of George Eliot*, 205.

characters who deliberately search for or serve as exemplars. Romola di'
Bardi does the former. When her father laments the loss of his son, whom
he hoped would become a great scholar, Romola cites Cassandra Fedele, the
most learned woman in the world, as evidence that she might become a great
scholar herself. Later, when Romola has been betrayed by her husband and
is wondering how to live her life on her own, she decides to make a pilgrim-
age to Venice so that she may meet Fedele and ask her "how an instructed
woman could support herself in a lonely life."[40] At this moment, she recalls
the equally desperate women who came to Eliot, the most learned woman of
her day, with similar requests. But in this case the exemplary woman is never
met. Romola is stopped at the outskirts of Florence by Savonarola, who
commands her to return to her husband and take up her cross as wife.

Where Romola searches for an exemplary figure, Felix Holt and *Middlemarch*'s Tertius Lydgate imagine themselves to be exemplary. And they
imagine that their exemplarity will serve the purposes of reform. Holt,
born to working-class parents but afforded a middle-class education, has
the opportunity of joining the middle class himself. But he rejects this
prospect and instead commits himself to serving as an example of what the
working class may, at its best, become. "If there's anything our people want
convincing of," he says, "it is, that there's some dignity and happiness for
a man other than changing his station" (401). Holt sets aside his medical
education and trains to become a watchmaker, in the hopes of showing his
"people" that it is possible to be an educated and cultivated artisan. As for
Lydgate, he intends to reform the medical profession and believes he can
do so by his own example. In Lydgate's view, medicine has been degraded
by the great physicians, who believe that a classical education is superior to
a scientific one, and by the more lowly surgeons, who support themselves
through the sale of useless patent drugs. He therefore intends to exem-
plify in his own practice the best features of both the surgeons and the
physicians, eschewing the worst. A gentleman born, he insists on getting a
scientific rather than a classical education; a surgeon trained, he insists on
being paid for his consultations, not for his prescriptions.

Through these two characters, Eliot explores both what exemplarity requires and what it can achieve. For Holt, the role of exemplary working man
requires that he forgo ambition and attachment, both of which would tempt
him to depart from his ideal. He must never marry, he believes, and never
have children, and when he is asked what his plans are, he invariably replies
that they are to leave the place where he is. These many renunciations are
the narrative correlate to what so many critics have remarked on, the odd

40. George Eliot, *Romola* (1862–64; London: Everyman, 1999), 330.

simplicity with which Holt is described.[41] Lydgate, of course, renounces almost nothing—not wife, not children, and certainly not ambition. But it is
for this reason that he fails to be an exemplary surgeon and becomes instead
a doctor for the rich at an exclusive spa.

Exemplarity is demanding, these novels show, and it is also less legible
than Holt and Lydgate expect. Lydgate imagines that his example will speak
for itself, and so he does not explain to his patients why he deviates from
customary practice. In the absence of explanation, however, his patients gen-
erate their own. Lydgate becomes a subject of gossip, as his patients become
increasingly willing to believe that he digs up bodies to experiment on them
or colludes in the murder of a patient. Holt, too, finds that his example is
often not understood. A few characters do notice that Holt is different from
other working men: the owner of a local pub notices that Holt seems unusually intelligent; a crowd of voters is struck by the disparity between Holt's
"educated expression" and his humble dress (270); the radical candidate recognizes that Holt is "superior to [his] fellows" (384). None of the men who
notice Holt's difference, however, are the workers for whom he hopes to set
an example. The radical candidate is a member of the gentry, the voters on
nomination day are all middle class, and even the publican is already eligible
to vote. And even though these characters remark on the difference, they are
unable to make sense of what it means. The publican suspects that Holt is
secretly working on behalf of one of the candidates, while the voters simply
stare at him in wonder.

Even this illegible exemplarity is obscured at the novel's climax, the riot
that breaks out on election day. When Holt sees the workers rioting, he
rushes to join them. He is taken, by the townspeople watching from the
windows above, to be the "leading spirit" of the mob (294). The narrator
hastens to emphasize that it is only "those with undiscerning eyes" who see
him as the leader (294), but the "eyes" of the townspeople are more discern-
ing than the narrator is willing to admit. After all, a leading spirit is precisely
what Holt intended to be. He joined the mob in an attempt to rechannel its
energies until the military should arrive to stop it. And yet once Holt joins
the mob, he quickly loses his power to act as its leader. Another voice cries

41. And not only Holt; the protagonists of all so-called industrial novels are subject to this
criticism. Raymond Williams was the first to identify the genre of the industrial novel—and the
failed characterizations that lie at its heart—in *Culture and Society, 1780–1850* (1958; New York:
Columbia University Press, 1983). Catherine Gallagher (*Industrial Reformation of English Fiction*) describes this problem with respect to Charles Kingsley's *Alton Locke;* Stephen J. Spector,
with respect to Charles Dickens's *Hard Times* ("Masters of Metonymy: *Hard Times* and Knowing the Working Class," *ELH* 51, no. 2 [Summer 1984]: 365–84); and Igor Webb, with respect
to *Hard Times* and Elizabeth Gaskell's *Mary Barton* (*From Custom to Capital: The English Novel
and the Industrial Revolution* [Ithaca, NY: Cornell University Press, 1981]).

out a new suggestion ("Let us go to Treby Manor!"), and Holt is reduced to simply one working man among others: "From that moment Felix was powerless. . . . Felix was carried along . . . he was pressed along with the multitude into Treby Park" (297–98). As he is "carried along," Holt knocks down a constable, without thinking much about it, only to learn, later on, that the constable was killed. The man who intended to be an exemplary worker ends up being tried for murder.

But Eliot's dissection of exemplarity, its requirements and its failures, did not stop her readers from wishing that she would create exemplary characters. Among the most exigent of these readers was Elizabeth Stuart Phelps, a U.S. novelist. Women novelists in Britain tended, as Elaine Showalter has shown, to either worship Eliot as a sibyl or feel oppressed by her example. "She was so consciously 'George Eliot,'" Eliza Lynn Linton complained, "so interpenetrated head and heel, inside and out, with the sense of her importance as the great novelist and profound thinker of her generation, as to make her society a little overwhelming."[42] Women novelists in the United States had a far easier time. They could approach the "great novelist" and "profound thinker" with an informality that they presented as characteristic of the United States, and they could imagine themselves less as Eliot's disciples than as her American counterparts.[43] In this context, we can begin to understand the remarkable letter that Phelps wrote to Eliot upon reading *Middlemarch*. She had never met Eliot or written to her before, and yet she begins this first letter with a peremptory request: "[I]t remains for you to finish what you have begun." What Eliot must do is write another novel, this one heralding the "Coming Woman." If she does not do this, then Phelps herself will.[44]

The novel that Phelps ended up writing, *The Story of Avis* (1877), revises Eliot's *Armgart*, as well as Elizabeth Barrett Browning's *Aurora Leigh* (1856). It does not depict an exemplary woman, however, but rather yet another woman who fails. Avis, a promising young artist, consents to marry and then discovers that she cannot devote herself to painting once she is married, or paint at all once she has children. Finally, when the finances of her family require that she paint again, she finds that she has lost her

42. Quoted in Elaine Showalter, *A Literature of Their Own: British Women Novelists from Brontë to Lessing* (1977; Princeton: Princeton University Press, 1999), 108.

43. For a discussion of Eliot's influence on women writers in the United States, see Sandra M. Gilbert and Susan Gubar, *The Madwoman in the Attic: The Woman Writer and the Nineteenth-Century Literary Imagination* (1977; New Haven: Yale University Press, 1989), and Jennifer Cognard-Black, *Narrative in the Professional Age: Trans-Atlantic Readings of Harriet Beecher Stowe, George Eliot and Elizabeth Stuart Phelps* (London: Routledge, 2004), 49–51.

44. George V. Griffith, "Elizabeth Stuart Phelps and George Eliot—An Epistolary Friendship," *Legacy* 18, no. 1 (2001): 96.

talent. The novel ends, as *Armgart* ended, with the would-be artist becoming a teacher. But the idea of teaching is here linked to the promise of the next generation. If it takes three generations to make a gentleman, the narrator observes, then it must take just as long to make a female artist. Avis is the middle generation, standing between the mother who dreamed of running off to the stage and then repressed those dreams to marry and the daughter, portentously named Waitstill, who will be an artist one day. And yet the novel does not merely postpone the creation of the exemplary figure; it also allegorizes the fact that women must create these figures for themselves. Avis paints one great work in her life, and it is a painting of a sphinx. The sphinx, whose riddle traditionally concerns the nature of man, here poses the question of woman. Phelps thus describes a woman who fails to be exemplary herself but nonetheless manages to create an image of woman's hidden potential—an image that slyly refers to the sibylline Eliot. In this way, Phelps's novel is a meditation on exemplarity, just as Eliot's own novels were.

The most generous account of Eliot's exemplarity comes, surprisingly enough, from Henry James. In his final review of Eliot, James announces that all those committed to the "'development' of woman" should "erect a monument to George Eliot," whose "example" has been and will be of the "highest value."[45] Unlike Eliot's female readers and female friends, James finds her example not in her life or in her characters but rather in the mastery that the novels themselves display. It is the novels, by showing what a woman novelist can do, that serve as woman's best example.[46]

Realism and Reform in Henry James

After a string of modestly successful novels of international manners, including *The American*, Henry James published *Daisy Miller* (1878), which proved to be far more popular than anything he had written before. James's letters from the era are filled with jubilant references to its success: he variously describes *Daisy Miller* as "a great hit," as "something of a hit," and as "a really quite extraordinary hit."[47] But these letters are also filled with James's

---

45. Hutchinson, *George Eliot*, 1:534.

46. Interestingly, Blake made much the same argument one hundred years later, identifying the exemplarity in *Middlemarch* with the narrator's voice ("*Middlemarch* and the Woman Question," 311).

47. Henry James to William James, 23 July 1878; James to Mrs. William Dean Howells, 14 August 1878; and James to Mrs. Henry James Sr., 18 January 1879, all in *Henry James Letters*, vol. 2: *1875–1883*, ed. Leon Edel (Cambridge: Harvard University Press, 1975), 179, 182, 213.

laments that he has not profited more from this success. He had been so pleased to learn that *Daisy Miller* had been accepted by the *Cornhill Magazine* that he forgot to make his usual provisions for securing the U.S. copyright by arranging for simultaneous publication in both nations. As a result, he earned only two hundred dollars from the novella that all of the United States was reading and arguing about. James was therefore all the more eager to repeat the success, and he set about writing a novel that would expand on *Daisy Miller* by once again describing the experiences in Europe of a young woman from the United States. But when this new novel, *The Portrait of a Lady* (1880–81), was published, it failed to arouse more than polite interest. This unexpected failure gave James considerable pause, prompting him to embark on what he called "a new era in my career."[48] This "new era" would consist of two novels, *The Bostonians* (1885–86) and *The Princess Casamassima* (1885–86), both of which were realist and both of which took up the subject of social reform.

Before the failure of *The Portrait of a Lady*, James was quite dismissive of realism, which he associated, in his reviews of the 1860s and 1870s, with unsavory subject matter. James follows other Anglo-American critics in identifying this subject matter as typically French. His 1875 review of Honoré de Balzac is typical in its claim that the "modesty" of the English tongue prevents him from translating Balzac's "lewd" French phrases.[49] He refers in much the same way to any British or U.S. novelist who takes up similar subject matter, even including George Eliot. In his 1866 review of "Janet's Repentance," one of the stories in *Scenes of Clerical Life*, James focuses on the fact that the heroine is a female drunkard. "The subject of this tale might almost be qualified by the French epithet *scabreux*," he observes, before going on to add, "it would be difficult for what is called *realism* to go further."[50] Here James aligns a still-foreign realism with scabrous subject matter and associates them both with France. In doing so, he fails to see what would later be clear to him, that Eliot's realism differs from Balzac's because its subject matter is embedded within—and justified by—an apparatus of reformist intention and effect. Eliot describes her heroine's drunkenness in order to bring her readers to repentance.

Toward the end of the 1870s, James began to acknowledge that realism is characterized by something more than a taste for the unsavory. In his

48. Henry James to Grace Norton, 19 January 1884, in *Henry James Letters: 1883–1895*, 21.

49. Henry James, *Henry James: Literary Criticism, Continental Writers*, ed. Leon Edel (New York: Library of America, 1984), 74.

50. Henry James, "The Novels of George Eliot," *Atlantic Monthly* 58 (October 1866): 479–92, reprinted in Hutchinson, *George Eliot*, 1:467.

French Poets and Novelists (1878), he describes realism, as Pierre Bourdieu would do, as a specific grouping within the literary field. Centered in Paris, realism is structured by a line of descent—from Balzac, through Gustave Flaubert, to Emile Zola—and is reinforced by its own codes and rituals of belonging.[51] James satirized these codes and rituals in an 1876 review that mocked aspiring novelists whose "highest ambition is to 'do' their Balzac or Flaubert."[52] But after the failure of *Portrait of a Lady* in 1881, realism became more appealing to James as a possible model for the "new era" he was embarking on. As a consequence, he began to discuss realism in new ways. He acknowledged for the first time, in an 1883 review of Alphonse Daudet, that realism entails a specific mode of perception, "an analytical consideration of appearances," as well as a specific mode of representation, a "closer notation."[53] And he also acknowledged that the realism of the French was not so much immoral as entirely unconcerned with morality—or, indeed, with any kind of purpose at all. He makes this point most fully in the 1884 essay he wrote upon the death of Ivan Turgenev. Recalling the visit he paid to the Turgenev circle nine years earlier, James writes:

> It would have been late in the day to propose among them any discussion of the relation of art to morality, any question as to the degree in which a novel might or might not concern itself with the teaching of a lesson. They had settled these preliminaries long ago. . . . The conviction that held them together was the conviction that art and morality are two perfectly different things, and that the former has no more to do with the latter than it has with astronomy or embryology. The only duty of a novel is to be well written; that merit included every other in which it was capable.[54]

This description implies an opposition between continental and Anglo-American realism that James would fully articulate two years later, in the review that would set Eliot's "moralizing" and "teaching" against Balzac's "picture" and "form."

By the mid-1880s, then, James had come to understand that continental realism was a specific mode of representation unconfined by purpose. And in 1884, he decisively aligned himself with it. He paid a well-publicized visit to

51. Henry James, *French Poets and Novelists* (1878; London: Macmillan, 1893), 198–99.

52. Henry James, "Charles de Bernard and Gustave Flaubert: The Minor French Novelists," *Galaxy* (February 1876), reprinted in *The Critical Muse: Selected Literary Criticism*, ed. Roger Gard (London: Penguin, 1987), 98.

53. Henry James, "Alphonse Daudet," *Century Magazine* (August 1883), reprinted in *Henry James: Literary Criticism*, ed. Leon Edel, 2 vols. (New York: Library of America, 1984), 2:229.

54. Henry James, "Ivan Turgenieff," *Atlantic Monthly*, January 1884, 46.

Turgenev's disciples, among them Alphonse Daudet, Edmond de Goncourt, and Zola. During this visit, he wrote to inform William Dean Howells that he had changed his opinion of their novels. Acknowledging that Zola and Daudet do depict "unclean things," James argues that such "things" honestly and strongly described are far better than the "floods of tepid soap and water" that are being "vomited forth in England."[55] In other letters, he began defending Zola against the kinds of criticisms that he himself used to make. Even more decisively, James, who a decade earlier had satirized those novelists who "did" their Balzac and Flaubert, began to do his own "bit" of Zola. It was at this moment in his career that he insisted on touring a prison and writing about it to his friends, informing them, with some irony, that he had become "quite the Naturalist."[56]

It is in the context of James's affiliation with the continental realists that we can best understand his famous debate with Walter Besant about the "art of fiction." An enormously popular late-century novelist, Besant exemplifies the union of realism and purposefulness. We can see this most clearly in his novel *All Sorts and Conditions of Men* (1882), which describes the efforts made by two reformers to improve working-class life in London's East End. Settling among the workers in order to understand them better, these reformers quickly find that the workers' greatest deprivation is the lack of culture and pleasure. And so they set out to establish what they call a "Palace of Delight." The question of what the novel intends in describing these reforms is raised and answered by the novel's subtitle and preface. The subtitle, "an impossible story," suggests that the novel does not seek to enact these reforms in the world, but the preface informs us otherwise. "I have been told by certain friendly advisers that this story is impossible," Besant informs his readers. "I have, therefore, stated the fact on the title-page, so that no one may complain of being taken in or deceived. But I have never been able to understand why it is impossible."[57] And, as it happened, the story proved to be possible after all. Besant's readers raised a collection and built a real-life Palace of Delight. In much the same way, a reader of a subsequent Besant novel, *Children of Gibeon* (1889), would establish a union of seamstresses like the one the novel describes.

55. Henry James to William Dean Howells, 21 February 1884, in *Henry James Letters: 1883–1895*, 28.

56. Henry James to Thomas Sargeant Perry, 12 December 1884, in *Henry James Letters: 1883–1895*, 61.

57. Walter Besant, *All Sorts and Conditions of Men: An Impossible Story* (1882; London: Chatto and Windus, 1924), viii.

Besant's *Art of Fiction* (1884), which he first gave as a lecture and later published as a pamphlet, sets out to argue, as its title suggests, that fiction is an art. From this first claim follow two others: that fiction is governed, like any other art form, by general laws; and that these laws can be taught, but only, as with any art form, to those who have already shown some talent. This insistence on the artfulness of the novel would seem to look forward to the late-century rise of aestheticism, but *The Art of Fiction* is everywhere underwritten by older presumptions about realism and purposefulness. Besant does dismiss the "preaching novel" as a genre whose time has passed, but he continues to presume that the novel in English will almost invariably take as its starting point a "conscious moral purpose."[58] He celebrates this purposefulness in much the same terms as George Eliot did thirty years before: "The novel . . . preaches a higher morality than is seen in the actual world . . . it creates and keeps alive the sense of sympathy; it is the universal teacher; . . . it is the only way in which people can learn what other men and women are like" (10). As for the realism that is put in the service of this purposefulness, Besant defines it in familiar terms. It entails a specific kind of subject matter, namely, characters and events that "might be met in actual life," as well as a specific mode of representation that relies on direct observation and copious note taking (18).

When James replies to Besant's *Art of Fiction* with an "Art of Fiction" of his own, he begins by agreeing with Besant that the novel is a form of art; indeed, he confesses to rubbing his eyes at the thought that anyone might argue the contrary. As for Besant's other explicit claims, that the novel has rules and that these rules can be taught, James first thanks him for making these claims a subject of debate—and, more generally, for making the novel *"discutable"*—and then goes on not to debate or discuss them at all.[59] This evasiveness is in keeping with James's own insistence that both the novel and the novelist must be left entirely free. But while James evades Besant's explicit claims, he repeatedly challenges what Besant takes entirely for granted, namely, the purposefulness of the novel. James at first responds to the presumption that the novel has a "moral purpose" by bundling it together with the rest of Besant's claims and rejecting them all as constraining the novel's freedom. But he then returns to the question of moral purpose a few pages later, in the midst of his discussion of

---

58. Walter Besant, *The Art of Fiction: A Lecture Delivered at the Royal Institution, April 25, 1884* (Boston: Cupples, Upham, 1884), 29. All further references to this edition will be marked in the text.

59. Henry James, "The *Art of Fiction*," *Critical Muse*, 186. All further references to this article will be marked in the text.

realism.[60] After insisting that nothing is as important as the novel's "air of reality," he goes on to add in parenthesis, not even the "conscious moral purpose" Besant takes for granted (195). At the end of the essay, James returns to the question of moral purpose once more. He identifies it as the most important question that Besant raises, and he professes himself disappointed that Besant does not discuss this question as fully as its "immense importance" deserves (203). But while James laments the fact that Besant does not discuss purpose in more depth, he hardly discusses it more fully himself. He has "left the question of morality . . . till the last," he tells us, and now finds that he has already "used up my space" (203, 204). He therefore leaves unargued his own almost Kantian view, that the "least dangerous" of all purposes is the "purpose of making a perfect work" (204). And this, of course, is a very different kind of purpose indeed.

After his "Art of Fiction" had been published, James confided in a letter to a friend that he had not yet said half of what he had intended to say.[61] He made the same confession a few months later, in a letter to Robert Louis Stevenson, who had written an essay of his own in response to those of James and Besant. James, of course, would never write the second half of the "Art of Fiction." What he wrote instead were *The Bostonians* and *The Princess Casamassima*, a pair of novels that seek to be realist without being purposeful. Given that this was James's intention, it is remarkable that he chose to focus in both of them on that most purposeful of all subjects, social reform. *The Bostonians* focuses on the campaign for women's rights, while *The Princess Casamassima* is set among reformers investigating the circumstances of the poor and revolutionaries conspiring toward an end that goes unnamed. Critics have tended to read these novels, particularly *The Bostonians*, as straightforwardly antireformist, and indeed there is much evidence that James was both ignorant of and hostile to the campaign for women's rights.[62] But to say that James was opposed to reform is not to say that his novels are antireformist. This becomes clear when we compare *The Bostonians* to those antireformist novels that take up the same subject matter, namely, women's rights and spiritualism. James is likely to have read at least some of these, including Orestes Brownson's

60. James's discussion of realism in "The *Art of Fiction*" is oddly inconsequential, given his contemporaneous interest in Turgenev and Zola. He speaks not about realism but about the "air of reality" (195), which he defines loosely enough to comprise characters as seemingly unreal as Mr. Micawber and Don Quixote (193). In response to Besant's more specific injunctions about realism, James is equally dismissive. There is no need to confine oneself to what one has seen, he says, so long as one has an imagination. And as for notes, the novelist "cannot possibly take too many" and "cannot possibly take enough" (195).

61. Henry James to Grace Norton, 3 November 1884, in *Henry James Letters: 1883–1895*, 53.

62. Alfred Habegger argues that James was opposed to the campaign for women's rights in his *Henry James and the "Woman Business"* (Cambridge: Cambridge University Press, 1989),

The Spirit Rapper: An Autobiography (1854), Fred Folio's *Lucy Boston; or, Women's Rights and Spiritualism, Illustrating the Follies and Delusions of the Nineteenth Century* (1855), and Bayard Taylor's *Hannah Thurston: A Story of American Life* (1864).[63] These novels are not merely critical of spiritualism and women's rights, as *The Bostonians* would be; they also actively seek to alter their readers' views about both. James, by contrast, is less interested in arguing against reform than in pursuing realism.

Having aligned himself with the continental realists, James wanted to show that he could "do" the cities he knew well as surely as Zola had done Paris.[64] As a consequence, the realism of *The Bostonians* is remarkably self-conscious, and never more so than when James is describing New York.[65] The novel marks its move from Boston to New York by offering an excessively detailed depiction of an ordinary city street, with a grocery store on the corner. James describes the exterior of the building, with its "red, rusty face" and "faded green shutters" and "fly-blown card" advertising rooms for rent; the sidewalk in front of it, with its "dislocated flags" and "dirty panniers" filled with "potatoes, carrots, and onions"; and the "red-faced, yellow-haired, bare-armed vendors" overlooking the scene. Having offered us this catalogue of details, James informs us that they are superfluous to the novel itself. He has described the scene not because it influenced any of the characters but simply for the sake "of local colour."[66]

What James registers, at this moment, is the extent to which he is self-consciously imitating his continental masters. He dedicates the rest of *The Bostonians* to describing more authentically U.S. subjects for realism. In doing so, James returns to a problem that he first took up in his critical study *Hawthorne* (1879). The most admired of U.S. novelists, Nathaniel Hawthorne was the only one of his countrymen to be included in the English Men of Letters series at Macmillan, and James was the only U.S. author asked to write for it. In his study of Hawthorne, James treats him with that mixture of reverence and condescension that marks the apprentice's confidence that he will soon overtake the master. This rivalry unfolds in terms of realism. Although James was not yet committed to realism himself, he was nonetheless quick to note

while Valerie Fulton argues that he was ignorant of the campaign in "Rewriting the Necessary Woman: Marriage and Professionalism in James, Jewett, and Phelps," *Henry James Review* 15, no. 3 (Fall 1994): 242–56.

63. Andrew Taylor argues that James likely read these in his *Henry James and the Father Question* (Cambridge: Cambridge University Press, 2002), 141.

64. Leon Edel, *Henry James: The Middle Years* (Philadelphia: J. B. Lippincott, 1962) 105.

65. Richard Brodhead describes the oddly ornamental quality of the novel's realism in his *The School of Hawthorne* (Oxford: Oxford University Press, 1984), 157.

66. Henry James, *The Bostonians* (1884–85; London: Penguin, 2000), 145.

that Hawthorne was unlikely to have "ever heard" of it.[67] Moreover, James goes on to suggest that Hawthorne could not have been a realist, even if he had wanted to, because there was simply not enough realist subject matter in the United States. What follows is a famous list of lacks: "no aristocracy, no church, no clergy . . . no country gentlemen . . . nor old country-houses, no parsonages . . . no cathedrals . . . nor public schools . . . no political society, no sporting class—no Epsom nor Ascot!" (34). These subjects are quite different from the ones that James associated with realism in his contemporary reviews, which focused instead on sex and drunkenness, but James is less interested here in describing realism accurately than in asserting his own cultural prerogatives. The list of what the United States lacks is a list of what his adopted Britain possesses, and it is also, to a remarkable extent, a list of what he would focus on in the next novel he would write, *The Portrait of a Lady*.

Still, James does not claim, in *Hawthorne*, that the United States is entirely lacking in subjects for realism. He concludes his famous list by confiding the secret that, he says, all U.S. authors know: even when all of these things are lacking, "a good deal remains" (35). What remains, in particular, is the subject of social reform. Discussing the time that Hawthorne spent at Brook Farm, James observes that utopian communities constituted the one source of variety in an otherwise monotonous social world. Here, too, James judges Hawthorne to have failed. Brook Farm would have been a worthy subject for realism, but Hawthorne evaded the challenge. The novel he wrote about the experience, *The Blithedale Romance* (1852), "get[s] too much out of reality" because Hawthorne was too little concerned with observing and recording the community that surrounded him (108). Once James had decided to write a realist novel himself, he sought to make concrete what Hawthorne had represented too abstractly. And so he took up almost exactly the same subjects: women's rights and mesmerism, set against a background of utopian living and the campaign against slavery.

The subjects are the same, but the era is degraded. *The Bostonians* sharply distinguishes the antebellum reform movements of Hawthorne's day from the postbellum reform movements of James's. Antebellum reform is represented in the figure of Miss Birdseye, whom James describes in a letter to his brother as the last "survivor of the New England Reform period."[68] Hers are the memories of an age of action, of sheltering foreigners and freeing slaves. There is, to be sure, some gentle irony in the narrator's suggestion

---

67. Henry James, *Nathaniel Hawthorne* (1879; Ithaca: Cornell University Press, 1997), 3. All further references to this edition will be marked in the text.

68. Henry James to William James, *The Letters of Henry James*, ed. Percy Lubbock (London: Macmillan, 1920), 1:117.

that she sometimes only imagined herself to be freeing a slave. But there is nonetheless far more nobility in her ineffectual delusions than in the opportunism of the new generation of reformers described in *The Bostonians*—the "mediums, communists, [and] vegetarians" (26), the publicists and inspirational speakers, the "witches and wizards, mediums, and spirit-rappers, and roaring radicals" (7) of the postbellum world. Like Eliot, James conceives of reform as an array of interrelated activities, but unlike Eliot, he is disgusted by them all. And in that disgust, he registers a humility in relation to Hawthorne, who may not have "heard" of the now-fashionable realism but who lived in a more dignified age of reform.

If Hawthorne shaped the writing of *The Bostonians*, Turgenev shaped the writing of *The Princess Casamassima*. In the poignant essay that he wrote after Turgenev's death, James admits that while he was embraced by Turgenev as a friend, he was never recognized by him as a novelist. James confesses, with considerable ruefulness, that he would send Turgenev copies of his books as soon as they were published, but that Turgenev never praised—or even finished reading—them. James surmises that his "reality" must have been a "good deal too thin" for Turgenev, that his novels must have seemed more concerned with "manner" than with "matter."[69] In *The Princess Casamassima*, James pays homage to Turgenev by borrowing the "matter" of one of Turgenev's own novels, *Virgin Soil* (1877). James takes Turgenev's revolutionaries and places them in the middle of the London slums amidst reformers of all kinds, and in doing so he makes possible a serious inquiry into the relation between realism and reform. In *The Bostonians*, James used reform as merely a subject matter for realism, but in *The Princess Casamassima* he explores the connections between reformist investigations and realist representations.[70]

The Princess Casamassima attempts to capture the place of reform within a continuum of social action that extends from charity to revolution. Prince Casamassima asks, upon hearing a discussion of poverty, whether English people do not give alms. His interlocutor informs him that they do, and, indeed, there is a great deal of charity in the novel, particularly in the gifts that Lady Aurora and the Princess Casamassima bring to the poor: the candles and dressing gowns and new couches, the nurses and serving women. But these isolated gifts are augmented by reformist efforts to understand the phenomenon of poverty as a whole. These efforts take the form of

69. Henry James, "Ivan Turgenieff," 45.

70. The result is a paradox, a putatively realist novel that derives its representations of the world from other literary texts. Brodhead has noted that *The Princess Casamassima* is the most allusive of all realist novels, with James borrowing from Honoré de Balzac, Charles Dickens, and Zola, as well as Turgenev (*School of Hawthorne*, 144).

investigatory visits. Members of the aristocracy and the gentry—no one in this novel is middle class—are eager to enter the homes of the poor in order to gather information about them. One such investigator is Captain Sholto, who begins asking questions immediately upon his arrival: "Now, how many families would there be in such a house as this," he begins, "and what should you say about the sanitary arrangements." His questions, which comprise "the position in life, the avocations and habits, of the other lodgers, the rent they paid, their relations with each other, both in and out of their family," are answered with many "statistics and anecdotes."[71] In this way, James shows us the origins of reformist writings such as the ones Eliot called for in her review of Wilhelm Riehl. But he is also showing us the origins of the realist novel. James proved himself to be a realist, after all, by touring a prison and taking notes.

Scenes like this are central to those critics who argue that realism and reform are both discourses of social control, an argument that has been made most forcibly by Mark Selzer. Noting the parallels between reformist investigation and realist representation, Selzer claims that "the realist project operates through a comprehensive surveillance and policing of the real."[72] But if James shows us the similarities between the would-be reformer and the realist novelist, it is surely significant that he also accuses the reformer of a vulgar want of tact. Sholto is far from alone in his tactlessness. All reform-minded Englishwomen are guilty of presuming, in the words of one of the novel's working-class émigrés, that they "may thrust themselves into your apartment because you have the *désagrément* of being poor" (129). Indeed, James goes further in criticizing the reformers than even present-day critics do. Where they focus on the disciplinary impulses behind reform, he unfolds in the reformers he describes a fuller and more distasteful array of motives. Sholto, for instance, is merely feigning an interest in the poor in order to pursue the Princess. As for the Princess, she is motivated by a desire to see a reality that she believes resides only in the poor, in the suffering and filth that she insists on calling the "real London" (201). Reform offers her an excuse for satisfying her curiosity, but it becomes increasingly clear that she is far more committed to seeing suffering than to ameliorating what she sees. She exults, at the end of the novel, that "in the depths of this huge, luxurious, wanton, wasteful city we have seen sights of unspeakable misery and horror" (464). *The Bostonians* briefly explores a similar desire. One character is licensed by her service in the "Associated Charities" to

71. Henry James, *The Princess Casamassima* (1885–86; London: Penguin, 1987), 227–28. All further references to this edition will be marked in the text.

72. Mark Seltzer, *Henry James and the Art of Power* (Ithaca: Cornell University Press, 1984) 18.

visit the "alleys and slums of Boston," but these visits seem to serve no other function than allowing her to announce that there is "no foulness of disease or misery she feared to look in the face" (134–35). In this way, James shows us all that reformist investigation can, at its worst, be: not only intrusive and patronizing but also voyeuristic and falsely vicarious. Nor does James fail to emphasize that what is true of reformers is true of realist novelists—and true of their readers as well.

On the other side of reform, there is revolution, which is figured in this novel as a kind of going beyond. The phrase "going far" is a kind of code for revolutionary plotting, and the characters compulsively question one another to see how far each has gone. One of the most insistent is the novel's protagonist, Hyacinth Robinson, who senses that he is on the periphery of a conspiracy he would like to join. He should be admitted into this conspiracy, he argues, because he has already gone quite far on his own. What follows is typical of many conversations in the novel. "I didn't know you were so advanced!" exclaims one of the revolutionaries, to which Hyacinth replies, "You didn't know I was advanced? . . . I think I go about as far as it is possible to go" (138). At this point, a charitable noblewoman interjects, "I should like so very much to know—it would be so interesting—if you don't mind—how far exactly you do go" (138). But this question never does admit of an "exact" answer. Instead, Hyacinth replies, "I think I see my way to conclusions from which . . . [others] would shrink" (138). So abstract are these discussions that the novel's readers are left to speculate about what going far might actually mean—revolution? anarchy? terrorism? And it comes as a shock when one of the novel's more cynical observers names at least one possibility, namely, throwing a bomb into a crowd.

Revolution carries with it a new form of representation, one that goes further than a reformist realism by seeing beneath the surfaces of things. We can see the difference when we pair two descriptions of the London streets. When Hyacinth is still part of the world of reformist investigation, he walks the streets and finds the people legible through observation:

He liked the people who looked as if they had got their week's wage and were prepared to lay it out discreetly; and even those whose use of it would plainly be extravagant and intemperate; and best of all, those who evidently hadn't received it at all and who wandered about disinterestedly, vaguely, with their hands in empty pockets, watching others make their bargains and fill their satchels, or staring at the striated sides of bacon, at the golden cubes and triangles of cheese, at the graceful festoons of sausage, in the most brilliant of the windows. (106)

Hyacinth's "liking" for all the people he sees should not obscure the fact that he is surveilling them in ways that Selzer describes, identifying, for instance, the ones who would "plainly be extravagant and intemperate." Here, too, James is showing us the disciplinary power of reformist investigation. But Hyacinth's perceptions are interestingly different after he joins the revolutionary conspiracy:

> It is more strange than I can say. Nothing of it appears above the surface; but there is an immense underworld, peopled with a thousand forms of revolutionary passion and devotion. . . . And on top of it all, society lives! People go and come, and buy and sell, and drink and dance, and make money and make love, and seem to know nothing and suspect nothing and think of nothing. . . . All that is one-half of it; the other half is that everything is doomed! In silence, in darkness, but under the feet of each one of us, the revolution lives and works. It is a wonderful, immeasurable trap, on the lid of which society performs its antics. (330)

What Hyacinth presents as an account of revolution is an account of representation as well. On the surface, there are the experiences that realism makes available to the sight, already abstracted here into a set of genres and tropes: arrivals and departures; celebrations and exchanges; the marriage plot and the narrative of prosperity achieved. But below this surface are the workings of conspiracy, which realism cannot perceive and which realism is imperiled by. The "trap" will be "sprung" at the moment of revolution, but already realism has been undermined. Hyacinth has entered a domain of abstraction, of inference, of deictic gestures as compulsive as they are incomplete, a mode appropriate to political conspiracy and characteristic of late James.

Hyacinth's perceptions become newly abstract at the very moment when he joins the revolutionary conspiracy. And it is at this moment that James's novel begins to draw most heavily on Turgenev. *The Princess Casamassima* reiterates *Virgin Soil* at many points. Both focus on a protagonist who is divided between his love for the people and his love for high culture, between his commitment to and his skepticism about revolution, and in both novels this division within the protagonist is attributed to a divided inheritance: both are the illegitimate children of noblemen. Both novels also take place in a world of revolutionary conspiracy, with letters arriving from unseen figures ordering that assassinations be performed. But *Virgin Soil* begins at a point that *Princess* will reach only halfway through. On our first glimpse of Turgenev's protagonist, he is already a member of the conspiracy and he has already grown skeptical of its usefulness. James's protagonist, on the other hand, spends the first half of *Princess* sensing the presence of just such a conspiracy but not knowing how to join in—or whether it exists at all. He does manage to join, at the precise midpoint of the novel, by making a vow to assassinate someone when he is commanded to do so. But at this moment, when *Princess* reaches the point where *Virgin Soil* began, the protagonist moves out of a realist domain.

In this way, James pays homage to a departed master and also signals that realism will not be his own mode. James would write no more realist novels, and he would retrospectively efface the authorial self-presentation that went into this one. In the preface to the novel, written for the New York Edition of 1909, James accounts for its genesis by relying on that old trope of verisimilar writing, the walker in the city streets, calling the novel the "ripe, round fruit of perambulation" (33). What is explicitly disavowed here are the investigations he did—or at least performed—in the course of writing the novel. "I recall pulling no wires, knocking at no closed doors, applying for no 'authentic' information" (47), he tells us, and in doing so denies the letters he had earlier sent describing himself doing precisely that. This denial is James's final rejection of a realism whose limits were now clear to him.

Typical Americans

If Henry James was drawn to reform because it was the subject matter and method of realism, he was also drawn to it because he shared with reformist writers an interest in the type. The type was central to Henry James's career from its very beginnings. His early novels were read, particularly in Great Britain, as almost ethnographic accounts of typical men and women from the United States. The scientific language is appropriate, Alex Zwerdling has argued, because critics variously described James's characters as "specimens," his novels as "romantic sociology," and observed that he took "rather an anthropological than an artistic interest" in the scenes he described. And James was quite happy to conform to this view. He spoke of his works as "*études des moeurs*," and he carefully shaped his short story collections to emphasize the very saleable international theme.[73] The result was a series of works with such typifying titles as *The American*, *The Europeans*, and *Daisy Miller: A Study*. In Zwerdling's account, the intense typicality of James's early period is decisively rejected

<hr>

73. Alex Zwerdling, *Improvised Europeans: American Literary Expatriates and the Siege of London* (New York: Basic Books, 1998), 144.

in *The Portrait of a Lady*, whose characters free themselves to transcend type and live in a cosmopolitan world.[74] But the type again became significant, I argue, in the mid-1880s. In part, this was because James was aligning himself with the continental realists, who as they turned toward naturalism were emphasizing type more and more explicitly. But it was also because James found himself at the center of debates about his own typicality—specifically, debates about whether or not he himself was typical of the United States. It was in this context that he set about writing *The Bostonians* and *The Princess Casamassima*.

In 1882, in an ill-advised review, William Dean Howells held up James as proof that the American novel had at last superseded the British: James, Howells proclaimed, had advanced beyond Charles Dickens and William Thackeray as surely as Dickens and Thackeray had themselves advanced beyond Henry Fielding and Samuel Richardson.[75] Howells's review was unfortunate for James, and not only because it turned a number of British critics against him.[76] More importantly, it undermined James's attempt in his own critical writings to rise above national identity and speak more generally of literature in English. Eliot had been able to do this, but James could not so long as he was identified, for better or for worse, with the United States. At the same time, other cultural observers claimed that James was dangerously atypical of the nation. In 1884, he was publicly attacked by a young Theodore Roosevelt as unmanly and un-American. Roosevelt argued that James, along with the rest of the U.S. expatriates, should return to their homes in the United States.[77]

In the midst of these debates, James set out to write what he identified as a novel typical of the United States. In a letter that he wrote to his publishers and then copied into his notebook, he confided his desire to write a novel "as local, as American, as possible, and as full of Boston: an attempt to show that I can write an American story . . . the subject is very national, very typical . . . a very *American* tale, a tale very characteristic of our social conditions."[78] What James took to be "very characteristic" of those conditions was the campaign for women's rights. In this way, he identifies as typically

74. Zwerdling, *Improvised Europeans*, 150–51.

75. William Dean Howells, "Henry James, Jr.," *Century Magazine* 25, no. 1 (November 1882): 24–29.

76. Donald M. Murray discusses the British response in "Henry James and the English Reviewers, 1882–1890," *American Literature* 24, no. 1 (March 1952): 1–20.

77. "Mr. Roosevelt's Creed," *New York Times*, 19 October 1884, 2, quoted in Taylor, *Henry James and the Father Question*, 2.

78. Henry James, *The Complete Notebooks of Henry James: The Authoritative and Definitive Edition*, ed. Leon Edel and Lyall H. Powers (Oxford: Oxford University Press, 1987), 19–20.

"*American*" a movement that was not in fact unique to the United States
at all, as he very well knew. James was acquainted with some of the British
women active in the campaign for women's rights, and his novel would bear
a trace of that knowledge. Its two women's rights activists, Olive Chancellor and Verena Tarrant, go on a tour of Europe, during which they discover
that the cause is further advanced in Europe than in the United States. In
much the same way, James would deny the Anglo-American dimension of
the revolutionary conspiracy he describes in *The Princess Casamassima*. The
revolutionaries in that novel are explicitly identified with continental anarchists, even though they much more closely resemble, as Margaret Scanlan
has shown, a contemporary group of specifically Anglo-American significance: the Fenians, a group of Irish anarchists who opposed the British with
considerable U.S. support.[79] In both cases, the putative typicality of James's
realist novels depends on a denial of the Anglo-American world.

But reform is more than national subject matter for James. In both novels, it is also an activity that relies, no less than the writing of realist novels, on the finding or creating of representative figures. The women's rights
activists in *The Bostonians* and the reform-minded aristocrats in *The Princess Casamassima* are eager to find representative figures, figures capable of
representing women or the working class. The women's rights activists are
particularly interested in exemplary figures. One announces that it would
be good for the movement to be "personified in a bright young figure" (79),
while another resolves to live in such a way as to show the world that women
are animated as much by ideals as by love. The revolutionaries in *The Princess Casamassima* also think in terms of exemplarity at times, if with some
irony; one describes Hyacinth as "constituted to show that the revolution
was not necessarily brutal and illiterate" (390). But the reformers in that
novel are searching for figures who are not exemplary but typical. As the
Princess gets to know Hyacinth, she is disappointed because he is not typical enough: there is "nothing of the people" about him (249). For his part,
Hyacinth insists that he is entirely typical, "one of the many thousands of
young men" of his class (197).

The reformers in *The Bostonians* are not very interested in typicality, but the
novel is everywhere shaped by it—in its plot, its narration, and its dialogue.
The Bostonians recounts, after all, the battle between a former slave owner and
a former abolitionist for the love of a young woman who is associated with
the new. Again and again, the novel emphasizes what Lukács and Gallagher
draw attention to, the play between individual and type. The narrator thinks

---

79. Margaret Scanlan, "Terrorism and the Realistic Novel: Henry James and *The Princess
Casamassima*," *Texas Studies in Literature and Language* 34, no. 3 (Fall 1992): 384.

in terms of type, but so do the characters. Olive Chancellor sees a pair of characters not as "individuals" but as a "type, a deplorable one" (86), she recognizes "the type" to which another character belongs (237), and she is troubled by the "type" of suitors coming to court Verena (115), one of whom will later be described as the "type of the reactionary" (224). Verena is dismissed by another character for being "of that kind" (126), while Olive herself is described as "a representative woman" and an "important Bostonian" (222).

The question of typicality also shaped the novel's reception. Within *The Bostonians*, there is an explicit debate about what Boston in particular is meant to represent. When one character refers to Boston as "the city of reform," his cynical interlocutor insists that "it isn't the city; it's just Olive Chancellor" (7). Olive herself offers a third account: "It isn't Boston—it's humanity" (19). This debate would soon be joined by James's readers, who also argued over whether Olive and Verena were typical of Boston. The closer reviewers were to Boston, the less likely they were to think so. The British *Pall Mall Gazette* read Olive as "a Bostonian *par excellence*," and the *Chicago Tribune* also found her to be representative, while the *Boston Evening Transcript* argued that Olive and Verena were "in no wise exponents of the women suffrage movement, or representative of its prominent workers," and the *Boston Beacon* concurred, arguing that "it is to be hoped" that most reformers are "infinitely better and less trivial than are the people in this novel." The *Springfield (Mass.) Republican* complained that James's " 'Bostonians' are all of them 'cranks.' " Only the (London) *Critic* took a less absolute position, suggesting that "Mr. James really meant *some* Bostonians, not Bostonians in entirety."[80] Most vociferous were the protests of women's rights activists. A writer in the *Woman's Journal* (Boston) dismissed Olive and Verena together as the "most impossible personages in modern fiction" and singled out Olive for particular critique, proclaiming that she belonged "neither to Boston nor to any other city." The novel itself should have been called, the review concludes, not *The Bostonians* but rather *"The Cranks."*[81] Another writer, Celia B. Whitehead, responded to James's work with one of her own, a pamphlet entitled "Another Chapter of *The Bostonians*, by Henrietta James" (1887).

80. *Pall Mall Gazette*, 15 March 1886; *Chicago Tribune*, 3 April 1886; *Boston Evening Transcript*, 19 March 1866; *Boston Beacon* 27 (March 1886); *Springfield (Mass.) Republican*, 18 April 1886; " '*The Bostonians*' as Mr. Henry James Sees Them," *Critic* (London), 17 April 1886, all reprinted in *Henry James: The Contemporary Reviews*, ed. Kevin J. Hayes (Cambridge: Cambridge University Press, 1996), 156, 161, 157, 160, 165–66, 164.

81. L. T. A., review of *The Bostonians*, by Henry James, *Woman's Journal* (1884), quoted in Habegger, *Henry James and the "Woman Business,"* 228.

In this way, *The Bostonians* reproduces the debates surrounding James's typicality—first by capturing them in its pages and then by reproducing them in its readers. *The Princess Casamassima*, by contrast, begins to imagine an alternative: characters who are in a given situation but not of it. Such characters are common enough in reformist novels, which often depend on displaced middle-class persons to serve as protagonists. Besant's *All Sorts and Conditions of Men* focuses, for instance, on an heiress in disguise and an orphan brought up to be a gentleman, both of whom choose to return and live among the poor. These characters are best equipped to represent the poor because they seem to be "one of [the workers'] own class" but none-theless can look and talk "like a swell."[82] Moreover, these characters are best able to feel what the poor themselves have been deadened to. James would make a similar point in his preface to *The Princess Casamassima*. Characters are compelling, he says, only insofar as "they feel their respective situation," but the very consciousness that enables them to feel it separates them from all the others in the same circumstances (35). These characters "know too much" and "feel too much" ever to be "natural or typical" (36–37). James is here describing Hyacinth Robinson, who is not at all typical, no matter what he sometimes claims. Hyacinth's difference from other working men is not, as in Besant, a function of plot, but is instead explained by a naturalist thematics of inheritance: the son of an English nobleman and the grandson of a French revolutionary, Hyacinth replicates in his consciousness the divi-sion of his birth. As a consequence of this division, he is typical only when he is out of context. He seems like an aristocrat when he is among the work-ers, like a Frenchman when he is among Englishman (102), like an "actor in private life" (104).

And what is true of Hyacinth was true of James as well. He felt that he was most typical of his nation when he was living abroad, and his brother felt the same. William James, as Zwerdling describes him, "was under the spell of Europe when he was in America—and was 'most ardently American when on European soil.'" This may have been a James family peculiarity, but Henry James elevated it to a novelistic principle. His greatest hope, he confided in 1888, was to write in such a way that no one would be able to tell whether he was "an American writing about England or an Englishman writing about America."[83] This is a remarkable conception of cosmopoli-tanism, one that envisions not transcending national boundaries but rather always remaining on their other side.

---

82. Besant, *All Sorts and Conditions of Men*, 261.
83. Zwerdling, *Improvised Europeans*, 128.

Of all the authors I discuss in this book, James is the one who is most commonly seen as challenging the categories of national literature. His decision to renounce his U.S. citizenship at the end of his life and become a British subject has prompted generations of critics to ask, as his contemporary readers had done, whether James should be read as a British or a U.S. author. The answer, his novels of the mid-1880s suggest, is neither. In this way, he rejected the typicality that shaped his brief experiment with realism and reform.

Chapter 6

Mark Twain
Reformers and Other Con Artists

When Mark Twain arrived for the first time in Great Britain, in 1872, he was already a famous traveler. In 1866 he had gone to Hawaii as a correspondent for the *Sacramento Union*, and in 1867 he had traveled through parts of Europe and the Middle East for the *Daily Alta California*. These two trips together launched Twain's career as a performer and a writer. After publishing his travel letters in the *Union* and the *Daily Alta*, Twain used the Hawaiian letters as material for his first public lectures and the European and Middle Eastern letters as material for his first book, *The Innocents Abroad* (1869). Both the lectures and the book were a resounding success, the former selling out in towns across California and Nevada and the latter selling eighty-five thousand copies within its first year and a half of publication. And so it is hardly surprising that Twain came to Britain at least vaguely intending to write a second travel book.

Britain, however, differed in important ways from the other places Twain had visited. It was not only a potential source of material for his books and lectures but also a crucial part of the literary world in which he was making a career. Simply put, the British were, for Twain, not only people who could be written about but also people who could write—as well as publish, read, and review what Twain himself had written. More immediately for Twain in the early 1870s, Britain was also the site of a literary market that interacted in complicated ways with the literary market of the United States. In the absence of international copyright law, British publishing firms were able to reprint Twain's work without offering compensation. Indeed, it was the fact of such reprinting and his intention of doing something about it that prompted Twain's visit to Britain. In this way, his trip both repeats Charles Dickens's first tour of the United States and also demonstrates how much the publishing relations between the two nations changed in the interim.

In Dickens's day, the U.S. literary market was oriented almost exclusively toward the reprinting of British books. What Dickens was campaigning against, then, was a set of relations that uniformly harmed British authors, at least financially, while uniformly benefiting U.S. publishers and readers—and stifling U.S. authors at the same time. In the years since Dickens's tour, however, the literary markets of the two nations had become more or less symmetrical, with publishers on both sides of the Atlantic printing works by authors from their own nation and reprinting works by authors in the other. The benefits and damages of this system were shared by publishers and readers in both nations, and authors, while still suffering some losses, had learned to manipulate the system at least to some extent. And so Twain came less to protest reprinting in general than to secure for himself the most favorable terms that he could. In a letter that he published in the London *Spectator* shortly after his arrival, Twain attacks one of the publishers who has been reprinting his work, John Camden Hotten. Hotten, Twain notes, not only reprinted three of Twain's books without offering compensation but also combined pieces written by Twain with pieces Hotten himself had written—or, as Twain puts it, "drooled"—and then offered the collection under Twain's name and a title of Hotten's own making, *Screamers and Eye-Openers*. Twain presents himself, through much of the *Spectator* letter, as being distressed on artistic grounds, in particular by the "vile" title that Hotten invented. His letter concludes, however, with a keen attention to the bottom line. Hotten, Twain reminds his British readers, is not the only British publisher reprinting his works. Routledge and Sons are doing so as well, and paying voluntary royalties to Twain for the privilege. And so Twain urges his readers to buy from them instead.[1]

Twain's situation differed from Dickens's in another way. In Dickens's day, English-language publishing was almost exclusively confined to Britain and the United States. But the expansion of the British Empire expanded the reach of the British literary marketplace. And this expansion intensified, at least for U.S. authors, the tradeoff that reprinting had always entailed between profit and fame. On the one hand, the emergence of a publishing industry in Canada made it all the more likely that a U.S. book would

1. Mark Twain to the London *Spectator*, 20 September 1872, reprinted in *Mark Twain's Letters*, vol. 5: *1872–1873*, ed. Lin Salamo and Harriet Elinor Smith (Berkeley: University of California Press, 1997), 164.

be reprinted and all the easier for these reprints to circulate in the United States, thus reducing the author's profits. On the other hand, a reprinted U.S. book had access to readers not only in Britain but throughout the British Empire. And so Twain arrived in England knowing that he was already famous in India and Australia as well. Recognizing Britain's imperial reach, Twain addressed London as "the metropolis of the world."[2] What he found in London was a kind of status that only a metropolis could confer. Upon his arrival in London, he was immediately embraced as a celebrity and introduced to artists (James Whistler and Sir John Millais), politicians (Sir Charles Dilke), and literary figures (Charles Reade, Charles Kingsley, Charles Dodgson, Matthew Arnold, and Robert Browning). His reception in Britain was widely reported in the U.S. press. An old friend described the coverage to Twain while Twain was still in Britain: "They are treating you handsomely in England—we are glad—everybody is watching you here."[3] In much the same way, U.S. reviewers would keep watching, throughout Twain's careers, to see how "handsomely" he was being treated in the British reviews. They would often cite the praise of British reviewers in support of their own, even, as Louis J. Budd has observed, if they had to invent the British reviews that they were claiming to cite.[4]

The U.S. attentiveness to Britain's response to Twain demonstrates the cultural authority that Britain continued to exert in the United States. Indeed, this attentiveness is one of the lingering traces of what Lawrence Buell has identified as the postcolonial relation between Britain and its former colonies.[5] But Twain also demonstrates that the relations between the two nations were complicated by regional differences. Twain was seen, at the time of his trip to Britain, not as a representative of the United States but rather as a representative of the South, of the West, of the frontier. All of these regions were viewed with some disdain by the publishing centers of Boston and New York. But in London the frontier was enjoying a vogue. The frontier humorist Artemus Ward had been particularly popular in London, and his sudden death had left the British eager to embrace a successor. Twain was recognized as this successor almost at once. The very first reviews of his *Innocents Abroad* condemned him for his "boorishness" and ignorance of European culture, but subsequent reviewers quickly recognized that these

2. London *Daily News* (19 October 1873, quoted in Howard G. Baetzhold, *Mark Twain and John Bull: The British Connection* (Bloomington: Indiana University Press, 1970), 16.

3. Quoted in Andrew Hoffman, *Inventing Mark Twain: The Lives of Samuel Langhorne Clemens* (New York: William Morrow, 1997). 203.

4. Louis J. Budd, introduction to *Mark Twain: The Contemporary Reviews*, ed. Budd (Cambridge: Cambridge University Press, 1999), 9.

5. Lawrence Buell, "American Literary Emergence as a Postcolonial Phenomenon," *American Literary History* 4, no. 3 (Autumn 1992): 411–42.

were part of Twain's persona as frontier exotic.[6] As a consequence, Twain was celebrated in Britain for precisely those things that most appalled the genteel Northeast, and yet nothing carried more weight in the Northeast than British approval. Only in London could the young Twain have been introduced, as he was, to a figure like Henry James. After his return from Britain, Twain cannily leveraged his reception in London into greater acceptance back in Boston and New York. And yet, over the next twenty years, he continued to bridle at what Boston and New York expected, namely, that he become a novelist of purpose. His response to this expectation gave rise, in the 1880s, to his two greatest novels, *The Adventures of Huckleberry Finn* (1885) and *A Connecticut Yankee in King Arthur's Court* (1889).

Mark Twain and the Novel of Purpose

In November of 1884, Mark Twain embarked on a four-month reading tour with the New Orleans writer George Washington Cable. The two were billed the "twins of genius," and the joke was that there was nothing twinlike about them at all. They differed in appearance and in temperament: Twain was large, disheveled, and irreverent, while Cable was small, fastidious, and pious. They differed in their modes of performance, with Twain speaking in his characteristic halting drawl and Cable deploying the wider—if less distinctive—range of the trained elocutionist. And they differed in their literary reputations. Twain had published three novels to Cable's two, as well as several travel books and short story collections, but he was nonetheless considered a humorist and Cable a novelist.[7] This difference was one measure of the fact that, at the time of the tour, Cable stood at the center of the literary world, while Twain's position was far more equivocal. Cable represented the kind of writer that Twain both wanted and refused to become: a novelist of purpose.

The postbellum U.S. publishing world was centered in Boston and New York, and as Nancy Glazener has shown, it was dominated by roughly a dozen elite magazines.[8] The most glamorous of these, at least in the 1880s, was the *Century*, but it was the *Atlantic Monthly* that set the tone for the rest. The *Atlantic*'s influence came in part from the fact that it was identified with

6. Baetzhold, *Mark Twain and John Bull*, 5.

7. By 1884, Twain had published *The Innocents Abroad* (1869), *The Gilded Age* (1874), *The Adventures of Tom Sawyer* (1876), *A Tramp Abroad* (1880), *The Prince and the Pauper* (1882), and *Life on the Mississippi* (1883). Cable, for his part, had published a short story collection, *Old Creole Days* (1879), as well as two novels, *The Grandissimes* (1880) and *Dr. Sevier* (1884). Guy A. Cardwell discusses the relative status of the two in his *Twins of Genius* (Lansing: Michigan State College Press, 1953), 3.

8. Nancy Glazener, *Reading for Realism: The History of a U.S. Literary Institution* (Durham, NC: Duke University Press, 1997).

the leading figures of antebellum literature, such as Ralph Waldo Emerson, John Greenleaf Whittier, and Oliver Wendell Holmes, and in part from the fact that it was subsequently edited by William Dean Howells, the most important man of letters in the postbellum era. Howells was unusually cosmopolitan in his literary tastes, and under his influence the *Atlantic* and later *Harper's* championed Spanish, Russian, Italian, and Norwegian writers, as well as writers working in English. But, as I argued in my second chapter, Howells championed these writers in terms that were recognizably Anglo-American, claiming that their realism was in the service of some purpose.

For the *Atlantic* and other elite northeastern magazines, purposefulness was grounded in social reform. These magazines therefore published reformist novelists, such as Rebecca Harding Davis, Elizabeth Stuart Phelps, and Hamlin Garland. They also published articles advocating reforms of all kinds, from changes in the administration of Indian reservations to improvements in the conditions of urban slums. In their advocacy of reformist writing and of reform itself, these magazines resembled their British counterparts, such as the *Edinburgh* and *Westminster* reviews. But these magazines also took up a purpose specific to the United States, namely, national reconciliation. The military occupation of the southern states had ended in 1877, but the northern and southern states were far from reconciled. In this context, Howells's exhortation that the novel "portray men and women as they really are" so that that they may know one another in their common humanity takes on a new resonance.[9] He is thinking, as George Eliot was thinking when she made a similar claim, of a humanity that transcends class, but he is also thinking of a humanity that transcends race and region as well. Committed to making the nation's regions known to one another, the elite northeastern magazines championed the genre of regional fiction, or "local color" writing, publishing the works of Sarah Orne Jewett, Charles Chesnutt, Kate Chopin, and Mary E. Wilkins Freeman. Such fiction celebrated and preserved regional differences, even as it demonstrated that such differences need not threaten national union. And in publishing such fiction, the elite northeastern magazines underscored their own centrality in mediating the relations between the nation and its unruly regions.

Cable was perfectly suited to succeed in this literary world because he was equally interested in old Creole customs and in contemporary social reform. As a young reporter for the *New Orleans Picayune*, he wrote a series of articles titled "The Churches and Charities of New Orleans," as well as sketches of old Creole life. He found that readers in New York and Boston were more receptive to Creole stories than were the Creoles themselves, and he

9. William Dean Howells, *Criticism and Fiction* (1891; New York: New York University Press, 1959), 51.

began publishing short stories in *Scribner's*, one of the northeastern literary magazines; these stories were later reissued in a single volume as *Old Creole Days* (1879). A year later, Cable published his first novel, *The Grandissimes* (1880), which also took the Creoles as its subject. But Cable's development as a novelist did not interrupt his engagements with actual social reforms. In the early 1880s, Cable became involved in the reform of institutions. He led an investigation into the conditions of prisons and asylums in New Orleans, and he was so horrified by what he found that he established both an official commission to oversee these institutions and a citizens' committee to monitor the commission's actions. *Scribner's*, now renamed the *Century*, was receptive to this project as well, and Cable published "The Convict-Lease System in the South" (1884) with them. The *Century* was equally receptive to the presence of reformist concerns in his second novel, *Dr. Sevier* (1884), whose hero dies because his health is destroyed in prison.

Cable's most famous reformist work was "The Freedman's Case in Equity" (1885), which he published just before setting out on his lecture tour with Twain. Most immediately, the essay is an argument against the segregation of public accommodations, in particular trains. Cable protests against such segregation because he finds race to be less significant than respectability. Not all white persons are respectable, he observes, and more and more black persons are. If train compartments are to be segregated, then they should be segregated by what Cable refers to as "caste." But this particular argument is embedded within a broader discussion of the treatment of African Americans more generally. They have been twice freed, Cable famously proclaims, and yet they are still not free. Neither emancipation nor Reconstruction has achieved its end, and so there must be a "voluntary reconstruction," which will rely on the spirit of equity.[10] "The Freedman's Case in Equity" outraged many white southern readers, and the *Century* gave one of them, Henry W. Grady, the opportunity to reply. The editor of the *Atlanta Constitution*, Grady was the unofficial spokesman for the so-called New South, and his essay articulated what would come to be the consensus white southern view. Slavery was wrong, he acknowledges, and secession misguided, but race relations must nonetheless be left to those who best understand them, namely, the former slave owners.[11]

Twain, like Cable, was a regional writer, but he was also a frontier humorist, a popular showman, and a literary entrepreneur. As an entrepreneur,

---

10. George Washington Cable, "The Freedman's Case in Equity," *Century Magazine* 29, no. 3 (January 1885): 412.

11. Henry W. Grady, "In Plain Black and White," *Century Magazine* 29, no. 6 (April 1885): 909–17.

he had realized that it was in the sale of subscription books that the real profits were to be found. Subscription publishing houses relied on agents to travel the country and show prospectuses of forthcoming work to potential customers; the books were printed only after a given number of subscriptions had been secured. Since there was little risk to the publisher, the author received a far higher proportion of the profits than more conventional forms of publishing would yield. By choosing to publish by subscription, Twain ensured that he would be one of the richest authors of the postbellum era. Subscription agents were particularly welcome in rural areas and small towns, and subscription books therefore reached what Twain proudly and a bit defiantly described, in an 1896 letter, as his true audience, "factory hands and farmers. . . . people who don't visit bookstores."[12] For such readers, prestige took a tangible form. Subscription books were extravagantly bound and lavishly illustrated, making the book itself an object of significance irrespective of its contents. But while subscription books conferred one kind of prestige on their buyers, subscription publishing denied another kind of prestige to the books' authors. They were rarely if ever reviewed by the elite northeastern magazines.

Twain was drawn to those magazines, almost in spite of himself. He recognized that the *Atlantic* had the power, as he later put it, to "make any novel respectable and any author noteworthy."[13] At the same time, he turned down a proposal from Houghton, a publishing house associated with the *Atlantic*, because he liked, as he said, "everything" about the offer "except the money side of it."[14] A number of biographers and critics, most prominently Justin Kaplan, Andrew Hoffman, and Richard S. Lowry, have observed that Twain was divided between his desire for prestige and his desire for profit. This division shaped, I argue, his views on the purposeful novel and social reform. We can see this most clearly in his negotiations with Howells. In 1869, the *Atlantic* had identified Twain as a writer worth watching, and Howells began reviewing him, despite Twain's status as a subscription author. Howells would soon become not only Twain's closest friend but also his most stalwart champion. Throughout the 1870s and 1880s he urged Twain to submit pieces to the *Atlantic* and, more generally, to write in the mode favored by the elite northeastern magazines. But much of what Twain did submit Howells rejected as unsuitable. Twain's comic stories, travel writings, and

12. Mark Twain to Henry Rogers, November 1896, *Mark Twain's Letters to His Publishers, 1867–1894*, ed. Hamlin Hill (Berkeley: University of California Press, 1967), 7.

13. Mark Twain, *Mark Twain's Own Autobiography: The Chapters from the North American Review*, ed. Michael J. Kiskis (Madison: University of Wisconsin Press, 1999), 235.

14. Quoted in Richard S. Lowry, *"Littery Man": Mark Twain and Modern Authorship* (Oxford: Oxford University Press, 1996), 36.

boys' books were all very well for subscription publication, but the *Atlantic* required something more like the writing Cable was doing for the *Century*, writing with a purpose.

After five years of failed submissions, Twain finally wrote something that the *Atlantic* would accept. It was, significantly, a work with recognizably reformist subject matter, a persona piece in the voice of a former slave woman entitled "A True Story, Repeated Word for Word As I Heard It" (1874). The piece begins with Twain, here referring to himself as Mr. C____, remarking on the unflagging good spirits of his family housekeeper and asking her how she managed to live sixty years without ever seeming to have suffered any trouble. The servant is taken aback by this question, and she informs Mr. C____ that she once stood on an auction platform watching as her husband and all seven of her children were sold away. She then goes on to relate that after thirteen years had passed and emancipation had come, her youngest son, now a soldier in the Union army, was miraculously returned to her. Her narration concludes with a poignant ironizing of Mr. C____'s first fatuous question: "Oh, no, Mista C____, I hain't had no trouble. An no joy!"[15] Twain submitted this story to Howells with a show of humility, warning that "it has not humor in it . . . it is rather out of my line," but this, of course, is why Howells was willing to take it.[16] Howells would also take Twain's work in other purposeful genres: both regional writing, as with the series of sketches that would later be expanded into *Life on the Mississippi* (1883), and explicitly political writing, as with "The Curious Republic of Gondour" (1875), a utopian fantasy that argued for suffrage reform.

On occasion, the *Atlantic* would accept a piece from Twain that was written in a less obviously purposeful genre, but Howells would then work very hard to insist that the piece had a purpose after all. We can see this in Howells's discussion of "The Facts concerning the Recent Carnival of Crime in Connecticut" (1876), a darkly comic story in which a man struggles with his conscience, which is represented by a shrunken and deformed version of himself. In the end, the man kills his conscience, leaving himself free to do as he likes, and what he likes to do, it turns out, is kill those persons who once annoyed him—thirty-eight of them in the first two weeks—as well as swindle a widow and her young children out of their last cow. A few years later, in 1882, Howells discussed this story in a review essay on Twain that he wrote for the *Century* magazine. Acknowledging that Twain is mostly thought of as a comic writer, Howells seeks to ground Twain's reputation in a more prestigious mode. He briefly argues for Twain's artistry but also, and far more extensively,

15. Mark Twain, "A True Story, Repeated Word for Word As I Heard It," *Atlantic Monthly* 34, no. 205 (November 1874): 594.
16. Quoted in Hoffman, *Inventing Mark Twain*, 222.

for Twain's purposefulness. As evidence for this claim, Howells mentions the obviously purposeful "A True Story," but he devotes considerably more space to reframing "The Recent Carnival of Crime" as a moral tale. "It is hardly practicable to establish [Twain] in people's mind as a moralist," Howells begins, before trying to do precisely that. He does acknowledge that very few readers have noticed the "ethical intelligence" that underlies the story, but he then cites one reader who has, a minister who finished the story and offered to hand his pulpit over to Twain at once. The extent to which Howells needs Twain's story to be moral, and thus purposeful, is perhaps best measured by the tenuousness of the claims he can actually make for it. What he calls the story's "ethical intelligence" seems to comprise nothing more precise than a "scorn of all affectation and pretense" and an "ardent hate of meanness and injustice," neither of which features very prominently in the story at all.[17]

In the early 1880s, then, Twain was drawn both to the profitable periphery of the literary world and, with some considerable pushing from Howells, to its prestigious center. These divided ambitions left their traces on the novel Twain was writing during those years, *The Adventures of Huckleberry Finn*. Twain began writing *Huckleberry Finn* in 1876, intending to capitalize on the success of his recently published boys' book, *The Adventures of Tom Sawyer* (1876). But its composition wore on for nearly a decade, and it began to touch on the adult world that *Tom Sawyer* excludes. It does so most importantly in its serious attention to race and racism and its awareness of social reform. Abolitionists lurk everywhere on the margins of the novel, even though they are condemned as slave stealers by the respectable persons Huck Finn meets, and the novel itself offers an account of slavery from the slave's own point of view. Through this engagement with the subject matter of reformist writing, *Huckleberry Finn* conforms to what is expected from a novel of purpose.

This is not to say that *Huckleberry Finn* was actually read as purposeful, at least not at first. On the contrary, critics continued to read the novel in terms of Twain's earlier works. The majority of reviewers praised it, and those who did uniformly discussed it as either comic or a boys' book. Those critics who acknowledged that the novel does take up some reformist subjects would then cite its famous prefatory "Warning" ("persons attempting to find a motive in the narrative will be prosecuted; persons attempting to find a moral in it will be banished") as license for reading it as a novel with no purpose at all.[18] A reviewer for the *Illustrated London News* recognized the novel's interest in slavery, for instance, but argued that *Huckleberry Finn* was a better

17. William Dean Howells, "Mark Twain," *Century Magazine* 24, no. 5 (September 1882): 782.

18. Mark Twain, *The Adventures of Huckleberry Finn*, in *Mark Twain* (1885; New York: Library of America, 2000). All further references to this edition will be marked in the text.

novel than *Uncle Tom's Cabin* because it was "written without partisanship, and without 'a purpose'."[19] And Walter Besant felt obliged to apologize for attending to the question of slavery at all: "[T]hough the book has no moral, one is pleased to find the 'nigger' receiving his freedom at the end."[20]

A handful of reviewers did criticize *Huckleberry Finn*, on the grounds that it was artless, too episodic and protracted, or, more often, that it was quite simply vulgar. It was an attack on the novel's vulgarity that ultimately changed the terms of the novel's reception. In 1885, the Concord Public Library expelled *Huckleberry Finn* from its collections as "trash of the veriest sort," which is to say, as failing to appeal to "respectable people" and instead appealing to the "slums."[21] Twain replied to the news with bravado, calling the library's condemnation "a rattling tip-top puff" certain to sell an additional twenty-five thousand copies.[22] Whether or not the library's condemnation did in fact improve Twain's sales, it certainly called forth defenses of the novel's respectability. And since respectability was so thoroughly aligned with purposefulness, these defenses sought to identify, however belatedly, the purpose of *Huckleberry Finn*.[23] The *San Francisco Chronicle* felt compelled to review the novel a second time, this time attacking the Concord Public Library for failing to recognize that *Huckleberry Finn* is a serious novel on the subject of slavery.[24] The particular terms of this defense are all the more striking since the first *Chronicle* review had made no reference to slavery at all.[25] The *Springfield Republican* went further in its defense of the novel's respectability, identifying a number of reformist topics that it takes up. *Huckleberry Finn* is, the review argues, "an argument against negro-slavery, lynching, whisky-drinking, family feuds, [and] promiscuous shooting."[26]

19. Andrew Lang, "The Art of Mark Twain," *Illustrated London News* 222 (14 February 1891), reprinted in *Mark Twain: The Critical Heritage*, ed. Frederick Anderson and Kenneth M. Sanderson (New York: Barnes and Noble, 1971), 134.

20. Walter Besant, "My Favorite Novelist and His Best Book," *Munsey's Magazine* 18 (February 1898), reprinted in Anderson and Sanderson, *Mark Twain*, 142.

21. Quoted in Lowry, *"Littery Man,"* 116, where there is an interesting discussion of the library's attempt to define the literary.

22. Quoted in Hoffman, *Inventing Mark Twain*, 322.

23. The one exception was Joel Chandler Harris, author of the Uncle Remus stories, who sought to defend the novel on the basis of its artistry rather than its purposefulness—and called on British critics to assist him in doing so. "Huckleberry Finn and His Critics," *Atlanta Constitution*, 26 May 1885, 4; reprinted in Budd, *Mark Twain: The Contemporary Reviews*, 279.

24. "Mark Twain's Readable New Story," *San Francisco Chronicle*, 29 March 1885, 4, reprinted in Budd, *Mark Twain: The Contemporary Reviews*, 274.

25. "Ruling Out Humor," *San Francisco Chronicle*, 15 March 1885, 6, reprinted in Budd, *Mark Twain: The Contemporary Reviews*, 271.

26. "Mark Twain and Lord Lytton," *Springfield (Mass.) Republican*, 27 April 1885, 2–3, reprinted in Budd, *Mark Twain: The Contemporary Reviews*, 276.

While all of these reviews reveal a great deal about how status was assigned within the Anglo-American literary world, they all misread *Huckleberry Finn* in a crucial way. *Huckleberry Finn* is neither a nonpurposeful novel nor a purposeful one, but rather a novel that is divided by the very question of purposefulness. And this division expresses itself through the novel's attack on reform. In saying this, I do not mean to suggest that Twain was untroubled by the slavery and racism the novel describes. He had long campaigned against racism, as Shelley Fisher Fishkin has eloquently shown, and his novelistic career is framed by protests against lynching: the 1869 editorial "Only a Nigger" and a 1901 essay, "The United States of Lyncherdom."[27] But even though Twain was opposed to racism, even though he spoke out against lynching, he was nonetheless skeptical of reform—and even more skeptical of those persons who fell under a reformer's influence. Reform, Twain suspected, was a kind of con.

The Con Artistry of Reform: *The Adventures of Huckleberry Finn*

In 1867, just returned from his European travels, Mark Twain invited a fellow humorist, Petroleum V. Nasby, to join him on a lecture tour. More specifically, Twain asked Nasby to perform the piece for which he had become famous, an antislavery lecture entitled "Cussed Be Canaan." The letter Nasby wrote in response to this request expresses a quite reasonable puzzlement. Because slavery had already been abolished, first by the Emancipation Proclamation and then by constitutional amendment, Nasby could see no reason to go on attacking wrongs that had already been redressed, nor could he see a market for doing so:

> You know that lemon, our African brother, juicy as he was in his day, has been squeezed dry. Why howl about his wrongs after said wrongs have been redressed. . . . You see, friend Twain, the Fifteenth Amendment busted 'Cussed be Canaan.' I howled feelingly on the subject while it was a living issue . . . but now that we have won our fight, why dance frantically on the dead corpse of our enemy.[28]

27. See, in particular, Shelley Fisher Fishkin's *Lighting Out for the Territories: Reflections on Mark Twain and American Culture* (Oxford: Oxford University Press, 1996); Mark Twain, "Only a Nigger," *Buffalo Express,* 26 August 1869, 2; Mark Twain, "The United States of Lyncherdom," in *Europe and Elsewhere* (New York: Harpers, 1923), 239–49.

28. Quoted in Philip S. Foner, *Mark Twain: Social Critic* (New York: International Publishers, 1958), 216. Evan Carton discusses this passage in an essay that raises some of the questions I will raise about the belatedness of Twain's abolitionist writings. For Carton, this belatedness is one instance of the lie that he takes to be constitutive of all performance in Twain. "Speech Acts and Social Action: Mark Twain and the Politics of Literary Performance," in *The Cambridge Companion to Mark Twain,* ed. Forrest G. Robinson (Cambridge: Cambridge University Press, 1995).

Nasby is responding here both as a once-committed reformer and as a popular lecturer with long experience in what audiences want. But Twain's sense of the market would prove to be cannier. Nearly twenty years after Nasby reminded him that antislavery discourse had been "busted" by the Fifteenth Amendment, Twain wrote a novel about the freeing of a slave, *The Adventures of Huckleberry Finn*. In doing so, he demonstrated that audiences were quite willing to listen to "howling about wrongs" that had already been redressed. And this, in turn, prompted him to ask what other functions such howlings might be fulfilling—and what pleasures such howlings might provide.

Huckleberry Finn first conforms to and then undermines the conventions of antislavery narratives. That the novel conforms to these narratives is most clear in its plot, which recounts, as so many abolitionist texts had done, a slave's attempt to escape to freedom. But the more important connection between *Huckleberry Finn* and antislavery narratives lies in the novel's use of sentimentalism. Antislavery reformers drew on a number of discourses, from Enlightenment appeals to the Constitution to religious appeals to the Bible. But none of these discourses were as influential as sentimentalism.[29] Sentimentalism derives its authority not from preexisting texts but rather from interior states that all humans putatively share, thus relying on sympathy. Sentimentalism understands sympathy to be both an affective experience and an ethical claim. To feel with the sufferings of another is to recognize that he or she is capable of suffering and thus a person like oneself. In this way, sympathy prompts what Philip Fisher has described as the "experimental extension of normality," by which he means the provisional attribution of humanness to persons in whom humanness has been previously denied—children, the old, the poor, the insane, the enslaved.[30] We can see sentimentalism most powerfully at work in Stowe's *Uncle Tom's Cabin* (1851–52). For Stowe, the paradigmatic instance of sentimental identification comes when a free woman realizes that a slave woman is a mother like herself. The novel describes a slave woman who is helped in her flight by free women who sympathize with her desire to save her son, and the novel seeks to create a similar sympathy for its characters among its readers. In the midst of describing the slave woman's heroic exertions, the narrator pauses to address her readers as mothers: what would you do, the narrator asks, if it were "*your* Harry,

29. Indeed, David Brion Davis argues that it was the emergence of sentimentalism that made it no longer possible to justify slavery (*The Problem of Slavery in the Age of Revolution, 1770–1823* [Ithaca: Cornell University Press, 1975], 45).

30. Philip Fisher, *Hard Facts: Setting and Form in the American Novel* (Oxford: Oxford University Press, 1987), 98.

mother, or your Willie," who would be sold down the Mississippi the next day.[31]

Twain is not often considered to be a sentimental writer. He is most often categorized as a realist, if only by virtue of his Cervantes-like attack on modes less verisimilar than his own, chief among them sentimentalism, as well as chivalric romance. And yet some of Twain's own writings are nonetheless sentimental, in particular, his antivivisectionist pieces of the early 1900s.[32] Similarly sentimental, I would add, is his earlier *Atlantic* piece about slavery. "A True Story" follows *Uncle Tom's Cabin* quite closely when the freedwoman reminds the narrator that "we loved dem chil'en jist de same as you loves yo' chil'en." Indeed, Twain goes even further than Stowe and has the freedwoman herself articulate the central presumption of sentimentalism, namely, that there is an essential humanness, gauged by affective bonds, that underlies the accidents of race: "de Lord can't make no chil'en so black but what day mother loves 'em."[33]

What these texts suggest is that Twain, while generally contemptuous of sentimentalism, is nonetheless willing to use it toward reformist ends. And this distinction holds true in *Huckleberry Finn* as well. Some instances of sentimentalism are satirized, most obviously in the episodes at the Grangerfords. Huck Finn is naively impressed by the lachrymose engravings memorializing lost loves and lost canaries made by the Grangerford women, but he is stunned by their readiness to weep over fictional losses while their brothers and sons fall one by one in an unexplained feud with the neighboring Shepherdsons. Other instances of sentimentalism are celebrated, however, in particular those that are connected with slavery. Another of the young women Huck Finn meets earns his undying regard when he sees her and the slaves sold away from her family "hanging around each other's necks and crying," and he later finds her crying on her own because she knows "that the mother and the children warn't ever going to see each other no more" (188, 191). And the most powerful instance of sentimentalism in the novel is the sympathy that develops between Huck and the fugitive slave, Jim.

Because we see Jim through Huck Finn's eyes, he is at first a racist stereotype. In the early chapters, Jim is credulous and deceptive at the same time, quick to believe in witches and ghosts and ready to embroider his supernatural adventures in order to raise his status among the other slaves in the neighborhood. It is only when the two separately flee this neighborhood and

31. Stowe, *Uncle Tom's Cabin*, 43.

32. Gregg Camfield discusses these stories in "Sentimental Liberalism and the Problem of Race in Huckleberry Finn," *Nineteenth-Century Literature* 46, no. 1 (June 1991): 97.

33. Twain, "True Story," 591.

end up together on a raft floating down the Mississippi that Huck begins to perceive other aspects of Jim's character, and the novel's characterization of Jim becomes correspondingly more complex. In particular, Huck learns, and readers learn through him, that Jim has a wife and children. And, in typical sentimental fashion, this discovery prompts Huck's recognition, and the readers' recognition, of Jim as a human being with griefs, hopes, and commitments like those of any other person. Waking in the middle of the night to the sound of Jim's tears, Huck reflects that Jim must care "just as much for his people as white folks does for their'n." "It don't seem natural," Huck concludes, "but I reckon it's so" (161).

But the sentimental vision of Jim proves to be fragile. His humanness is acknowledged only in the first third of the novel; in the middle third, it is largely ignored, and in the final third, it is actively denied. The novel's final third begins when Jim is captured and held so that he can be returned to his masters. Tom Sawyer, who has suddenly appeared on the scene, resolves at once to free Jim, but he does so not out of sympathy with Jim's plight but rather in a quest for adventures of his own. Not for him the circumspect wisdom of Huck Finn, who proposes that they steal the key to the shed in which Jim is imprisoned, wait until the slave guarding him has fallen asleep, and then escape down the river by raft. Tom insists on following the "best authorities," by which he means the stories of such famous prisoners as Baron Trenck, Casanova, Lady Jane Grey, and, above all else, the eponymous hero of Alexandre Dumas's *The Count of Monte Cristo* (1844–45). Disappointed that Jim's imprisonment does not resemble these more illustrious ones, Tom sets about inventing "*all* the difficulties" (242). He and Huck dig tunnels rather than unlocking doors, make ropes when there is no need of them, and saw through chains that could easily be slipped off. Thrilled by all that he and Huck are doing, Tom has only one regret, that he cannot keep rescuing Jim for the next eighty years and then bequeath Jim to his children for them to free at last. Tom realizes, however, that he must free Jim before Jim is sold to a slave trader, but first he invents one final difficulty: he alerts the neighboring farms to the possibility of a rescue and thereby ensures that he, Jim, and Huck will be pursued in their flight. As a consequence, Tom is shot and Jim recaptured.

This series of events has long troubled critics. While contemporary reviewers had only rarely remarked on the novel's final third, one of Twain's most important early critics, Bernard de Voto, observed a few decades later that "in the whole reach of the English novel there is no more abrupt or more chilling descent."[34] And from that point on, the novel's ending has

---

34. Bernard de Voto, *Mark Twain at Work* (Cambridge: Harvard University Press, 1942), 92.

been recognized as a problem. Lionel Trilling and T. S. Eliot separately sought to resolve this problem by arguing that the ending makes a necessary, and formally pleasing, return to the very first chapters of the novel, in which Tom Sawyer leads Huck Finn in a similar set of chivalric adventures. But ever since Leo Marx's angry response to Trilling and Eliot, critics have agreed that this return marks a retreat from the novel's prior extension of sympathy.[35] One way of describing this retreat is to observe that Huck seems to have forgotten whatever sympathy he once felt for Jim: he objects from time to time to the impracticality of Tom's plans, but he never objects to their cruelty, not even the cruelty of Tom's wishing to keep Jim enslaved for eighty more years. Another way of describing this retreat is to observe that Twain too seems to have forgotten his own novel's foray into sympathy as he eagerly returns to his favorite sport of attacking chivalric romance.

But what I want to argue is that Twain's parody of chivalric romance at the end of the novel is not a manifestation of, but rather a commentary on, the novel's withdrawal of sympathy from Jim. The parody reflects on the sympathy because chivalric romance is, for Twain, a collection of sentimental as well as heroic tropes. This became clear during the visit Twain paid, many years earlier, to the castle in which the Count of Monte Cristo had been held. Describing this visit in *The Innocents Abroad,* Twain is already skeptical of the heroic tropes of romance, the facility with which prisoners dig tunnels through stone walls with their cutlery and make candles out of the grease from their food. But Twain is genuinely moved by the traces of their interior suffering. He is taken to see cells whose walls have been covered by fantastic designs, original verses, or merely names carved by prisoners destined to die imprisoned but refusing to die forgotten. These carvings offer Twain harrowing access to the subjectivity of the imprisoned. He imagines the minutes that feel like hours, the hours that feel like weeks, when one is imprisoned for a lifetime.

These sentimental tropes return at the end of *Huckleberry Finn.* Tom Sawyer insists not only that he and Huck Finn display as much heroism as possible in rescuing Jim but also that Jim display as much sorrow as possible in his imprisonment. Toward this end, Tom smuggles in rats, snakes, and spiders for Jim to tame and befriend and talks of finding a flower for Jim to water with his tears. He also instructs Jim to keep a journal, preferably one written in rust and tears on a scrap of stolen shirt. Jim follows Tom's instructions as

35. Lionel Trilling, *The Liberal Imagination* (New York: Charles Scribner's Sons, 1950); T. S. Eliot, introduction to *The Adventures of Huckleberry Finn* (New York: Chanticleer Press, 1950); Leo Marx, "Mr. Eliot, Mr. Trilling, and *Huckleberry Finn*," *American Scholar* 22 (Autumn 1953): 423–40.

closely as he can. But in doing so he is not revealing his own interiority but rather performing the interiority that Tom wants to see. The result is often grotesque, as when Jim makes ink out of the blood from his rat bites, but the purpose of Twain's parody is not to show that sentimentalism is grotesque or ridiculous. It is to show that sentimentalism can be performed. And in showing this, the novel begins to sever the connections that sentimentalism draws between suffering and circumstance, as well as the connections between the one who suffers and the one who sympathizes.

We see the effects of this dismantling when Jim explains that he cannot water a flower as Tom would like since he "doan' skasely ever cry" and Tom responds that Jim should make do with an onion (267). The many tears that Jim earlier wept are thus forgotten, while tears themselves are redefined as a response to physical stimuli rather than a confirmation of humanness. In this way, not only is Jim excluded from the community of sympathy, but the very basis for that community is undermined. Another kind of dismantling is at work when Tom Sawyer writes a sentimental text of his own. Writing posed problems for the rescue from the very beginning, when Tom first insisted that Jim must keep a journal and Huck replied, "Journal your granny—Jim can't write" (244). For a time, Tom was content to have Jim make meaningless marks, but he soon decides that there must be a "mournful inscription" of the kind that Twain saw in Europe (263). And so Tom sets about composing an inscription for Jim to copy. He ends up composing four, each of which is more removed than the last from the real circumstances of Jim's sufferings. They range from "1. *Here a captive heart busted*" to "4. *Here, homeless and friendless, after thirty-seven years of bitter captivity, perished a noble stranger, natural son of Louis XIV*" (263). Having composed these inscriptions, Tom reads them aloud in order to decide which is best, and as he reads them a remarkable thing happens: Tom's voice trembles, Huck reports, and he almost breaks down in tears. He decides that he cannot choose between them and that Jim must carve all four.

This is sentimentalism made decadent. It no longer serves to communicate one person's experiences to another. Jim can neither write nor even weep for himself, while the person whose sufferings do prompt Tom Sawyer's tears, the "natural son of Louis XIV," does not even exist. And it serves no longer as a mode of intervening in the world but only as a mode of stimulating the self. Tom is the only one to weep over the texts that he himself has written, and these texts have nothing to do with the world around him.

The separation between text and world becomes total with the novel's final revelation: Jim has been free all along. He was freed two months earlier by his repentant owner, and Tom has suppressed the fact because he wants to enjoy the excitement of rescuing Jim himself. This revelation has troubled generations of the novel's readers, and it troubles the novel's characters as well. When Tom announces that Jim has been free all along, his aunt is astonished and cries out, "Then what on earth did *you* want to set him free for, seeing he was already free?" (292). Huck, too, cannot believe that "Tom Sawyer had gone and took all that trouble and bother to set a free nigger free!" (293), and he later asks Tom, as soon as the two are alone, what Tom was intending to do after setting "a nigger free that was already free before?" (295). This thrice-repeated description of Tom's actions as freeing a slave who was already free echoes Cable's famous claim that the freedman has been "twice freed" and is not yet free.[36] But even as this echo connects Twain and Cable, it also measures the distance between them: unlike Cable's essay, Twain's novel is not straightforwardly reformist.

Indeed, the question of why Tom would free a slave who is already free prompts us to ask in turn why Twain would write a novel attacking an institution that had been abolished long ago. Like Tom, Twain is making a seemingly reformist intervention that is certain to have no reformist effect. It is not simply the belatedness of Twain's attacks on slavery that ensures this. After all, many reformist writings describe the injustices of the past in order to attack the injustices of the present. A number of Cable's works, for instance, assert the continuities between past and present social problems. In *The Grandissimes*, the incorporation of New Orleans into the United States following the Louisiana Purchase looks forward to the second such incorporation, not yet fully achieved, following the Civil War. And in "The Convict-Lease System," the sentencing of African Americans to long periods of field labor for relatively minor offenses looks back to the institution of slavery. At times Twain too uses antebellum scenes to reflect on postbellum circumstances. Early in the novel, Huck Finn's father encounters a free person of color and learns that this man cannot be bought or sold in a slave state and can even vote in a free state. Responding to these facts with a half-crazed rant, Pap Finn predicts the resistance that Reconstruction would face.

With this in mind, we might read the novel's attack on (antebellum) slavery as an attack on (postbellum) racism more generally. But it is precisely the belatedness of Tom's action that renders it meaningless, and this calls into question the meaning of Twain's novel as well. The false freeing of Jim is doing something other than the work of reform. When Tom Sawyer is asked why he freed a slave who was already free, he replies that he "wanted the *adventure* of it" (292). Twain's own motives were not much more complex. Like Tom dreaming of a slave who could be freed over an entire lifetime, Twain

36. Cable read the proofs of *Huckleberry Finn* while he was composing "The Freedman's Case," and so if there is any direct influence at work here, it runs from Twain to Cable.

wants Nasby's "lemon," slavery, to remain a continuous source of juice. Indeed, from Twain's perspective, the subject of slavery is all the more useful now that slavery has been abolished. It signals purpose, but a purpose that has become increasingly uncontroversial, and thus increasingly marketable, in the postbellum era. Even Grady, in his debate with Cable, is willing to say that the abolition of slavery was a good thing.

But Nasby's letter raises another and more interesting question. We may be able to understand why Twain would want to write a belated attack on slavery, but why would readers—in his own day and in ours—be so eager to read it? Twain addressed this question earlier in *Huckleberry Finn*, through his depiction of two con artist reformers, the Duke and the Dauphin. Con artists are, of necessity, attentive to the desires of their dupes, and the success of the Duke and the Dauphin's reformist cons therefore throws into relief the desires that audiences bring to a reformist performance and readers bring to a reformist text. In this way, con artistry defamiliarizes the conventions of reform, as do the pranks of two young boys playing at setting a slave free.

The Duke and the Dauphin dominate the middle section of the novel, a section that most critics tend to overlook. But it was central to Twain's conception of the novel. The prospectus he wrote for his subscription agents to circulate focuses on it almost exclusively. Here is the prospectus in full:

> the adventures of Huckleberry Finn, Tom Sawyer and a negro named Jim, who in their travels fall in with two tramps engaged in *taking in* the different country towns through which they pass, by means of the missionary dodge, the temperance crusade, or under any pretext that offers to *easily* raise a dishonest dollar. The writer follows these characters through their various adventures, until finally, we find the tramps properly and warmly clothed,—*with a coat of tar and feathers,*—and the boys and Jim escape their persecutions and return safely to their friends.[37]

To be sure, the contents of this prospectus were partly driven by the needs of advertisement, as Jonathan Arac has suggested. The prospectus therefore recalls some of Twain's more popular early works, in particular *The Adventures of Tom Sawyer* and the stories of frontier humor, and implies that the new novel will provide more of the same.[38] But Twain continued to use this prospectus even after the novel had been published and reviewed and its

37. Quoted in Jonathan Arac, *Huckleberry Finn as Idol and Target: The Functions of Criticism in Our Time* (Madison: University of Wisconsin Press, 1997), 143.
38. Arac, *Huckleberry Finn as Idol and Target*, 143.

other subjects were widely known. Of all of these reviews, he singled out as the most perceptive the one that identified the "swindling schemes of the two river sharpers" as the novel's best episodes.[39] Clearly, then, the prospectus reveals something important about Twain's own conception of *Huckleberry Finn*. And so it is worth noting that the prospectus focuses not simply on cons but on two cons that are connected with reform: the "temperance crusade" and the "missionary dodge."

Con artists, and the subject of fraud more generally, pervade Twain's work. More important, they long shaped his conception of himself as a performer and writer. Twain advertised his first public lectures with a series of placards that gestured toward the kind of cons that the Duke and the Dauphin would subsequently perform. "THE CELEBRATED BEARDED WOMAN! . . . is not with this circus," read one, and another read, "MAGNIFICENT FIRE WORKS . . . were in contemplation for this occasion, but the idea has been abandoned."[40] At the end of the tour, Twain's manager exulted that Twain had "taken in over two hundred dollars," and Twain replied that he had "taken in over two hundred people" as well.[41] And when Twain planned subsequent tours he spoke of them in much the same terms as the Duke and Dauphin would speak of their schemes: where they "lay out a campaign" (134), Twain said he had to "plan a raid." Identifying with con artists in this way, Twain emphasizes that he is in it for the money, every bit as much as they are.

But if con artistry names the motivations of the con artist, it also, and more interestingly, throws into relief the motivations of the dupe. Indeed, it is the dupe's motivations, not the con artist's, that are inscribed in the name of the con game itself. The term "confidence man" was first applied to a man named William Thompson, who would approach prosperous-looking men on the streets of New York and ask them if they had confidence enough to lend him their watch for a day. A surprising number did. In these encounters, there was an element of deception, with the dupes expecting that their watches would be returned the next day. But there was more importantly a structure of exchange. What Thompson got from this exchange is obvious, nearly a dozen watches, but what the dupes got is no less significant: a confirmation of their status as openhearted, unsuspicious men. These dupes were buying, with their watches, a certain sense of themselves. In this way, the confidence man reveals not only his own—rather banal—desire for money but also the rarely acknowledged and often surprising desires of his dupes.

---

39. *San Francisco Chronicle*, 15 March 1885, reprinted in Budd, *Mark Twain: The Contemporary Reviews*, 271.
40. Hoffman describes these signs (*Inventing Mark Twain*, 114, 112).
41. Quoted in Hoffman, *Inventing Mark Twain*, 114.

And so we can turn to the reformist con artists, the Duke and the Dauphin, in order to see what Twain takes to be the true motivations of those who attend reformist performances or read reformist texts.

The Duke and the Dauphin enter the novel as each is separately fleeing a mob of enraged townspeople. The Duke has angered some people by selling a patent toothpaste that removes the enamel as well as the tartar, while the Dauphin has angered others by giving temperance lectures and then spending the proceeds on a large jug of drink. Huck Finn catches sight of the two and invites them aboard the raft he shares with Jim. Once aboard, they inform one another of their specialties. The Duke is a journeyman printer by trade and a tragic actor by avocation. He acts scenes from Shakespeare and offers lectures on mesmerism and phrenology, as well as performing an indescribable something he calls the "Royal Nonesuch." The Dauphin, for his part, is the master of temperance crusades, as well as "general missionarying" around (128). When the two decide to join forces, then, they reenact in comic form the historic dependence of reform on both performance and print. Having joined forces, the two play a number of cons, the most elaborate of which is cheating three orphan girls out of an inheritance and the most damaging of which is pretending that Jim belongs to them so that they can sell him back into slavery. But it is the "missionary dodge" and the "temperance crusade" to which the prospectus draws our attention.

The "missionary dodge" begins when the Duke and the Dauphin land at a river town and find that everyone has gone into the woods for a camp meeting. The Dauphin sets out for this meeting with Huck, leaving the Duke to his own devices in an abandoned print shop. When they arrive at the meeting, Huck is struck by the hymn singing and even more by the effect that it has on the singers, some of whom groan and shout. When the singing stops and the preaching begins, the groaning and shouting spread, until one person after another rises up and runs to the mourner's bench to be saved. Suddenly, the Dauphin runs up and joins the others, singing and groaning louder than all the rest. Once the Dauphin has attracted the preacher's attention, he climbs onto the platform and begins to speak. The passage is worth quoting in full, channeling as it does the Dauphin's extravagant performance through Huck's deadpan narration:

> He told them he was a pirate—been a pirate for thirty years, out in the Indian Ocean, and his crew was thinned out considerable, last spring, in a fight, and he was home now, to take out some fresh men, and thanks to goodness he'd been robbed last night, and put ashore off of a steamboat without a cent, and he was glad of it, it was the blessedest thing that ever happened to him, because he

was a changed man now, and happy for the first time in his life; and poor as he
was, he was going to start right off and work his way back to the Indian Ocean
and put in the rest of his life trying to turn the pirates into the true path; for
he could do it better than anybody else, being acquainted with all the pirate
crews in that ocean; and though it would take him a long time to get there,
without money, he would get there anyway, and every time he convinced a
pirate he would say to him, "Don't you thank me, don't you give me no credit,
it all belongs to them dear people in Pikeville camp-meeting, natural brothers
and benefactors of the race—and that dear preacher there, the truest friend a
pirate ever had!" (137–38)

The Dauphin's audience insists that he raise a collection, as if the idea
originated with them, and he goes through the audience passing his hat,
wiping his eyes, and kissing the pretty young women five or six times. Back
on the raft, the Dauphin counts his money and finds that he has made
eighty-seven dollars and seventy-five cents. He then gives Huck an excellent
piece of con artist advice: "[H]eathens don't amount to shucks, alongside of
pirates, to work a camp-meeting with" (138).

What this scene demonstrates is that reform can be a kind of popular entertainment. The Dauphin describes his "temperance crusade" as if it were a
traveling theatrical, complete with ticket price (ten cents a head), box office
(five or six dollars a night), and length of run (six nights in the same town).
Huck watches the camp meeting as if it were a performance as well, noting the size of the crowd (large) and the range of refreshments being sold
(lemonade and gingerbread, watermelon and green corn). And the townspeople also respond to the Dauphin as if he were a performer rather than an
evangelist. No one runs to the mourner's bench while he is speaking; they
are entertained mightily, but they are not saved. The preacher's words may
prompt them to be born again en masse, but the Dauphin's words prompt
only money and kisses.

In presenting a camp meeting as popular entertainment, Twain is drawing
on a long tradition of southwestern humor writers, for whom such meetings
were a familiar comic topos.[42] But he is also drawing on his own memories. Twain grew up in a river town much like the ones that the Duke and
Dauphin visit, where camp meetings were common and not easily distinguished from the carnivals that also traveled up and down the river. Twain

---

42. Hennig Cohen and William B. Dillingham offer a taxonomy of these topoi, twenty in all.
The ninth is "sermons, camp meetings, and religious experiences." *Humor of the Old Southwest*
(Athens: University of Georgia Press, 1975), xvii. Leland Krauth describes how Twain selects
among these topoi, ignoring those that have to do with violence or sexuality ("Mark Twain: The
Victorian of Southwestern Humor," *American Literature* 54, no. 3 [October 1982]: 368–84).

attended these meetings with great enthusiasm, and Hoffman has argued that these preachers were his first models for compelling public speaking.[43] When Twain was an adolescent, he joined the Cadets of Temperance, solely, Hoffman tells us, because he was entranced by the costumes and pageantry. His own father had renounced alcohol and occasionally sought to reform other drunkards, but for Twain himself the appeal of temperance lay in the parades. He joined right before Memorial Day, achieved a relatively high rank, and then quit as soon as the Fourth of July had passed and no more parades were in the offing.[44] What Twain's own history and other southwestern humorists demonstrate is that reform of all kinds was embedded in the popular culture of the time. And so it is hardly surprising that the novel does not condemn the Dauphin's reformist con. Indeed, it almost seems to delight in his virtuosity.

The camp meeting episode does more than demonstrate that reformist performances can entertain. It also anatomizes the pleasures that such entertainment entails. Some of these pleasures, at least, have little or nothing to do with reform. If, as the Dauphin suggests, pirates are more profitable than heathens, it is because they are more exciting, more exotic. In making this point, Twain echoes contemporary critics of reform who feared that reformist performances and texts might satisfy desires that have little to do with reform, desires for the lurid, the violent, or the sexual. But there are other pleasures that are provided by reform itself, and it is these mostly unacknowledged pleasures that Twain is alone in observing. These pleasures, too, are at work in the camp meeting. The Dauphin concludes his speech by announcing that he will forever attribute both his own salvation and any good he might do to the "dear people in Pikeville camp-meeting" and "that dear preacher there." In saying this, the Dauphin interpellates his listeners not only as virtuous people but as people whose virtue has the power to transform others' lives. And when his listeners respond with such wild enthusiasm, they are responding, at least in part, to this. When reform is working properly, the pleasures of such interpellation are masked by the effects the reform is having on the world. We might not notice the audience's readiness to be congratulated, and its readiness to congratulate itself, if we believed that the Dauphin had actually been saved and that his fellow pirates would soon be redeemed. But because we do not believe this, the audience's other motivations are thrown into relief. And what we see is a desire for the pleasures of self-congratulation.

43. Hoffman, *Inventing Mark Twain*, 14.
44. Hoffman, *Inventing Mark Twain*, 26.

Much nineteenth-century reform depended on the presumption that a text or performance would act on its audience and that this audience in turn would act on the world. But Twain uses the Dauphin to show that this process can be halted halfway through. The young girls at the camp meeting cry, the women at the temperance crusade cheer, but the pirates are not saved, the "rum-mies" are not made sober, the world is not changed. In much the same way, the Dauphin's temperance crusade was repeated over six nights because the "womens-folk" never tired of listening to him "making it mighty warm for the rummies" (127), even though there was no sign that any "rummy," cer-tainly not the Dauphin himself, had been persuaded to give up drink. What these scenes suggest, then, is that the reformist con is a profitable one because people like to feel that they are acting upon the world even—or, perhaps, especially—when they are not. It is in this way that Twain differs from that earlier creator of hard-drinking temperance reformers, Dickens. Dickens used con artistry as a way of highlighting the cynicism of the reformer, while Twain, though his Dauphin is surely a great cynic, is more interested in attacking the easy self-congratulation of the reformer's audience.

With this in mind, we can better understand both Tom Sawyer's belated rescue of Jim and Twain's own belated attack on slavery. Here, too, affects are produced that do not—because they cannot—change the world. Chief among these, for Tom, are the thrill of power that comes from rescue, a thrill to be extended, if possible, for eighty years, and the more rarefied delights of a sympathy disconnected from real persons, a sympathy to be indulged in, ideally, four times in a row. To some extent, the novel produces these affects in its readers as well. Certainly Tom's weeping over his "mournful inscrip-tions" bears an uncomfortable resemblance to whatever tears Jim's suffering might prompt in us. But the novel also produces, as the Dauphin's perfor-mances produce, a too easy self-congratulation.

In his searching inquiry into *Huckleberry Finn*'s reception, Arac has ar-gued that the novel has long been celebrated for teaching us lessons that we should already have learned. Arac focuses on the novel's twentieth-century reception, which he divides into two main phases. The first, which he calls "hypercanonization," took place in the 1940s as academic critics argued for the novel's greatness on the grounds of its formal perfection, as in Trilling's and Eliot's discussions of the ending. The second, which he calls "idolatry," began in the 1980s and continues into the present day, as academic critics join school officials and the press in dismissing the protests of those students and parents who object to the novel's vocabulary and depiction of race. The "idolators" dismiss these objections in much the same way as nineteenth-century reviewers dismissed the objections of the Concord Public Library, by adducing the novel's purpose as its defense. And the purpose identified by the novel's defenders has remained much the same. In the late nineteenth century, the novel was defended as a serious account of slavery; in the late twentieth, as proof that African Americans are human beings. But this, Arac notes, is hardly a lesson that still needs to be taught: "Is this all it means to fight racism in the 1990s?" he asks. "Must students be taught that even white boys at the verge of puberty can treat African Americans as human? If this premise of humanity is not already shared, what can a single book do?"[45] What Arac's questions suggest is that *Huckleberry Finn* no longer functions as a novel of purpose. The teaching of it has become nothing but the performance of a phony purposefulness, one that distracts from the very real reformist work that remains to be done.

But if we recognize that *Huckleberry Finn* no longer functions as a novel of purpose, then we must also recognize that it did not function as one even in its own day. It was, rather, a novel that displayed its virtuosity at one mode of reformist writing, antislavery sentimentalism, while also casting a skeptical light on both the writing and the reading of reformist texts. And what this light reveals, in the elite magazines of the 1880s as in the classrooms of the 1990s and 2000s, are the self-congratulatory pleasures of a seeming iconoclasm. "All right, then, I'll *go* to hell," Huck famously says to himself as he decides to violate the moral standards of respectable society and rescue Jim, now his friend, from slavery (219). But while his decision violates the moral standards of the antebellum South, it conforms to and even affirms the moral standards of the postbellum United States—the New South as well as the northern states, as Grady's response to Cable reminds us. Generations of readers have identified with Huck and have in the process congratulated themselves as if they were alone in recognizing that slavery was wrong, that African Americans are human beings. And this, Twain suggests, is the worst con of all.

Mark Twain in Anglo-America: *A Connecticut Yankee in King Arthur's Court*

Despite its deep ambivalence about purposeful writing, *Huckleberry Finn* was published at a moment when Mark Twain himself was becoming more and more aligned with the elite northeastern magazines. His fiftieth birthday, which came several months after *Huckleberry Finn*, was marked by an elaborate dinner held in his honor by the *Atlantic*, and Oliver Wendell Holmes wrote a poem for the occasion. Twain's transformation from frontier humorist

45. Arac, *Huckleberry Finn as Idol and Target*, 11.

to genteel man of letters was reflected, in part, by his growing involvement in U.S. political life.[46] He campaigned in 1884 for Grover Cleveland, who would be the first Democratic president since the Civil War, because he was appalled by the corruption of the Republican candidate and persuaded of the need for civil service reform. At the same time, Twain's own newly established subscription publishing firm became famous for publishing the memoirs of Ulysses S. Grant, whose phenomenal popularity underscored the continuing centrality of the Civil War in the postbellum imagination.

Twain's transformation into a genteel man of letters was also reflected in his growing engagement with social reform. Indeed, his next novel, *A Connecticut Yankee in King Arthur's Court* (1889), is a kind of fantasy of reform: its protagonist is endowed not only with what he takes to be en-lightened social views but also with the knowledge and authority to impose them on others at will. When the nineteenth-century Yankee finds himself in Arthurian Britain, he vows to "boss the whole country inside of three months."[47] He soon has himself knighted Sir Boss, and in that role he imposes an array of reforms, many of them resembling the reforms then being debated in the United States, such as state universities, lower tariffs, and civil service reform. Much of this is comic, but *Connecticut Yankee*, unlike *Huckleberry Finn*, is not a satire of reform. On the contrary, it is a serious and sustained inquiry into what reform entails. It not only expands Twain's critique of sentimentalism, but also explores the potential—and the limits—of institutional reform as well.

Connecticut Yankee critiques sentimentalism in two ways. First, it shows that sentimentalism does not lead to social change because sympathy itself is fleeting. We see this in the Yankee's visit to the castle of Morgan le Fay. He is shocked to see her casually dirk a page who inadvertently brushed against her and, later, to hear her order that the castle composer be hanged for writing bad music. In the latter case the Yankee is moved to intervene, and he commands that she spare the composer. But his compassion passes as soon as he hears the music once more, and he urges her to hang the entire band. The Yankee does not reflect on this action, but elsewhere in the novel he will speculate that sympathy does not last because imagina-tion is a poor substitute for experience: "[W]ords realise nothing, vivify nothing to you, unless you have suffered in your own person the thing which the words try to describe" (264). Having come to this conclusion, he decides that the conditions of the poor will not be improved in Arthurian

46. Budd makes this point in "Mark Twain as an American Icon," in *The Cambridge Companion to Mark Twain*, ed. Forrest G. Robinson (Cambridge: Cambridge University Press, 1995), 15.

47. Mark Twain, *A Connecticut Yankee in King Arthur's Court* (1889; London: Penguin, 1986), 50. All further references to this edition will be marked in the text.

Britain until King Arthur has experienced those conditions for himself. He therefore dresses the King in a yeoman's tunic and cuts the King's hair in a yeoman's bangs, and the two go traveling in disguise among the King's people.

This is not the first time that royalty has disguised itself in Twain. The prince and the pauper from Twain's eponymous 1882 novel exchange clothing at the prince's command. They then look at themselves in the mirror, and the prince observes that "fared we forth naked, there is none could say which was you and which the Prince of Wales."[48] As it happens, this is not quite true. The novel has already acknowledged that while the two boys are remarkably similar in feature, they are less so in body. The prince is "tanned and brown with sturdy outdoor sports and exercises" (13), while the pauper is "frail and little" (15). And yet the novel must insist on bodily similarity at the moment of the clothing exchange because the very purpose of this exchange is to demonstrate that paupers and princes differ only in their clothing, which is to say, in the accidents of their birth. The novel began with brief descriptions of the two boys on the day of their birth: the prince was "lapped in silks and satins" (5), while the pauper was "lapped in his poor rags" (6), and the difference in fabric here figures all other differences in their circumstances. In much the same way, then, the identical bodies figure the shared humanness on which sentimentalism relies. And *The Prince and the Pauper* does, in fact, proceed along recognizably sentimental lines.[49] The pauper quickly assumes the "port and manner" of a prince (35), and the prince, having experienced for himself the cruelty of the kingdom's laws, vows to reverse them as soon as he ascends the throne. His reign, Twain tells us, was one of the most merciful that England has ever known.

The Yankee is motivated by a similar faith that there is no essential difference between nobles and commoners. He scours the nation looking for men who might help him in abolishing the monarchy and establishing a democracy, and one of the most promising is a commoner who has been imprisoned for saying, in the Yankee's vernacular translation, that a king could not be distinguished from a quack doctor, or a duke from a hotel

48. Mark Twain, *The Prince and the Pauper* (1882; New York: Modern Library Editions, 2003), 17. All further references to this edition will be marked in the text.

49. The sentimentalism here is best understood in light of Audrey Jaffe's study, *Scenes of Sympathy: Identity and Representation in Victorian Fiction* (Ithaca: Cornell University Press, 2000). Where Fisher follows Jean-Jacques Rousseau in conceiving of sympathy as the experimental extension of subjectivity to another, Jaffe follows Adam Smith in conceiving of sympathy as the replacement of the other with an image of one's own self—with all the bodily peril that substitution might imaginatively entail. Where my reading of *Huckleberry Finn* draws primarily on Fisher, my reading of *Connecticut Yankee* draws primarily on Jaffe.

clerk, if the nation were stripped naked. And yet the Yankee finds that the stripping naked and the donning of new clothes are far more difficult than he anticipated. The King can be dressed as a commoner, but he continues to look like a king. Acknowledging the discrepancy between "clothes and bearing" (261), the Yankee attempts to alter the King's bearing by asking him to imagine that he is a commoner. But even the Yankee's descriptions of a commoner who is "in debt, and eaten up by relentless creditors . . . out of work . . . and can get none," with a sick wife and children who are "crying because they are hungry," cannot subdue the proud head and erect back of the King (263–64). It is at this moment that the Yankee realizes that words "vivify nothing."

In time, the King will experience such privations for himself. The Yankee and the King, dressed as commoners, are captured by a slave trader and sold as slaves. And yet the King does not experience these privations as the other slaves do. He plots escapes while the others submit, and he returns the blows that are dealt him, just as he alone among the yeoman farmers dared to enter a house infected with smallpox and comfort the dying within. In the end, when the King is standing on a gallows in his rags, the Yankee is compelled to admit that "really there *is* something peculiarly grand about the gait and bearing of a king, after all" (352). In part, the Yankee's admission reflects his own ambivalence about authority; he can never decide whether he would prefer that Arthurian Britain be made a democracy or an autocracy under his own rule. But the Yankee's admission also points to what Twain takes to be the second failure of sentimentalism: sentimentalism posits a shared humanness that does not in fact exist. Twain shows that while the accidents of our birth may be nothing but accidents, they nonetheless determine who we are. In time, the trivial differences between the prince's silken swaddlings and the pauper's rags will cause the more significant differences between a strong and healthy body and a sickly one.

Environments determine, and while Twain suppresses this recognition in *The Prince and the Pauper*, he confronts it directly in *Connecticut Yankee*. It is for this reason that the reforms in the latter novel focus not on recognizing personhood but rather on producing or transforming it; and it is for this reason that the reforms in *Connecticut Yankee* take place not between persons, as in the nighttime conversations between Huck and Jim, but rather within institutions. The Yankee is an avid founder of schools, which he refers to as "man-factories" (130), and this phrase emphasizes their function as environments that produce a certain kind of personhood. In this way, Twain looks forward to the late-century return to the reformist institutions of the 1830s, evidenced most clearly in the settlement house movement of the 1890s. Because such reforms do not rely on affective responses, such as sympathy, they do not depend as much on the novel, nor do they fit as easily into it. The Yankee's "man-factories" remain on the novel's periphery, referred to but never described, and the periods of the Yankee's greatest reforms are elided in the narration. "Consider the three years sped," the Yankee tells us, and then mentions the schools and colleges, the newspapers and publishing houses that have been founded, the slavery that has been abolished and the laws that have been reformed in that time (364).

In the end, however, these institutions prove to be as ineffectual as the sentimental reforms they seek to replace. When the Church places the nation under an interdict in response to the death of Arthur, the people of Britain quickly renounce all of the Yankee's improvements and reforms. The Yankee realizes that he has not, in fact, "educated the superstition out" of them (384). Only fifty-two persons stand with him. These are the young men who have spent nearly their entire lives within one of his "man-factories." Anything less comprehensive seems to have no lasting effect. And fifty-two reformed young men are not enough to stand against all of England. The novel, which began as a fantasy of reform, culminates in reform's tragedy.

Connecticut Yankee was published to a mixed response. It was very popular in the United States, much less so among the British, in part because it was presented and read as an attack on Great Britain. Twain had grown disenchanted with Britain in the years following his first triumphant visit, and so he was ready to claim, in a newspaper interview that he gave at the moment of the novel's publication, that his British publishers were delaying the release of the novel because of its critiques of monarchy.[50] In truth, the British publishers had asked for some changes, but they had honored his refusal to make them. By circulating this misleading story, Twain ensured that *Connecticut Yankee* would be read in terms of conflict between the two nations. Howells subtly reinforced this reading in his review of the novel, which argued that Twain was the apotheosis of a tradition of humor, "the American kind," that puts itself in the service of "democracy" and "humanity."[51]

As for the British, they were quick to read the novel in terms of national conflict because they were not alert to its regional meanings. They did not see that Twain's satire of feudalism was an attack less on Britain than on the southern states. In the early nineteenth century, as the increasingly commercial northern states were newly connected to the western territories first by canal and then by railway, the still agrarian southern states began to fear that they were losing their preeminence within the United States.

50. Baetzhold discusses this episode in *Mark Twain and John Bull*, 131.
51. *Harper's Magazine* 80 (January 1890): 319–21, reprinted in Anderson and Sanderson, *Mark Twain*, 153.

They responded to this fear by aligning themselves all the more closely with Britain, to whom they were already connected through the cotton trade, by imitating an imagined Britain of the cavaliers. This gave rise to what the historian W. J. Cash has described as an idea of the southern states as "wholly dominated by ideals of honor and chivalry and *noblesse*."[52] This southern Anglophilia was the counterpart and rival to the transatlantic ties that connected antislavery campaigners in both nations. As a result of these competing identifications, Great Britain would be divided, during the U.S. Civil War, between its reformist alignments with the northern states and its cultural, as well as economic, alignments with the southern states. In this context, we can see that Twain's parody of Arthurian romance, like his ongoing attacks on Sir Walter Scott, has less to do with the U.S. War of Independence than with the U.S. Civil War.[53] But Twain's British readers did not fully grasp the significance of these regional rivalries, as we can see from the novel's British title. *A Connecticut Yankee in King Arthur's Court* was published in Britain as *A Yankee at the Court of King Arthur*, with the Yankee thereby transformed from a representative of a particular region of the United States into a representative of the United States as a whole.

To read *Connecticut Yankee* in terms of national conflict is to miss not only its regional but also its Anglo-American aspects, in particular its immersion in an Anglo-American culture of reform. One sign of this immersion is the fact that the novel's critiques invariably cut both ways. To be sure, the novel does criticize the aristocrats for their unthinking allegiance to the old ways, but it also criticizes the Yankee for his unthinking faith in the new. It does condemn monarchical privileges, established churches, and other specifically British practices, but it also, and far more extensively, condemns antebellum slavery. Nor does it deny that abuses much like slavery continue in the United States of the present day: to Twain's great delight, the novel's slave trader was drawn with the face of the U.S. industrialist Jay Gould.

Twain's own political views were quite close to those of the Liberal party in Britain, and he shared the party's views as to what reforms were needed in both nations.[54] In fact, some of the reforms that the Yankee contemplates were being debated in Parliament as Twain was writing, in particular, reforms of officer training and primary schools, as well as the reform—or even

52. W. J. Cash, *The Mind of the South* (New York: Knopf, 1941), xi.

53. For a full account of the transatlantic complexities of the relation between Twain and Scott, see Susan Manning, "Did Mark Twain Bring Down the Temple on Scott's Shoulders?" in *Special Relationships: Anglo-American Affinities and Antagonisms, 1854–1936*, ed. Janet Beer and Bridget Bennett (New York: Palgrave, 2002).

54. Louis J. Budd makes this argument in *Mark Twain: Social Philosopher* (Bloomington: Indiana University Press, 1962).

the abolition—of the House of Lords.[55] This last reminds us that attacks on the British aristocracy are hardly limited to the citizens of the United States. To be sure, Huck Finn offered a homegrown critique of the monarchy when he observed of the Duke and Dauphin that "all kings is mostly rapscallions" (159). But the critiques in *Connecticut Yankee* are for the most part derived from British sources, in particular from the writings of George Standring, a London radical who contributed to many liberal and freethinking journals.[56] In all of these ways, the novel is less a distinctively U.S. attack on the British monarchy than an Anglo-American collaboration in reformist concerns.

British reviewers, however, were reluctant to accept Twain as a reformer. In the U.S. reviews, Twain was everywhere celebrated for his new purpose-fulness. Howells begins his by referring to Twain as "Mr. Clemens" and explains that he is doing so because the "arch-humorist" Mark Twain has been replaced by a writer who hates injustice and loves equality, that is to say, by a novelist of purpose.[57] The *Atlantic* referred to the novel's "moral purpose," as did the *San Francisco American Standard*; the *San Francisco Ar-gonaut*, to its "serious purpose"; the *Boston Herald* to its "earnest purpose"; the *New York Examiner*, to its "earnestness of purpose"; and the *Boston Literary World* spoke of its "serious aims."[58] There was widespread agreement that the novel was purposeful, even as there was little agreement as to what its purpose might be. British reviewers, by contrast, also recognized that *Connecticut Yankee* was a novel of purpose, but they did not share the U.S. view that this fact conferred respectability on Twain's career. On the contrary, they lamented that Twain was abandoning his true strengths. To be sure, Matthew Arnold had adduced Twain the year before as a prime instance of what he called a "national misfortune," namely, the national "addiction to 'the funny man'."[59] But most British reviewers continued to value Twain for his peripheral status, as both a humorist and a man of the frontier, and were therefore not impressed by his attempt to move to the center of the literary world. The *Athenaeum* gingerly described the novel as "a rather la-borious piece of fun with a sort of purpose in it," while the *Scots Observer*

55. Baetzhold, *Mark Twain and John Bull*, 126.

56. Baetzhold, *Mark Twain and John Bull*, 111.

57. *Harper's Magazine* 80 (January 1890), reprinted in Anderson and Sanderson, *Mark Twain*, 153.

58. "Books of the Month," *Atlantic Monthly* 65 (February 1890): 286; "Literary Gossip," *San Francisco American Standard* 17 (May 1890); "Mark Twain's New Book," *San Francisco Argonaut* 25 (23 December 1889); *Boston Sunday Herald* 17 (15 December 1889); *New York Examiner* (6 April 1893); *Boston Literary World* 21 (15 February 1890), all reprinted in Budd, *Mark Twain: The Contemporary Reviews*.

59. Matthew Arnold, "Civilization in the United States," *Nineteenth Century* 23, no. 134 (April 1888): 498.

described it as "bewrayed with seriousness and bedevilled with a purpose."[60]
And the *Speaker* deplored the fact that Twain had given in to the "Spirit of
his Time," which it identified as "didactic." "We had expected to laugh a
little," the review concludes, "but instead we have learned much—much that
we knew."[61]

The British reception of *Connecticut Yankee* is further complicated by the
fact that British reviewers were offended less by the novel's political satire
than by its parody of the King Arthur legends. The nineteenth-century Arthurian revival had been prompted by two texts: the 1861 translation of Sir
Thomas Malory's *Morte d'Arthur* (1485) into contemporary English, and
the Arthurian poems that Alfred Lord Tennyson intermittently published
between 1832 and 1869. The thought that Twain might participate in this
revival shocked the British reviews. "Is nothing to be safe from the Yankee
humorist?" asked the *Pall Mall Gazette*, while the *Spectator* argued that the
Arthurian legends were the proper inheritance of Britain, not the United
States.[62] Certainly, the nineteenth-century Arthurian revival was over-
whelmingly British. The Arthurian legends were taken up by poets such as
Dante Gabriel Rossetti, Algernon Swinburne, and William Morris; by visual
artists such as the Pre-Raphaelites and Aubrey Beardsley; and by a number
of 1890s closet dramatists.[63] But if it is striking that all of these artists or
authors are British, it is equally striking that none of them are novelists.[64]

Genre is significant because Twain rewrote the Arthurian legends not simply to appropriate British subject matter for U.S. literature but also to represent that subject matter in the contemporary novel's most characteristic mode.
At least some of what the British took to be irreverence was actually Twain's
attempt at realism. Twain had been introduced to the *Morte d'Arthur* by Cable
during their reading tour. He had delighted in its language, even going so far
as to speak a mock archaic English to Cable between performances, but he
also formed the intention of rewriting the story to include all the things that
Malory had left out. For Twain, this meant bodily realities, as it had done for

---

60. *Athenaeum* 3251 (15 February 1890); *Scots Observer*, 18 January 1890, reprinted in Budd,
Mark Twain: The Contemporary Reviews, 170, 164.

61. *Speaker* 1 (11 January 1890), reprinted in Budd, *Mark Twain: The Contemporary Reviews*.

62. "Mark Twain and King Arthur," *Pall Mall Gazette*, 21 December 1889; "Mark Twain's
Camelot," *Spectator*, 5 April 1890, reprinted in Budd, *Mark Twain: The Contemporary Reviews*,
287, 316.

63. Benjamin Fisher Franklin discusses the 1890s plays in his "King Arthur Plays from the
1890s," *Victorian Poetry* 28, nos. 3–4 (Autumn 1986): 153–76.

64. It was David Staines who observed the absence of the novel from Arthurian art, and
his discussion of this absence remains very illuminating even though it entirely ignores *Connecticut Yankee*. "King Arthur in Victorian Fiction," in *The Worlds of Victorian Fiction*, ed. Jerome
H. Buckley (Cambridge: Harvard University Press, 1975), 267–94.

Miguel de Cervantes nearly three hundred years before. Twain's first notes toward *Connecticut Yankee* make this bodily focus quite clear: "Dream of being a knight errant in armor in the Middle Ages . . . No way to manage certain requirements of nature. Can't scratch. Cold in the head—can't blow—can't get a handkerchief, can't use iron sleeve."[65] British reviewers, and a few American ones, dismissed this focus on the body as burlesque, because they were unwilling to recognize Cervantesque realism in the depiction of subject matter they continued to associate with the lyric or the lyric drama.

But when this seeming irreverence is stripped away, what remains is Twain's complex, and rather poignant, relation to British literature. His two British predecessors, Malory and Tennyson, are both present in the novel from the beginning. The illustrator gave Tennyson's face to the Yankee's archenemy, Merlin, a charlatan who proves to be deadly. As a magician, Merlin is as impotent as he is fraudulent, and he is humiliated by the Yankee in each of their encounters. And yet, while the Yankee's innovations (dynamite and guns) give him the temporary advantage over Merlin, Merlin's magic, hitherto useless, prevails in the end. The Yankee is wounded in the final battle of Camelot, and Merlin, disguised as an old nurse, gives him a drug that condemns him to perpetual sleep. The sudden potency of Merlin's magic can only be explained as an effect of the sudden potency of the Arthurian legends that the Yankee—and Twain—have been trying to rewrite. In the end, what brings the Yankee's reforms to naught is the resurgence of the Arthurian plot. His schools are closed, his factories are abandoned, his people turn away from enlightenment and back to monarchy and the established church—and all because Launcelot is in love with Guinevere, because the inherited plot, the British tradition, must in the end have its way.

But if Tennyson as Merlin enacts the killing power of inherited culture, the novel's use of Malory conjures up the possibility of a happier relation between Britain and the United States. Malory is present in the novel through the tedious and unending stories that the Yankee is forced to listen to at every turn. The text of these stories is taken directly from the *Morte d'Arthur;* it is Malory, then, who repeatedly puts the Yankee to sleep. And yet the Yankee ultimately marries the most egregious of these storytellers.[66] Moreover, he ultimately comes to value Maloryesque narration over his own. As the founder of the first newspaper in Britain, the Yankee trains his staff to write like newspaper reporters in the nineteenth-century United States, and the

---

65. Quoted in Bruce Michelson, "Realism, Romance, and Dynamite: The Quarrel of *A Connecticut Yankee in King Arthur's Court,*" *New England Quarterly* 64, no. 4 (December 1991): 612.

66. Michelson makes an illuminating distinction between romance as practiced by Sandy and romance as practiced by Merlin ("Realism, Romance, and Dynamite," 620).

novel is punctuated by his staff's half-successful attempts, which are filled with slang and exclamation points and type set upside down. Over time, however, this style no longer seems appropriate to the Yankee: "[I]t was good Arkansas journalism," he thinks, "but this was not Arkansas" (246–47). Only at the end of the novel does the Yankee's star reporter write in a style that the Yankee entirely approves, and this happens at the moment when the whole Arthurian world is coming undone. The King is dead, killed in a battle with his illegitimate son, and Camelot is doomed. The Yankee reads about these events in one of his newspapers, in a story that opens with these words: "Then the king looked about him, and then he was ware of all his host and of all his good knights" (383). The text has been taken from the *Morte d'Arthur*, and this, the last of the novel's interpolations from Malory, compels the Yankee's assent. "That," he announces, "is a good piece of war correspondence" (384). The moment is a remarkable one because it reveals that the Yankee, who had been working to alter institutions in order to alter people, has himself been shaped by Arthurian England in ways that he does not fully understand. He thinks he has failed as a reformer, but it is he who has, in an older sense of the word, been reformed.

In paying tribute to the power of British culture, the ending of *Connecticut Yankee* recalls those heady days of the late 1860s when metropolitan London was the making of a young man from the frontier. Since then, Twain had come to conform more and more to the expectations of the genteel Northeast, in ways that would disappoint and offend his first champions. But if the publication of *Connecticut Yankee* marks the low point of Twain's relations with Great Britain, it does not mark their end. The next stage, which I will touch on in my epilogue, would involve him in one of the last Anglo-American reformist campaigns.

Chapter 7

Thomas Hardy
New Women, Old Purposes

Thomas Hardy is unlike the other novelists in this book. He was not a realist but rather the great nineteenth-century author of pastoral and tragedy. He had nothing to do with reform, at least not until after his novel-writing career was done. And he had no interest in, or even much awareness of, the Anglo-American world. A handful of his characters think briefly about emigrating to the United States, but it is just as exotic and remote to them as the Brazil or New Zealand or Australia to which a few other characters actually do travel.[1] They have heard that the United States is a place where an ingenious man can make a fortune, but they are very reluctant to venture to what one of them describes as "the other side of the warrld."[2] Registered in that phrase is the insistent localness that characterizes Hardy's fiction and accounts for his lack of interest in Anglo-America.

In all of these ways, Hardy stood on the periphery of the literary world I have sought to describe. And yet when this world began to fragment at the end of the century, it was Hardy who would reflect on its fragmentation in the richest and most illuminating ways. He did so in his final novel, *Jude the Obscure* (1895). *Jude* is, or at least seems to be, a reformist novel: it describes

1. Simon Gatrell makes this argument in "England, Europe, and Empire: Hardy, Meredith, and Gissing," in *The Ends of the Earth: 1876–1918*, ed. Gatrell (London: Ashfield Press, 1992), 69.
2. Thomas Hardy, *The Mayor of Casterbridge* (1886; Oxford: Oxford University Press, 1987), 47.

the injustices of marriage law, as well as the impediments to working-class education. In the end, however, it shows that reform is not enough. And in doing so, it points beyond the novel of purpose to something more utopian and visionary.

Pastoral, Tragedy, Reform

In 1867, Hardy completed his first manuscript, which was entitled "The Poor Man and the Lady: By the Poor Man." He sent it off to publishers in great confidence, only to have it be rejected again and again. In the letters he sent with the manuscript, we can see his early bravado give way to a growing willingness to do anything at all in order to be published.[3] "Would you mind suggesting the sort of story you think I could do best," he asked in a fol-low-up letter to a press that had received his manuscript in silence, "or any literary work I should do well to go upon?"[4] Two publishing houses replied with some advice. The reader at Macmillan, John Morley, told Hardy that his manuscript was strongest in its rural scenes, while the reader at Chapman and Hall, George Meredith, advised him to "attempt a novel with a purely artistic purpose."[5]

Hardy would be given a great deal of direction over the course of his ca-reer, and at this early stage he was eager to accept it. We can see in Morley's and Meredith's advice the first references to the two literary modes that would characterize Hardy's career. Hardy would focus on the rural in a se-ries of pastorals, among them *Under the Greenwood Tree* (1872), *Far from the Madding Crowd* (1874), and *The Woodlanders* (1887). In other novels, he would write in what seemed to him, a largely self-taught scholar of clas-sics, the most "artistic" mode of all: tragedy. He would become the one great tragic novelist in English, writing *The Return of the Native* (1878), *The Mayor of Casterbridge* (1886), and *Tess of the d'Urbervilles* (1891). But Hardy would increasingly come to resent, as Peter Widdowsdown has shown, the expectation that he write only tragedy and pastoral. He would rebel, in the middle of his career, by publishing a string of experimental novels: *The Hand*

---

3. J. A. Sutherland offers a searching discussion of Hardy's early negotiations with his pub-lishers in *Victorian Novelists and Publishers* (Chicago: University of Chicago Press, 1976).

4. Thomas Hardy to Alexander Macmillan, 10 September 1868, in *The Collected Letters of Thomas Hardy: 1840–1892*, ed. Richard Little Purdy and Michael Millgate (Oxford: Oxford University Press, 1978), 8.

5. [Thomas Hardy], *The Early Life of Thomas Hardy, 1840–1891* (London: Macmillan, 1928), reprinted, along with *The Later Years of Thomas Hardy, 1892–1928* (London: Macmillan, 1930), as *The Life of Thomas Hardy* (London: Studio Editions, 1994), 82.

of Ethelberta (1876), *A Laodicean* (1881), and *Two on a Tower* (1882). These experimental novels were as unpopular with readers as with critics, however, and Hardy soon returned to the modes that had made his career.[6]

Hardy received even more direction with respect to his subject matter. His first three novels were published by minor publishing houses, but his fourth, *Far from the Madding Crowd*, was serialized in the prestigious *Cornhill Magazine*. The *Cornhill* was edited by Leslie Stephen, who took it upon himself to instruct Hardy in which subjects were acceptable and which were not. Hardy professed himself to be baffled by these distinctions, so much so that his most important biographer, Michael Millgate, has argued that Hardy was simply unable to understand what his publishers and readers would find shocking.[7] But T. R. Wright has more recently argued that Hardy knew very well indeed. In the early years of his career, Hardy would negotiate a serial contract on the basis of a few chapters and then introduce sexual subject matter once the serial was under way. The editor of the *Atlantic Monthly* was not alone in complaining that Hardy had promised him "a family story" and delivered a "story in the family way." Hardy defended himself from the charge of duplicity by insisting that his characters had surprised him as well when they suddenly took it into their heads to behave in scandalous ways. Over time, Hardy would become even more canny. He would write each novel in two versions—one for the magazines and one for the circulating libraries—and the skill with which he distinguished between the two versions demonstrates how sensitive he had become to precisely what subject matter each audience would allow.[8]

Hardy's career was shaped by another injunction as well: that he not write novels of purpose. So thoroughly did Hardy conform to this injunction that he alludes to it only once, in the autobiography that he wrote under his wife's name and arranged to have published after his death. In this autobiography, he informs his readers for the first time that his career began with a manuscript that was never published and subsequently lost, "The Poor Man and the Lady." Hardy describes this manuscript as recognizably reformist. It was "socialistic, not to say revolutionary," written by a "a young man with a passion for reforming the world," and it culminated in what he called his

---

6. Peter Widdowsdown, *Hardy in History: A Study in Literary Sociology* (London: Routledge, 1989), 16.

7. Michael Millgate, *Thomas Hardy: A Biography* (New York: Random House, 1982), 305–6, 371.

8. Indeed, so different were the magazine and library versions that I depart in this chapter from my usual practice of citing the serialization dates as the date of publication and instead cite the date of the three-volume edition. T. R. Wright, *Hardy and His Readers* (London: Palgrave, 2003), 136 (negotiations with Stephen), 136 (negotiations with the *Atlantic Monthly*), 149 (two versions of novel).

"speech to the working man."[9] All of this would have been common enough at the time, and yet this was the manuscript that prompted Meredith's advice that Hardy abandon politics and attempt a "purely artistic purpose" instead. It is impossible to tell whether Hardy's manuscript failed on purely literary grounds or whether "speeches to working men" were more welcome when coming from established metropolitan novelists like George Eliot than from aspiring young men of the rural laboring class. Whatever the real cause of the manuscript's failure might have been, however, it is clear that the lesson that Hardy learned from it was to abandon any reformist purposes—or any purposes at all. He would follow this lesson until the very end of his novel-writing career.

From the late 1860s into the 1890s, Hardy took great care to hide anything "socialistic, not to say revolutionary" from view. In his public persona, he did so by refusing to take any political stands. Although he was a committed Liberal, he maintained a posture of public neutrality. He was prone to announcing that his "politics really are neither Tory or radical" and to decrying "democratic" as well as "aristocratic privilege," and he refused to lend public support to a friend's campaign for Parliament.[10] When asked to make the formal nomination of a Liberal candidate, he insisted that his role as an artist prohibited him from doing so because an artist must view the world from an "absolutely unpledged point."[11] In much the same way, Hardy refused to take up any political topics in his writings—even after his status as a prominent novelist had been secured, even on issues closest to his own heart. "The Dorsetshire Labourer" (1883) is a case in point. *Longman's Magazine* commissioned this essay in the midst of the Liberal campaign to extend the suffrage to the very farm workers who were Hardy's particular literary domain. But while the essay describes these farm workers with equal respect and sympathy, it mentions neither the suffrage campaign nor the more general question of their political representation. And when Hardy was asked later in the year to write another piece dealing specifically with the question of suffrage, he evasively refused.

In his novels, Hardy similarly masked any "passion for reforming the world." He did so in large part through his characteristic literary modes. Tragedy, of course, is necessarily opposed to reform. It attributes suffering to individual or cosmic, rather than social, causes, and it discharges through catharsis the readerly response that reformist texts instead seek to transform

9. [Thomas Hardy], *Life*, 81.
10. Quoted in Widdowsdown, *Hardy in History*, 71; quoted in Millgate, *Thomas Hardy*, 272.
11. Thomas Hardy to Joseph Eldridge, 8 June 1892, in *Collected Letters of Thomas Hardy: 1840–1892*, 272.

into social action. Pastoral, by contrast, had been a reformist mode in the past. In Philip Sidney's *Arcadia* (1590, 1593) and William Shakespeare's *As You Like It* (1598–1600), the temporary retreat to a simplified natural space makes possible the renovation of the existing social and political world. But in Hardy, the simplified natural space is discontinuous with the existing world and so does not admit of reformist thinking. In all of Hardy's novels until the last, potentially reformist subject matter is contained within modes that either distance or rechannel readerly response.

This is most clear in those novels that take as their subject what Hardy calls "matrimonial divergence."[12] Few marriages in Hardy are without their "divergences," as Eustacia Vye and Tess Durbeyfield can attest, but Hardy uses the term to single out the three novels in which marital unhappiness leads to fairly formal separations: *The Mayor of Casterbridge* and *The Woodlanders*, as well as *Jude the Obscure*, which I discuss more fully at the end of the chapter. The subject matter of these novels has obvious reformist potential. Throughout the nineteenth century, novels about unhappy marriages greatly contributed to the reform of marriage law. Such novels as Anne Brontë's *Tenant of Wildfell Hall* (1848) and Charles Dickens's *Hard Times* (1854) altered public thinking about marriage and divorce and made possible the passage of the Matrimonial Causes Act of 1857. The 1857 act made divorce a matter for the courts rather than Parliament, thereby expanding access to divorce dramatically.[13] Still, important restrictions remained. Divorces were granted only in the case of adultery, but husbands could sue for divorce on the grounds of adultery alone, while wives could sue only when adultery was compounded by at least one other violation, such as incest, sodomy, bestiality, cruelty, or abandonment for two years. Moreover, the cost of divorce made it less accessible to the poor.

Passed at least partly in response to the reformist novels that had already been written, the 1857 act went on to influence future novels in turn. The 1860s vogue for sensation fiction was made possible, Elaine Showalter has argued, by the newspaper reporting on divorce trials that involved charges of cruelty.[14] And the cruelty provision also gave rise, Andrew K. Dowling has argued, to a more serious and longer-lasting novelistic inquiry into what constitutes suffering in marriage. The legal definition of cruelty had been expanded, by the 1870 decision in *Kelly v. Kelly*, from discrete "bodily

12. Thomas Hardy, "[1895] Preface," in *The Woodlanders* (1887; Oxford: Oxford University Press, 1996), 3.

13. Stone, *Road to Divorce*, 379.

14. Elaine Showalter, "Family Secrets and Domestic Subversion: Rebellion in the Novels of the 1860s," in *The Victorian Family: Structure and Stresses*, ed. Anthony S. Wohl (New York: St. Martin's Press, 1978), 101.

injuries" to a more pervasive "injury to health." The novel would go further, however, and attend to a suffering that was not limited to the body, as in the unhappy marriages in Anthony Trollope and George Meredith and, most chillingly, in George Eliot's *Daniel Deronda* (1874–76) and Henry James's *Portrait of a Lady* (1880–81).[15]

In this context, we can see that Hardy's depiction of unhappy marriages might make a particularly radical case for the reform of marriage law. Michael and Susan Henchard in *The Mayor of Casterbridge*, Grace Melbury and Evered Fitzpiers in *The Woodlanders*, Jude Fawley and Arabella Donn and Sue Bridehead and Richard Phillotson in *Jude the Obscure*—all are couples, we are invited to feel, whose marriages should be ended. These marriages should be ended even though the actual sufferings each comprises are far from what readers might be ready to call cruel: a vague sense of unsuitedness; a longing for an earlier, better lover; a quixotic ambition now thwarted by marriage; a fastidious unwillingness to have sex with even the kindest of husbands. Most poignantly, and in the context of the nineteenth-century novel, most radically, these novels even invite us to sympathize not only with sufferings but also with desire, as when we are invited to imagine better second marriages for certain characters. And yet while *The Mayor of Casterbridge*, *The Woodlanders*, and *Jude the Obscure* do much to expand our conception of marital suffering, none of them ends up arguing for the further reform of marriage law. They are constrained from doing so by literary mode.

In *The Mayor of Casterbridge*, divorce does not exist and husbands and wives separate through wife sales. The other characters disapprove when Michael Henchard sells his wife, but they do not find it extraordinary. When asked about it later, one witness distinguishes the sale of a wife from truly memorable events like fistfights or pickpocketings. The historian E. P. Thompson helps us to make sense of this nonchalance. Noting that nearly four hundred wife sales were described in provincial newspapers between 1800 and 1850 and speculating that many more may have gone unrecorded, Thompson argues that wife sales were understood as a form of rural divorce.[16] While in Hardy's novel a wife is sold in a drunken fit of pique, in reality wives were more often sold to their acknowledged lovers and only with the consent of all three parties. The sale would take place in public, so that the community would witness the change, and it would be permanently recorded

15. Andrew Dowling, "'The Other Side of Silence': Matrimonial Conflict and the Divorce Court in George Eliot's Fiction," *Nineteenth-Century Literature* 50, no. 3 (December 1995): 322–36.

16. E. P. Thompson, *Customs in Common* (London: Penguin Books, 1991), 428. Stone disputes this conclusion, arguing that wife sales were rare (*Road to Divorce*, 147).

in the form of a sales receipt. These receipts were as carefully preserved, Thompson notes, as if they had been actual divorce decrees.[17]

And yet while *Casterbridge* is set in a world in which husband and wife are capable of parting, it nonetheless shows that true separation is more difficult than it might at first seem. The marriage vow proves to have an unexpected force. *Casterbridge* is a novel structured by the speech acts of its protagonist. In the beginning, Henchard promises not to drink for twenty-one years; in the middle, he curses the man who has become his rival; and at the end he bleakly refuses to bequeath. But the novel is dominated by the one speech act it does not depict, Henchard's vow to marry. The selling of the wife is the novel's originary crime, and the consequences of this crime work themselves out through the irrevocability of the marriage. The sold wife remains a wife, and she inevitably returns—in this case, at the moment of Henchard's greatest triumph, the public dinner honoring him as mayor of Casterbridge.

The Woodlanders comes closer to being a functioning reformist text because it imagines that marriages might be dissolvable under the right legal circumstances. But it limits the force of this reformist insight within the alternations of pastoral and tragedy. The novel begins as a pastoral, set in a world governed by the timeless round of the seasons. In this world, wife sales are not an option, but neither is divorce—or at least so it seems at first. And so we watch with some trepidation as the novel's pastoral gives way to impending marital tragedy. The novel's protagonist, Grace Melbury, is engaged to a glamorous young doctor, but she breaks off the engagement when she discovers that he is involved with another woman as well. She is forced to resume the engagement, however, by her father, who is proud of the excellent match. Just before the marriage takes place, a minor character suddenly arrives from the continent and refers in passing to the life he has made for himself in Italy since the end of the U.S. Civil War. He then vanishes from the novel without affecting its plot at all. His sole function, it seems, is to demonstrate in the most obtrusive way possible that this seemingly timeless story is in fact taking place at a relatively specific time: certainly between the 1865 of the war's ending and the 1887 of the novel's publication, and given the number of years that the character seems to have lived in Italy, most likely in the latter 1870s and 1880s. As a consequence, we know, although Grace does not, that divorce is now legally possible, and it is with this in mind that we watch her husband's subsequent adulteries.

Just as the sudden emergence of this one character (the continental traveler) informs the readers that divorce is possible, the sudden emergence of another, a drunken law clerk, informs the characters of the same thing.

17. Thompson, *Customs in Common*, 425.

He tells them about the 1857 Matrimonial Causes Act, even though he gets its provisions crucially wrong. Up until this point, no character in the novel has been able to imagine divorce, not even the most worldly. Even Grace's husband, who is freethinking enough to insist on a civil rather than religious wedding, does not seem to know that divorce is possible. But now Grace permits herself to imagine not only that she might divorce her husband but also that she might marry a former suitor afterward. In this way, we are invited to identify not only with Grace's sufferings but also with her extramarital desires. In the midst of these imaginings, Grace is finally informed of the full provisions of the law: as a woman, she needs not one cause for divorce but rather two. A London lawyer explains what the drunken law clerk did not know, that her husband's conduct has not been "sufficiently cruel" (285); when her father explains this to her, he bitterly repeats that her husband "has not done . . . *enough* harm" (289).

Not enough harm, insufficiently cruel—these phrases could galvanize a new reformist campaign to equalize the provisions of divorce. But instead the novel reverts to tragedy. Grace ends up returning to her husband in order to live out the consequences of her father's excessive pride. Once again, tragedy serves to limit or deny the possibility of reform. And yet the very heavy-handedness of the novel's tragedy is significant. In the midst of describing the woodlands for the first time, the narrator pauses to remind us that "dramas of a grandeur and unity truly Sophoclean" could nonetheless be enacted there (8). From that moment on, the tragic always seems like a forced imposition. We are left with a sense that there is a reformist intervention that Hardy would make if he could.

Through his public reticence and his careful use of literary modes, Hardy accommodated to a literary world that he believed would not embrace him as a novelist of purpose. By 1890, however, he had grown weary of accommodation. And so he wrote his final two novels, *Tess* and *Jude*, as an act of defiance. The novels most obviously defy the strictures on subject matter. The heroine of *Tess* gives birth to an illegitimate child and then murders its father; moreover, her actions are not framed, as they would be in a purposeful novel, by a reassuring narrative of judgment and redemption. On the contrary, Tess is identified, by the novel's subtitle, as "a pure woman" still. Hardy was also less willing to allow the novel to be bowdlerized for magazine publication. When the editors at *The Graphic* refused to publish the novel's two most shocking scenes, Hardy insisted on publishing them elsewhere, as freestanding sketches.

Not only did Hardy defy the literary world with the subject matter of *Tess*, but he also recorded the results of his defiance in the prefaces to the novel's subsequent editions. In his earlier novels, Hardy had used his prefaces to toy with his own claims of realism. He would cite the real-life source of a character's accent or suggest that certain places described in the novel either did or did not exist in reality. But the prefaces to *Tess* are interested less in the relation between the novel and the world than in the relation between the novel and its readers. The 1891 preface defies readers to be shocked by the novel's subject matter, warning them against being "too genteel."[18] The 1892 preface mocks those readers and critics who did in fact prove to be too genteel—or who at least pretended to be. One reader complained, for instance, that the novel's scandalous subject matter made it almost impossible "for him to read the book through three times" (38). This anecdote alludes to the fact that *Tess* was not only Hardy's most scandalous novel but also by far his most popular: his novels were typically published in editions of a thousand, of which at least a few hundred were usually remaindered, but *Tess* was in its fifth printing by the time he wrote the 1892 preface.[19] In this way, the later prefaces make the responses of contemporary readers a permanent part of the novel itself.

In *Jude*, too, Hardy set out to shock. Once again, he represents the sexually scandalous (frigidity and fornication), but he now adds to this the brutal (pig killings and child suicides). And once again Hardy defies his readers to be shocked by what he has written. "I am not aware," he blandly claims in the novel's first preface, "that there is anything in the handling [of this subject matter] to which exception can be taken."[20] But exception was taken indeed. "Hardy the Degenerate" and "Jude the Obscene" screamed the headlines of hostile reviews, while the bishop of Wakefield informed the press that he had burned his copy of *Jude*.[21] Hardy preserved these responses, too, in a subsequent preface, the one he wrote for the 1912 Wessex Edition. Nearly twenty years removed from the publication of *Jude*, he seems almost amused by those readers who were straightforward in either their prudery or their prurience, by the bishop who burned the book with such fanfare and by the man who demanded his money back because the novel was not nearly as sexually explicit as he had been led to believe. Hardy's contempt is reserved for those who condemned the book hypocritically. His chief target here is the U.S. author who wrote a damning review, complete with a full list of

18. Thomas Hardy, *Tess of the d'Urbervilles* (1891; London: Penguin, 1985), 35. All further references to this edition will be marked in the text.

19. Wright, *Hardy and His Readers*, 19.

20. Thomas Hardy, *Jude the Obscure*. (1895; London: Penguin, 1998), 3. All further references to this edition will be marked in the text.

21. Jeannette L. Gilder, "Hardy the Degenerate," *World*, 13 November 1895; "Jude the Obscene," *Pall Mall Gazette*, 12 November 1895; Bishop William Walsham How, letter to the editor, *Yorkshire Post*, 8 June 1896, all reprinted in *Thomas Hardy: The Critical Heritage*, ed. R. G. Cox (London: Routledge, 1970).

Jude's obscenities, and then asked to make Hardy's acquaintance when she next traveled to Britain.

In presenting shocking subject matter, defying readers to be shocked, and then coolly recording the spluttering indignation that ensued, *Jude* repeats the pattern that *Tess* established. But it differs from *Tess* in one crucial way. It was not only shocking but also controversial. *Jude* was written in what was the most popular and notorious reformist genre of the day, New Woman fiction. Hardy's late entry into purposeful writing was his other great act of literary defiance, but this seemingly individual act was made possible by contemporary changes in the literary world.

The End of the Novel of Purpose

In the mid-1880s, the novel of purpose came under attack in Great Britain. This attack was inspired by the translation of Emile Zola's novels into English, an event that prompted British novelists and critics to articulate their own dissatisfactions with the contemporary literary world. U.S. novelists followed them a decade later. Some called for a new realism along specifically continental lines.[22] Others called for an end to the expectation that all novels be written for family reading, under the imagined gaze of a censorious "Mrs. Grundy." Still others called for an end to purposefulness itself. The debate about continental realism and naturalism, the debate about Mrs. Grundy, and the debate about purposefulness were all expressions of the same phenomenon: the demise of a specifically Anglo-American realism that justified its representations in the name of a purpose understood in reformist terms. By the end of the century, realism, subject matter, and purpose would all be up for debate. And the novel of purpose would no longer be the predominant literary genre.

Some of the critics and novelists who attacked purposefulness did so because they believed that it deformed the very realism it enabled, a point that Charles Dickens had made in his early writings and George Eliot in her literary reviews. The novel of purpose subordinates, in Clarence Darrow's

---

22. Terminology is slippery here. As with realism, naturalism was not theorized in the United States and Great Britain as thoroughly as it was theorized in France. The term was used most often by those writers who wanted to distinguish themselves from the Anglo-American realists whom they were attacking. Or at least this is how the term functioned in the United States, when it was taken up by writers such as Theodore Dreiser and Frank Norris to attack the Anglo-American realism of William Dean Howells. See Bell, *Problem of American Realism*, 119. The situation was even more confused in Britain, where the terms realism and naturalism were used interchangeably. See P. J. Keating, *The Working Classes in Victorian Fiction* (New York: Barnes and Noble, 1971), 132.

view, "the doings of the men and women in the book" to "the views that
the author holds." For this reason, Darrow calls for an end to "novels on
religion, war, marriage, divorce, socialism, theosophy, [and] woman's rights"
and, more generally, for an end to the conception of novelists as "preachers and lecturers."[23] Where Darrow was skeptical of realism's entanglement
with purposefulness, other critics were simply wearied by it. In an essay entitled "The Artificiality of the Novel" (1890), D. F. Hannigan first attacks
the many contemporary novelists who refuse to represent any subject matter
that might bring a blush to a young person's cheek. He then goes on to attack even those few novelists who are willing to attempt a "bold piece of realism" on the grounds that they invariably accompany their realist passages
with "some irrelevant bit of didacticism." The only function of the didacticism is, he suspects, to contain the realism within a reassuringly moral frame
and thereby "appease the virtuous indignation of the Pharisaic middle-class
reader for whom the naked truth is unpalatable."[24] What Hannigan is suggesting is that purposefulness has become nothing but a convention—at best
merely ornamental, at worst deeply cynical. The convention was necessary,
Havelock Ellis argued, because the reading public remained lamentably suspicious of fiction: "[W]hereas children can only take their powders in jam,
the strenuous British public cannot be induced to devour their jam unless
convinced that it contains some strange and nauseous powder."[25] But while
readers may insist on purpose, purpose is, Ellis insists, inimical to art. True
artists must never allow themselves to be made "the tool of a merely moral
or immoral purpose."[26] In this way, Ellis looks forward to the emergence
of an autonomous sphere of art that would find its fullest expression in
modernism.

These attacks on the novel of purpose made little difference, however,
so long as the literary marketplace continued to be dominated by the great
circulating libraries. One of the first to make this point was Zola himself.
Interviewed on the subject of the British novel in 1884, he observed that
its subject matter was largely determined by its modes of circulation and its
intended audience. It has been shaped, indeed deformed, by "the monopoly
the circulating library holds, and its tendency to cater exclusively for young

23. Clarence Darrow, "Realism in Literature and Art," *Arena* 9 (December 1893): 98–113,
quoted in *Documents of American Realism and Naturalism*, ed. Donald Pizer (Carbondale: Southern Illinois University Press, 1998), 140.

24. D. F. Hannigan, "The Artificiality of the Novel," *Eclectic*, May 1890, quoted in William
C. Frierson, "The English Controversy over Realism in Fiction, 1885–1895," *PMLA* 49, no. 4
(December 1934): 543.

25. Havelock Ellis, "Concerning *Jude the Obscure*," *Savoy Magazine* 6 (October 1896): 35–49,
quoted in Cox, *Thomas Hardy*, 305–6.

26. Ellis, "Concerning *Jude the Obscure*," 309.

girls."[27] A year later, George Moore took up these two points and elaborated them in his *Literature at Nurse, or Circulating Morals* (1885). Zola and Moore focused on the circulating libraries, Mudie's Select Library in particular, because these libraries entirely dominated the literary marketplace in Britain. Novels in Britain had stabilized at a price much higher than most people could afford, and the circulating libraries arose in response to that fact: for roughly the price of a new novel, a family could subscribe to a library for the year and read as many novels as they liked. As a consequence, the circulating libraries were both the chief purveyors and the chief consumers of the British novel.[28]

As such, the circulating libraries were able to impose their preferences on publishers and novelists. Publishers were required to issue novels in three volumes, each of which could be lent separately, thus tripling the volumes in circulation. And novelists were required to write nothing that could not be read aloud in the family circle—nothing, that is to say, that would shock Mrs. Grundy or bring a blush to a young person's cheek. A few novelists, such as Robert Louis Stevenson and Rudyard Kipling, as well as Moore himself, evaded these requirements by writing in one, rather than three, volumes and selling these volumes directly to their readers. But most other novelists continued to follow the libraries' terms even as they protested against them. Nor did the libraries pose the only difficulty. The literary magazines were even more restrictive in the limits they set on subject matter, and this was as true in the United States as in Britain. In an 1887 essay entitled "Why We Have No Great Novelists," H. H. Boyeson argued that the "young American girl" for whom all novelists must write had become the "Iron Madonna who strangles in her fond embrace the American novelist."[29]

Despite the growing protests of authors, it seemed to many observers that little would ever change. But in 1894 Mudie's and its chief competitor, W. H. Smith, astonished the literary world by announcing that they would no longer pay more than four shillings a volume.[30] British publishing houses were suddenly forced to reconfigure themselves on a U.S. model, selling cheaper editions in larger numbers, directly to readers. As a consequence, it was suddenly possible for novelists to write on a broader array of topics in a broader variety of formats. With these new possibilities came a splitting of what had been a unified literary world. The result was an explosion of genres that identified themselves as "new": the new journalism,

27. Émile Zola, "Topics of the Day by Heroes of the Hour—My New Novel," *Pall Mall Gazette*, 3 May 1884, 6.

28. Saint-Amour, *Copywrights*, 60.

29. H. H. Boyeson, "Why We Have No Great Novelists," *Forum* 2 (1887): 615–22.

30. Guinevere Griest discusses the reasons for this in *Mudie's Circulating Library and the Victorian Novel* (Bloomington: Indiana University Press, 1970), 156–75.

championed by W. T. Stead, which prompted the writing of such investigative texts as Charles Booth's *Life and Labour of the People in London* (1892–97); the new drama, pioneered by Henrik Ibsen and George Bernard Shaw, which brought social problems to the formerly trivial British stage; the new fiction, exemplified by George Gissing, which described working-class experience in a naturalist mode; and New Woman fiction, which argued either for or against the social emancipation of women.[31] As even these brief descriptions demonstrate, the various new genres were, in one sense at least, not new at all. On the contrary, they variously carried on the reformist work that had been part of the Anglo-American novel since Dickens. Only now they did so from a newly marginal position within a newly fragmented literary world.

Shaw's new drama aspired to precisely the centrality that the novel of purpose no longer had, and in this way his aspirations serve as a kind of elegy for the genre. Before he turned to drama, Shaw had been writing novels because, as he would later confess, "everybody did so then."[32] But when he participated in an informal staging of Ibsen's *A Doll's House*, he realized that the drama could be a genre just as serious. For Shaw, seriousness was defined, as it had been defined for at least two generations of novelists, in terms of purposefulness—indeed, in terms of reform. Ibsen's play was in his view reformist because it exposed the infantilization of women within the middle-class home. And the play that Shaw wrote in response to it, *Mrs. Warren's Profession* (1893), intensifies this purposefulness by connecting the home to other sites familiar to reformist writing, namely, the brothel and the factory. The play's references to prostitution are quite restrained, and they would not have been at all shocking in a novel of purpose. But Shaw's play was censored for eight years because the theater was still expected to entertain, not reform. In his remarkably unapologetic "Author's Apology" (1902), Shaw notes that his critics pretended to be shocked by passages that merely reiterated the "moral commonplaces" of "the pulpit" and "the platform." And he goes on to imagine an ideal audience, one in which theater critics have been replaced by actual reformers: "Play *Mrs. Warren's Profession* to an audience of clerical members of the Christian Social Union and of women well experienced in Rescue, Temperance and Girl's Club work. . . . I should be quite content to have my play judged by, say, a joint committee of the Central Vigilance Society and

31. For the new journalism, see Arata, "1897," 55; for the new fiction, see Sally Ledger, *The New Woman: Fiction and Feminism at the Fin de Siècle* (New York: St. Martin's Press, 1997), 36.

32. Quoted in Katherine E. Kelly, "Imprinting the Stage: Shaw and the Publishing Trade, 1883–1903," in *The Cambridge Companion to George Bernard Shaw*, ed. Christopher Innes (Cambridge: Cambridge University Press, 1998), 28.

the Salvation Army."[33] But by the time Shaw wrote this "Apology," which was actually an attack on the theater, the genre with which he was comparing the novel no longer commanded a reform-minded audience itself, at least not as a matter of course.

If the attack on the novel of purpose took place on three fronts, Hardy joined the battle on two of them. He clearly shared the views of his literary contemporaries with respect to Mrs. Grundy. Even more than many of them, he wrangled with his publishers over how sexually explicit his novels could be. And when he was invited to contribute to a *New Review* symposium entitled "Candour in English Fiction" (1890), he offered a strong defense of a literature written for adult readers.[34] He also joined his contemporaries in protesting the censorship of Zola's novels, even though he remained skeptical of Zola's method and skeptical of Zola as a person.[35] With respect to purpose, however, Hardy was unique. When many of his contemporaries were expressing their skepticism of or boredom with purposefulness, he began to write in a purposeful—indeed, in an explicitly reformist—mode.

What enabled Hardy to make this last defiant gesture was another change in the literary marketplace, the 1891 ratification of an international copyright law. Hardy had long advocated for such a law. Early in his career, he campaigned for one with Charles Dickens and Wilkie Collins, and in 1880 he met with the U.S. consul to London, James Russell Lowell, and persuaded him to join the cause.[36] When the law was ratified at last, however, it made less of a difference for many novelists than they had hoped. It protected only those British novels that were separately typeset in the United States. Since a second typesetting would more than double the publishing costs, British publishers were reluctant to secure U.S. copyright for any but the best-known novelists. But they had secured copyright for Hardy.[37] As a consequence, the vast profits from the United States were his as well, and just in time for his most popular novel. Hardy ended up profiting so much from *Tess* that he no longer needed to support himself by novel writing. But before he abandoned novel writing entirely,

33. George Bernard Shaw, "Author's Apology," in *Plays by George Bernard Shaw* (1902; New York: Signet, 1960), 4–5.

34. Thomas Hardy, "Candour in English Fiction," *New Review* 2 (January–June 1890): 15–21.

35. For a full account of the trial of Zola's publishers, and the British reception of Zola more generally, see Frierson, "English Controversy over Realism in Fiction," 533–50.

36. Carl J. Weber, *Hardy in America: A Study of Thomas Hardy and His American Readers* (Waterville: Colby College Press, 1946), 34.

37. James L. W. West, "The Chace Act and Anglo-American Literary Relations," *Studies in Bibliography* 45 (1992): 303–11. For a fuller account of this, see chapter 1.

he provoked his readers one last time by writing what seemed to be a New Woman novel in *Jude*.

The New Woman and Thomas Hardy

The New Woman is both a sociological and a literary phenomenon.[38] As a sociological phenomenon, the New Woman was made possible by the expansion of female education in the second half of the nineteenth century—so much so, indeed, that her other name was the "Girton Girl."[39] As this name suggests, the expansion of female education was most dramatic with respect to the universities. Before 1848, the year in which Queen's College was founded, no woman was permitted to study in any British university; by 1895, the year in which *Jude* was published, women were studying at Oxford and Cambridge and even receiving degrees at nine other British universities. In the United States, a handful of colleges and universities admitted female students and even more were established solely for women. The opening of colleges and universities to women had a powerful symbolic effect, but of greater practical significance was the vast growth of secondary school education for girls. Not only did the number of girls receiving a secondary education increase exponentially, but the quality of this education was vastly improved. No longer finishing schools run by distressed gentlewomen, secondary schools for girls were remade by certified teachers and standardized exams.

With better education came a broadened sense of female possibility. In the name of the New Woman, women began bobbing their hair and wearing divided skirts while riding bicycles, as well as living independently in bed-sits of their own.[40] This vivid array of activities pointed toward the

---

38. The extent to which the New Woman is one or the other has been the subject of much debate. The earliest scholars of the New Woman, such as Gail Cunningham (*The New Woman and the Victorian Novel* [London: Macmillan, 1978]), focused on the sociological, while subsequent scholars, such as Sally Ledger (*New Woman*) and Ann Heilmann (*New Woman Fiction: Women Writing First-Wave Feminism* [New York: St. Martin's Press, 2000]), have focused on the literary. The debate continues today: Lyn Pykett notes that there is much new evidence that the readers of women's periodicals did think of themselves as living in new ways. Talia Schaffer, on the other hand, argues that both anti- and profeminist persons found it useful to transform real economic and social gains into a fictional representations. Lyn Pykett, Foreword, and Talia Schaffer, "'Nothing but Foolscap and Ink': Inventing the New Woman," in *The New Woman in Fiction and in Fact: Fin-de-Siècle Feminisms*, ed. Angelique Richardson and Chris Willis (London: Palgrave, 2001).

39. Ledger, *New Woman*, 17.

40. This list of activities points to the class specificity of New Woman agitation. As Sally Mitchell dryly notes, working-class women had lived alone, supported themselves, and managed their own sexual lives for quite some time ("New Women, Old and New," *Victorian Literature and Culture* 27, no. 2 [1999]: 579–88).

differences between New Woman feminism and earlier forms of women's rights activism. Some activists, such as Mary Wollstonecraft and John Stuart Mill, had focused on removing specific legal and political disabilities.[41] Others, such as Bessie Rayner Parkes and Barbara Bodichon, had also sought to expand professional and educational possibilities. The New Women were even more wide-ranging in their aims, advocating for a host of changes in social life—and often acting as if they had already achieved them. In particular, the New Women sought to reimagine childhood and maternity, but most of all marriage and sex.

The meaning of the term "New Woman" would evolve over time. In its very first usage, in an 1893 issue of the British feminist journal the *Woman's Herald*, the term "New Woman" named a new political identity for women. This New Woman was, as Michelle Tusan has shown, a model social reformer.[42] But the term did not become popular until 1894, when it resurfaced in an exchange of essays in a U.S. literary magazine, the *North American Review*. The exchange took place between a woman identified as a New Woman, Sarah Grand, and woman who had made herself one of the New Woman's chief detractors, Ouida, and it was in the debate between them that the term New Woman expanded to its present meaning.

Grand's essay is vague and oracular. She does not define the "new woman" except by distinguishing her from the dumbly maternal "cow woman" and the brutishly sexual "scum woman."[43] Nor does she articulate this "new woman's" intentions for the future except by condemning the past actions of men. Ouida responds to Grand's essay first of all by parodying Grand's language in portentous capitals: "the Woman," she begins and then pauses to correct herself, "the New Woman, be it remembered."[44] She then launches an almost incoherent battery of attacks: Grand, she says, is pompous, humorless, and self-deluding in her conception of female power; the New Women are ignorant, hypocritical, and cruel in their treatment of animals; and the essay's style is vulgar and inelegant, as are the New Women themselves. Both Grand's and Ouida's essays are an odd mix of their authors' familiar themes and idiosyncratic obsessions—in Grand's case, prostitution; in Ouida's, the wearing of feathers and furs. What matters in the end is less the content of the debate than the fact that it was through a debate that the New Woman was named.

41. Cunningham, *New Woman and the Victorian Novel*, 3.

42. Michelle Elizabeth Tusan, "Inventing the New Woman: Print Culture and Identity Politics during the Fin-de-Siècle," *Victorian Periodicals Review* 31, no. 2 (Summer 1998): 170.

43. Sarah Grand, "The New Aspect of the Woman Question," *North American Review* 158 (1894): 271.

44. Ouida, "The New Woman," *North American Review* 158 (1894): 610.

Because the term "New Woman" has always identified less a program than a controversy, the New Woman genre is a remarkably capacious one, including male as well as female writers; protomodernists and decadents as well as realists; essayists and playwrights as well as novelists; writers from the United States, South Africa, and Australia, as well as from Britain, all joined solely by their interest in the figure of the educated, independent, socially and sexually unconventional New Woman.[45] Their conceptions of what such a woman is or should be vary widely. The genre includes authors advocating free love (George Egerton), contractual marriage (Mona Caird), and chastity for men and women alike (Sarah Grand), and it also includes authors arguing against all of these things. Victoria Cross's *The Woman Who Didn't* (1895) and Lucas Cleeve's *The Woman Who Wouldn't* (1895) are as much a part of the genre as Grant Allen's *The Woman Who Did* (1895). Caird's essay on marriage is a New Woman text, but so too are the twenty-seven thousand letters, most of them hostile, that readers wrote in response to her essay when it was reprinted in the *Daily Telegraph* under the heading "Is Marriage a Failure?"[46]

To write about the New Woman was therefore to enter this field of controversy and necessarily to take either a reformist or an antireformist stance. And this is what Hardy did when he created the female protagonist of his final novel. Pale, nervous, and dressed in men's clothes, a "clever girl" and an "urban miss," Sue Bridehead is the paradigmatic New Woman (107, 139).[47] And so it was hardly surprising, although Hardy claimed to be surprised, that the first readers and reviewers of *Jude* identified the novel at once as a work of New Woman fiction and therefore took for granted that the novel had a purpose. "Unless it be regarded as a 'novel with a purpose,'" announced a hostile review for the *Morning Post*, "it is hard to imagine why it should have been written at all," while a defense of the novel began by recalling "Mr. Hardy's strenuous 'purpose' in *Jude the Obscure*."[48] Havelock Ellis remarked on this tendency in other reviews in the course of writing

45. The boundaries of this genre are contested, with some critics, such as Kate Flint, arguing that the genre contains only profeminist authors, while other critics, such as Cecelia Techi, arguing that any novel about an independent woman belongs. Kate Flint, *The Woman Reader, 1837–1914* (Oxford: Oxford University Press, 1993); Cecelia Techi, "Women Writers and the New Woman," in *The Columbia Literary History of the United States*, ed. Emory Elliot (New York: Columbia University Press, 1988). I would draw the boundaries around those texts that understand themselves to be participating in a public debate about female possibility.

46. Ledger discusses this incident, *New Woman*, 21–22.

47. For a comprehensive account of these parallels, see Ledger, *New Woman*, 182, and Cunningham, *New Woman and the Victorian Novel*, 103.

48. *Morning Post*, 7 November 1895; Richard Le Gallienne, review of *Jude the Obscure*, by Thomas Hardy, *Idler*, February 1896, both reprinted in Cox, *Thomas Hardy*.

his own. He observed that *Jude* was being read as "a book with a purpose, a moral or an immoral purpose, according to the standpoint of the critic."[49]

Hardy responded to the first round of reviews in a frantic spate of sometimes incoherent and often contradictory letters to his friends and literary companions. In some, he denied that he had written a novel of purpose at all. *Jude* is "not a novel with a purpose," he baldly insisted in a letter to Florence Henniker.[50] He wrote to Edmund Gosse on the same day to express his astonishment that *Jude* was being read as a "a manifesto on 'the marriage question.'"[51] In other letters, Hardy gave a number of reasons why *Jude* could not be such a "manifesto." In a letter to Lady Jeune, he claims that the novel's criticisms of marriage are voiced entirely by the characters, not by the narrator; this claim happens not to be true, but it is in any case largely beside the point.[52] He also has recourse to his old strategy of literary mode by noting that the novel is a tragedy and thus beyond the scope of possible reformist intervention. Indeed, he doubles the determinism by pairing tragedy with naturalism and referring to "the tragic issue of two bad marriages, owing in the main to a doom or curse of heredity temperament peculiar to the family of the parties."[53] And he also argues that the novel has no bearing on the "*general* marriage question" because it focuses exclusively on one idiosyncratic pair. Now that he has described them, he says, "the philanthropists must do the rest."[54] And finally, Hardy insists that if his novel has any purpose at all, that purpose lies entirely elsewhere; his primary interest in writing the novel, he says, was not marriage at all, but rather the struggles of a poor man to enter a university.[55]

In the course of these denials, Hardy also offered a remarkably disingenuous account of his relations to the New Woman writers. He has no connection to them at all, he implies, other than the coincidence of near-simultaneous publication. "Owing, I supposed, to the accident of its appearance just after the sheaf of purpose-novels we have had lately on the marriage question—though written long before them—some of the papers class mine

49. Havelock Ellis, review of *Jude the Obscure*, by Thomas Hardy, reprinted in Cox, *Thomas Hardy*.

50. Thomas Hardy to Florence Henniker, 10 November 1895, in *The Collected Letters of Thomas Hardy: 1893–1901*, ed. Richard Little Purdy and Michael Millgate (Oxford: Oxford University Press, 1980), 94.

51. Thomas Hardy to Edmund Gosse, 10 November 1895, in *Collected Letters of Thomas Hardy: 1893–1901*, 93.

52. See, for instance, Thomas Hardy to Lady Jeune, 17 November 1895, in *Collected Letters of Thomas Hardy: 1893–1901*, 97.

53. Thomas Hardy to Edmund Gosse, 10 November 1895.

54. Thomas Hardy to Edward Clodd, 10 November 1895, *Collected Letters of Thomas Hardy: 1893–1901*, 93.

55. Thomas Hardy Edmund Gosse, 10 November 1895.

with them."⁵⁶ But the relations between Hardy and the New Woman authors of that "sheaf of purpose-novels" were far more extensive than Hardy
is here willing to admit. He had dined with Caird and traveled with Allen.
Grand had sent him a copy of her *Heavenly Twins* (1893), with the inscription
"a very inadequate acknowledgment of all that she owes to his genius." Allen
had proclaimed in his *British Barbarians* (1895) that every woman in England
should be given a copy of *Tess*, and Hardy returned the compliment by sending Allen an inscribed copy of *Jude*. Finally, Hardy not only read Egerton's
Keynotes (1893) but also annotated his copy with provocative marginal notes
and sent it to Henniker, with whom he was then falling in love.⁵⁷

　　Hardy subsequently reproduced two of these letters in his autobiography, thereby transforming ephemeral semiprivate documents into a permanent part of his public self-presentation. What Hardy preserved, in doing
so, was both his repudiation of the reformist genre he had deliberately chosen to write in and his denial of any reformist intention at all. But even as
Hardy was issuing these denials, he was also attempting, for the first time,
to recast some of his other writings as reformist. The most straightforward
instance of this concerns *Jude*'s pig-killing scene. After *Jude* had been published, Hardy wrote to the Animal Protection League and invited them
to reprint this scene in their journal, the *Animal's Friend*. In this way, he
retrospectively and deliberately recast it as reformist. A more surprising
recasting involves the new preface that he wrote for *The Woodlanders* as
Jude was still appearing in serial form. It is in this preface that he refers to
those of his novels particularly concerned with "matrimonial divergence,"
and he suggests that "the present novel," *The Woodlanders*, belongs to this
category, along with "one or two others" (3). As the preface goes on, it
becomes clear that Hardy places *Jude* in that category, as well as *The Mayor
of Casterbridge*. This recasting of the three novels is doubly remarkable.
Three months before denying any connections to the New Women's "sheaf
of purpose-novels on the marriage question," Hardy is claiming that he
has written such a "sheaf" himself. And three months before he denying
any reformist intentions in *Jude*, he is retrospectively identifying reformist
intentions where no one has suspected them, in his most classical tragedy
and his most fully realized pastoral. In this way, Hardy throws his earlier
career into a new light.

　　The spate of denials that surrounded the publication of *Jude* point to
Hardy's real ambivalence about the novel of purpose. On the one hand,

---

56. Thomas Hardy to Edmund Gosse, 10 November 1895.
57. Millgate (*Thomas Hardy*) details Hardy's connections to Allen (359) and Egerton
(356, 375).

Hardy would like to be seen as preeminent in the New Woman genre, the author of "a sheaf of novels" extending back before the genre's emergence. On the other hand, he is reluctant to be identified as a New Woman writer at all. This may have been in part because of the critical opprobrium that was attaching itself to the genre. *Jude* tended to be praised when it was read on its own and condemned when read in conjunction with other works of New Woman fiction, as in Margaret Oliphant's notoriously vituperative review essay, "The Anti-Marriage League" (1896).[58] But Hardy's denials reflect something else as well, a real ambivalence about the reformist activity that he refused to engage in all those years. In *Jude*, he shows that reforms, when they come, do not make enough of a difference, and he begins to imagine radical alternatives.

Communities and Collectives: *Jude the Obscure*

From the moment of its publication, *Jude the Obscure* has been read as if it were two novels in one: a failed working-class bildungsroman, often referred to as the "Jude plot," uneasily entangled with a balked marriage plot, the "Sue plot." Contemporary reviewers debated which of the two plots was better, most often arguing for the bildungsroman, while genetic critics have since struggled to determine which of the two plots was conceived of earlier, finally deciding that the marriage plot came first.[59] More recently, however, feminist critics have asked what it means to imagine that the two plots can be parceled out so neatly, that education and ambition can be assigned to the working-class man, reproduction and sexuality to the middle-class woman. Such a parceling out constitutes, Penny Boumelha has shown, a grave misreading of the novel. Both of its protagonists are equally implicated in both of its plots: Sue, like Jude, is deformed by the education that is partly granted and partly denied her, while Jude, like Sue, falls victim to social conventions and the burdens of family life.[60]

In emphasizing that the story of a working-class man cannot be separated from the story of a middle-class woman, these critics point to one of

58. Cunningham, *New Woman and the Victorian Novel*, 116–17.

59. For an argument that the bildungsroman came first, see John Pasterson, "The Genesis of *Jude the Obscure*," *Studies in Philology* 57 (1960): 87–98. For what is now taken to be the decisive argument that the marriage plot was, in fact, the earlier one, see Patricia Ingham, "The Evolution of *Jude the Obscure*," *Review of English Studies* 27 (1976): 27–37.

60. Penny Boumelha, "Sexual Ideology and Narrative Form, in *New Casebooks: "Jude the Obscure*," ed. Boumelha (1991; London: St. Martin's, 2000), 56–57.

the most important points of contact between Hardy and the New Women. The New Women aspired to bring together the problems of gender and class. To be sure, this was an aspiration most often honored in the breach. The New Woman writers all too often forgot the concerns of the working classes, just as the New Drama lost sight of women in its concern for working-class men.[61] But traces of this aspiration remain visible. We can see them in the subtitle of the feminist newspaper *Shafts: A Paper for Women and the Working Classes,* and we can see them as well in Ouida's irritated dismissal of what she identifies as the greatest "bores" of contemporary literature: "The Workingman and the Woman. The Workingman and the Woman . . . meet us at every page of literature written in the English tongue."[62] The worker and the woman, the poor man and the lady—Hardy found in New Woman fiction a way of returning to the subject of his first, lost manuscript.

Jude takes up the two reformist causes most central to the New Women, educational reform and reform of married life. The first third of the novel is given over to Jude's early efforts to learn about Christminster University from scraps of provincial gossip and his later, more sustained efforts to make his way there himself—first by painstakingly teaching himself Latin and Greek, and then by learning stonemasonry so he can find work repairing the college buildings. At last, Jude feels ready to apply to Christminster, but his application is dismissed by the most patronizing of letters, which advises him to remain in his "own sphere" (117). Jude's response to this rejection, scrawling on the college walls and later falling into a drunken stupor, brings the first third of the novel to an end. What the novel has shown, quite vividly, is an educational system in need of reform.

But *Jude* then goes on to show an educational system that has been reformed already. While Jude is vaguely planning to devote himself to a life of Christian service, the *Bildung* plot is suddenly taken up by Sue. She receives a letter announcing that she has passed her scholarship examination and will be able to attend the Melchester Training School in order to certify as a normal school teacher. Christminster and Melchester are narratively contiguous, but they are structurally opposed. Christminster represents an older model of advancement wherein classical education provides the cultural capital that can then secure a professional life. Melchester, by contrast, is part of a rationalized system, whereby talent is identified and evaluated through Queen's examinations, supported by scholarships, and ratified by

61. Ellen Gainor makes the latter point in "G.B.S. and the New Woman," *New England Theatre Journal* 1, no. 1 (1990): 3.
62. Ouida, "New Woman," 610.

certification. The Melchester Training School is, then, the quintessential reformist institution, the kind of school that Harriet Martineau would have advocated and Charles Dickens would have toured. A training school is the very paradigm of the disciplinary institution. It is the place where such institutions learn to perpetuate themselves, where the teachers go to be trained. Hardy is quite aware of the benefits that such training can confer: Sue will have "twice as large an income" and "twice as much freedom" (103). Training to be a teacher would significantly increase her autonomy, as the Girton girls recognized. But it would do so, Hardy shows us, at considerable cost.

Hardy knew of such institutions both from his sisters, who had attended the Salisbury Training School as they prepared to be teachers, and from a tour he took of another training school a few years before he began writing *Jude*. Hardy's autobiography and his sisters' letters home emphasize the same two themes: female friendship and discipline. Hardy describes himself as touched by the thought of the friendships that the training school makes possible, and at least one of his sisters treasured the memory of the friendships she made there as well.[63] But no such friendships are depicted in the novel. Sue's fellow students do little more than gossip among themselves, and Sue looks down on them as vulgar and "mixed" (133). The novel concentrates exclusively on the disciplinary system that made Hardy's other sister feel that she had been "badly . . . used" at school.[64]

When Jude first visits Sue at the training school, he stands outside its walls and, in a scene that recalls his first arrival at Christminster, imagines the students within and envies them the education he is sure they do not value highly enough. But Jude soon realizes that he is mistaken. What happens inside the walls is not education but discipline. This becomes clear to him as soon as he sees Sue. She has changed in appearance, wearing plain dresses and pinning her hair back tightly, and she has changed in manner as well. All her exuberance is gone, and she is hungry, although she is ashamed to admit this at first. She has, Jude recognizes, "altogether the air of a woman clipped and pruned by severe discipline" (132). And she will be expected to discipline others in turn. When she is evaluated by a visiting government inspector, she is judged to be an excellent teacher because she is so good at governing her class.

63. Millgate, *Thomas Hardy*, 315, 352.
64. Millgate, *Thomas Hardy*, 352.

If *Jude*'s attention to education shows the coercive power of reformist institutions, its attention to marriage shows the inefficacy of legal reform. In its account of "matrimonial divergence," *Jude* begins in much the same way as *The Woodlanders*. We watch as Sue and Jude each marry the wrong person, we learn to empathize with their desire for a husband or wife better suited to them, and we imagine that their desires will be thwarted since divorce does not seem to be a possibility in the world of the novel.[65] Certainly, Jude and Sue do not seem to be aware that it exists. They continually debate the nature of marriage, with Jude claiming that it is a sacrament and Sue a contract. And yet, despite the worldliness of these conversations, neither Sue nor Jude can imagine any way to end their respective marriages—not even after Jude's wife has abandoned him to go to Australia, not even after she returns and announces that she has bigamously married for a second time. The two are made increasingly desperate by their inability to leave their spouses: Sue exclaims that some future world will look back on this one and be horrified by the barbarity of making people stay married, and Jude fervently agrees.

But then suddenly, two-thirds of the way through the novel, it becomes clear that Jude and Sue have been living in that future world all along. Jude's wife writes to him and asks for a divorce so that she can marry her second husband legally. The possibility of divorce intrudes on *Jude* as abruptly as it did in *The Woodlanders*, but this time the characters do not seem to be surprised. They already know about the provisions of the Matrimonial Causes Act, and none of these provisions prove to be a problem. The requirement that wives cite two causes rather than one does not prevent Sue from getting a divorce because her husband is complaisant enough to do the petitioning on her behalf. And Jude's status as a worker actually benefits them: his obscurity ensures that the courts and the press will not inquire too closely into their circumstances. A few pages after the word "divorce" is first mentioned

---

65. The time of the novel's setting has remained something of a critical crux, with Richard Dellamora following Robert Gittings in arguing that it is set in the 1860s and most other critics arguing that it is set in the 1890s ("Male Relations in Thomas Hardy's *Jude the Obscure*," *New Casebooks: "Jude the Obscure*," ed. Penny Boumelha [1991; New York: St. Martin's Press, 2000], 145–65). Boumelha has argued that this confusion is precisely the point, that Hardy is invoking two different moments at once in the activism for women's rights: the Comtean positivism of the 1860s and the woman of the period, and talk of degeneration and the new woman. Dale Kramer notes that the conflation of the two paints a devastating picture of reform, which presumes the possibility of progress through history. "Hardy and Readers: *Jude the Obscure*," in *The Cambridge Companion to Thomas Hardy*, ed. Kramer (Cambridge: Cambridge University Press, 1999), 171.

in the novel, the divorce decrees actually arrive in the mail, and Jude and Sue are free of the bond that has so oppressed them.

The odd casualness of this episode reflects Hardy's view of marriage law reform. The availability of divorce makes no difference in the lives of Sue and Jude because they want something more radical than what divorce can provide. Divorce frees them to marry one another, but they want to be free of marriage altogether. They cannot fully admit this desire, even to themselves, but they delay marrying for years, even after they have two children; twice they decide to marry, but both times they turn away from the marriage registry at the last minute. When their neighbors learn of this, the relatively happy life that Jude and Sue have created for themselves and their children is destroyed. Jude is expelled from an artisan's improvement society, that working-class alternative to Christminster, and he and Sue are both cast out, along with their children, from the street in which they have long been living. "The society of Spring Street," the narrator tells us, " . . . did not understand" (298). And thus begins their descent into poverty. In desperation, one of their children finally kills himself and his two siblings; later that night, their last child is stillborn. In the end, Jude and Sue each return to and remarry the spouses they divorced, and in this way the original marriages are reconstituted, even as Jude and Sue are themselves destroyed.

Jude attempts to account for these sufferings with reference to various literary modes. From the perspective of tragedy, Jude and Sue suffer because they are destined to do so. Sue announces, for instance, that a "tragic doom" overhangs them, just as it did over "the house of Atreus" (283). From the perspective of naturalism, Jude and Sue are simply superfluous. Jude is convinced, even as a child, that his life is "unnecessary" (17) and his existence "undemanded" (18), and his own children are destroyed because the oldest recognizes that they "*are too menny*" (336). Finally, from the perspective of a modernity that is aligned with the novel's protomodernism, Jude and Sue are simply the first victims of a modern disease, what their doctor refers to as "the coming universal wish not to live" (337). Tragedy, naturalism, modernity— these are the accounts that the narrator and the characters give. But there is something artificial in the invocation of each of these modes, and certainly something excessive in the invocation of so many.

Unacknowledged in the midst of these competing modes is the New Woman genre to which *Jude* clearly belongs. Hardy may have denied his participation in this genre, but his emphasis on the irrelevance of marriage law reform places him at the center of one of the most central New Woman debates. Whether he intends to or not, Hardy is taking a stand against the more liberal New Woman writers, such as Mona Caird, who understood marriage as a contract. In doing so, he aligns himself with the more radical ones, who sought to embed the family within more collective forms of life.

From this more radical perspective, Jude and Sue suffer because there is no collective to embrace and sustain them. The need for such a collective is most obvious at the moments when Jude and Sue are expelled from the artisan's society and from Spring Street. But collectives were equally lacking even when they were still able to live as a nuclear family. That there might be something beyond such families, an alternative to them, is something that Sue dimly perceives. When she agrees to take in the child of Jude and his first wife, she imagines this expansion of their household as the first step toward relations that will extend far beyond the family: "[A]ll the little ones of our time," she tells Jude, "are collectively the children of us adults of the time and entitled to our general care" (274). Sue was not alone in fantasizing about collective child rearing; contemporary socialists, such as Annie Besant and Eleanor Marx, were envisioning it as well, as was the feminist Charlotte Perkins Gilman. For this reason, Sue's fantasy of collectivity is presented less as an example of her eccentricity than as an example of her modernity. As she tells Jude in a related context, "everybody is getting to feel as we do, we are a little beforehand, that's all" (287).

In its attention to new forms of collectivity, then, *Jude* comes quite close to that strain of New Woman writing that was explicitly utopian, a strain that includes such texts as Olive Schreiner's *Dreams* (1891), Jane Hume Clapperton's *Margaret Dunmore; or, A Socialist Home* (1888), and Charlotte Perkins Gilman's *Herland* (1915). In some sense, utopians represent a turn away from reform, insisting as they do that society must be entirely remade. And yet a number of New Women made their own utopias, or at least their own female communities, in reformist institutions, such as settlement houses.[66] A number of late-century novels reflect this fact by representing, on their peripheries, various reformist communities that might serve as a possible refuge to the isolation that their protagonists endure. We can see this in such novels as William Dean Howells's *Annie Kilburn* (1888) and Henry Black Fuller's *With the Procession* (1895), both of which describe women who seek to establish communal spaces for factory workers. And we can see this as well in Edith Wharton's *House of Mirth* (1905), in which a young socialite helps to establish a club for working girls that might, in turn, have eased her own loneliness after she loses her money and descends to

66. Shannon Jackson has shown in her study of Hull House that settlement houses offered a permanent home for the settlement workers as well as a temporary home for the persons whom they had settled among. *Lines of Activity: Performance, Historiography, Hull-House Domesticity* (Ann Arbor: University of Michigan Press, 2000).

factory work and boarding houses herself. These reformist institutions offer an alternative both to the doll's house from which Nora Torvald escapes in Ibsen's play and to the doll's house that Edna Pontellier makes for herself in Kate Chopin's *The Awakening* (1899). Few women lived as reformers, but many more women lived as students in residential colleges and boarding schools, and these too sometimes became utopian. Boarding schools and colleges provided, as Martha Vicinus has shown, a temporary community for the women who attended them and a permanent community for the women who taught in them—women who were often unwilling to live in a heterosexual marriage.[67]

If the longing for a collective is connected to the utopian strain in New Woman writing, it is also connected to Hardy's own longstanding concern for community. Community is palpable everywhere in Hardy, as Simon Gatrell has eloquently shown. Hardy's main characters are almost always set against the background of an organic community, whether it be the woodland workers in *The Woodlanders* or the gossips of Mixen Lane in *The Mayor of Casterbridge*. The main characters may suffer from their alienation from these communities, which no longer contain them comfortably. But communities nonetheless remain as a model, however archaic, of a rich and sustaining way of life.[68] In *Jude*, however, these old communities no longer function. The novel opens in Marygreen, a village whose church has already been torn down and whose schoolmaster is about to leave. In the absence of community, there is nothing to hold the characters to any particular place. The extent to which Jude and Sue wander is captured in the titles of the novel's six books: "At Marygreen, At Christminster, At Melchester, At Shaston, At Aldbrickham and Elsewhere, At Christminster Again."

In the midst of their wanderings, Jude and Sue dream of communities. The most obvious of these dreams is Jude's dream of Christminster. Before the young Jude learns that Christminster is a place of classical learning, he thinks of it as the place where the schoolmaster went and the place where he and the schoolmaster may one day be reunited.[69] As Jude attempts to prepare himself for Christminster, he joins the imagined community of educated men, but he remains excluded from the actual community of university students. On the night of his arrival, he feels that he is walking among

67. Martha Vicinus, *Independent Women: Work and Community for Single Women, 1850–1920* (Chicago: University of Chicago Press, 1985).

68. Simon Gatrell, "Wessex," in *The Cambridge Companion to Thomas Hardy*, ed. Dale Kramer (Cambridge: Cambridge University Press, 1999), 28.

69. Dellamora ("Male Relations in Thomas Hardy's *Jude the Obscure*") discusses the homoerotics of this wish in the context of the homosociality of Victorian education.

the ghosts of Ben Jonson, Robert Browning, Arthur Swinburne, Thomas Hobbes, Edmund Gibbon, and Walter Pater. But the university students whom he passes on the streets fail to recognize the fellow scholar in the artisan's garb.

The novel also presents two other fantasies of community: the itinerant fair workers who come to Shaston and Sue's seventy fellow students at the Melchester Training School. Each of these communities appears only briefly, in a set piece of less than a page, and neither of them has any effect on the events of the novel. For these reasons, both communities have been almost entirely ignored by critics.[70] And yet the two scenes are extraordinary, fantastic expressions of a longing that pervades the novel as a whole. Both communities appear in response to an act of expulsion. The first appears after Sue's husband, Richard Phillotson, is asked to resign his position as headmaster because he has permitted Sue to leave him and go live with another man. He refuses to resign and is called to a public meeting. At the meeting, he argues that his private life is of no public concern, but he fails to persuade the school's managers. At this moment, support arrives from an entirely unexpected source:

> It has been stated that Shaston was the anchorage of a curious and interesting group of itinerants, who frequented the numerous fairs and markets held up and down Wessex during the summer and autumn months. Although Phillotson had never spoken to one of these gentlemen, they now nobly led the forlorn hope in his defense. The body included two cheap-jacks, a shooting-gallery proprietor and the ladies who loaded the guns, a pair of boxing-masters, a steam-roundabout manager, two travelling broom-makers, who called themselves widows, a gingerbread-stall keeper, a swing-boat owner, and a "test-your-strength" man.
>
> This generous phalanx of supporters, and a few others of independent judgment, whose own domestic experiences had been not without vicissitude, came up and warmly shook hands with Phillotson; after which they expressed their thoughts so strongly to the meeting that issue was joined, the result being a general scuffle, wherein a blackboard was split, three panes of school-windows were broken, an inkbottle spilled over a town-councillor's shirt-front, and some black eyes and bleeding noses given, one of which, to everybody's horror,

70. Laura Green is the only critic to remark on this very remarkable scene in her important discussion of education in the novel (*Educating Women: Cultural Conflict and Victorian Literature* [Athens: Ohio University Press, 2001). I depart from her account in one important respect: she focuses on the punishing of Sue by the school authorities, pairing it with Jude's subsequent expulsion from the Artisan's Improvement Society; I focus instead on the defense of Sue by her fellow students.

was the venerable incumbent's, owing to the zeal of an emancipated chimney-sweep, who took the side of Phillotson's party. When Phillotson saw the blood running down the rector's face he deplored almost in groans the untoward and degrading circumstances, regretted that he had not resigned when called upon, and went home so ill that the next morning he could not leave his bed. (248)

With this, the "curious and interesting group of itinerants" depart from the novel, never to return.

When the "itinerants" shake Phillotson's hand and confess to their own marital vicissitudes, they offer the fellowship that is otherwise so signally lacking in *Jude*. And yet it is clear that whatever community they conjure up is entirely nostalgic and therefore no real solution to the characters' isolation. The appearance of the itinerants in Shaston every summer is simply one of the town's many wonders, along with the graveyard higher than the church steeple and the water more expensive than beer. Moreover, their fellowship, although warm-hearted, leads only to injury and humiliation.

The fellow students whom Sue found vulgar and "mixed" are transformed into something quite different when she is temporarily isolated from them. Sue, who has been walking in the countryside with Jude, fails to return to the school when she should. When she does return, she is sent immediately to the principal. The other students have been warned not to speak to her, an injunction that they all obey without question. At breakfast, however, they learn that Sue has been condemned to a week of solitary confinement, and to this punishment they refuse to acquiesce:

[T]he seventy [students] murmured, the sentence being, they thought, too severe. A round robin was prepared and sent in to the Principal, asking for a remission of Sue's punishment. No notice was taken. Towards evening, when the geography mistress began dictating her subject, the girls in the class sat with folded arms.

"You mean that you are not going to work?" said the mistress at last. "I may as well tell you that it has been ascertained that the young man [Sue] Bridehead stayed out with was not her cousin, for the very good reason that she has no such relative. We have written to Christminster to ascertain."

"We are willing to take her word," said the head girl.

"This young man was discharged from his work at Christminster for drunkenness and blasphemy in public-houses, and he had come here to live, entirely to be near her."

However, they remained stolid and motionless, and the mistress left the room to inquire from her superiors what was to be done. (142)

This is the counterpart to and revision of the earlier scene: where the "itinerants" were full of action, the "seventy" are entirely still; where the itinerants broke windows and bloodied noses, the seventy refuse to act. The "stolid and motionless" resistance of the seventy brings not only their own training, but the novel itself, to a halt.

The seventy bring radical possibilities into the world of the novel. They are a community that recalls the existence of those real-world alternatives for women like Sue, the schools and settlement houses in which many women found refuge from heterosexual marriage. At the same time, the seventy also allude to alternate modes of writing, in particular, the utopia. It would be going too far to call the geography classroom a utopia, but the seventy, through their motionlessness and through their silence, hold the space of the classroom open within the narrative by refusing to allow any plot to fill it. It thus remains a purely empty space that a true collectivist utopia might one day fill. And this space will remain open forever because the novel never returns to the seventy. The geography mistress asks for further instructions, but in the very next paragraph, Sue stages an individual act of resistance. She climbs out of a window and fords the river that demarcates the training school's ground, thus mooting the act of collective resistance that is being staged by the seventy on her behalf. But for this reason, the seventy continue to exist beyond the novel's end, as an enduring model of collectivity. It is at this moment that *Jude* most clearly moves beyond the reformist novel, and at this moment that Hardy aligns himself with the most radical of the New Woman writers. In doing so, he also remains faithful to that younger Hardy, the "socialist" and even the "revolutionary," committed to the poor man and the lady.

The publication of *Jude* marked a double turning point in Hardy's career. When he abandoned novel writing for poetry, he also took up public advocacy of various kinds. In the midst of writing *The Dynasts*, his verse drama about the British involvement in the Napoleonic Wars, he signed one open letter protesting the imprisonment of Maxim Gorky and another advocating warmer relations between Great Britain and Germany, as well as writing an open letter himself in support of a Jewish state in Palestine. He also became increasingly involved in a number of reformist causes, in particular ones concerning animals. It is in this context that Hardy returned to reflect upon *Jude* as he wrote the new preface for the 1912 edition.

Nearly twenty years after the publication of *Jude*, Hardy is now quite willing to be identified as a New Woman writer—indeed, he is willing to be seen as the first. He recalls that after *Jude* was published in Germany, an "experienced reviewer of that country informed the writer" that Sue was the first New Woman (468). There is some irony, to be sure, in the "experienced" and the "informed," but Hardy nonetheless allows this false attribution of priority to stand as his last statement about his relation to the New Women. Hardy is now equally willing for *Jude* to be identified as a reformist text. With respect to the reform of marriage law, he comes close to disclosing what his own views might be. Conjuring up critics who feared that *Jude* was part of an "unholy antimarriage league," Hardy notes, with some ruefulness, that "the famous contract—sacrament I mean—is doing fairly well still" (468). With this slip from "sacrament" to "contract," Hardy alludes to the pro-divorce arguments he made earlier that year in a magazine symposium entitled "How Shall We Solve the Divorce Problem?"[71] But Hardy goes even further with respect to the novel's other reform, the reform of education. He has been "informed," he says, "that some readers thought" that the novel's attacks on Christminster were really attacks on Oxford and Cambridge. And these readers also think, Hardy goes on to say, that Ruskin College, the college since founded at Oxford for working-class men, should instead have been called "the College of Jude the Obscure" (467).

At this moment, Hardy resembles no one so much as Charles Dickens, in his retrospective preface to *The Pickwick Papers* (1836–37). Looking back from a distance of ten years, Dickens laid claim to reforms he had not dreamed of while writing, such as the abolition of debtors' prisons. Dickens's claim was necessarily retrospective because he had largely invented the reformist novel in the course of writing it. He learned from his readers that his novels might act on the world. With Hardy, of course, the retrospective claim works quite differently. He was not permitted to be a novelist of purpose at the moment when that was what nearly all novelists sought to be. On the contrary, he laid claim to the status only after he was no longer a novelist at all—and after the novel of purpose itself was no longer preeminent.

71. Thomas Hardy, "How Shall We Solve the Divorce Problem?" *Nash's Magazine*, March 1912, 683.

Epilogue

The Novel of Purpose has focused on the transatlantic relations made possible by print culture and social reform. These relations tended to be collaborations or, at worst, friendly rivalries. But alongside this history of shared reform is a more violent history of war and imperial conquest. The U.S. War of Independence (1776–81) is only the first event in a surprisingly long history of military conflicts between the United States and Great Britain, a history that extends through the War of 1812 (1812–14) and a subsequent series of near wars over borders in New York (1837), Maine (1839), and, most seriously, over the Oregon territories (1841–46). Even as Britain and the United States were still fighting against one another, however, they were also beginning to imperialize in tandem. The withdrawal from the North American colonies may have been a humiliating defeat for the British, and the War of Independence remains the only war that the British have lost. But, as the historian Linda Colley has shown, the loss of their first empire taught the British lessons that would help them hold onto their second.[1] Moreover, the British soon found that they had left behind in North America what the historian Michael Bellesiles has called "a successor empire in the republican United States."[2]

1. Linda Colley, *Britons: Forging the Nation, 1701–1837* (New Haven: Yale University Press, 1992).
2. Michael Bellesiles, "Creating Empires," *Journal of British Studies* 40, no. 4 (October 2001): 586.

This imperial succession was understood in specifically racial terms. In 1845, the United States was on the verge of war both with Britain over Oregon and with Mexico over Texas. At the height of this conflict, Ralph Waldo Emerson wrote in his journal that the "strong British race" was certain, in both cases, to prevail.[3] The phrase is brilliantly ambiguous, as Paul Giles has observed. It refers to the British themselves in the first conflict and to their American successors in the second. In this way, it looks forward to a possible future in which the United States and Britain will no longer fight against one another but instead work together to subdue other, weaker races. Within another generation, this possible future had become reality. In 1868, Charles Wentworth Dilke, a future leader of the Labour Party, published an account of his travels through what he was the first to call "Greater Britain." Greater Britain encompassed Canada, India, Australia, New Zealand, and southern Africa, but it was specifically in the United States that Dilke saw the future of the Anglo-American world. The United States, he argued, was gathering together the world's peoples and remaking them as British: "[I]n America, the people of the world are being fused together, but they are run into an English mould." Dilke was an anti-imperialist for his time, and he hoped that the United States might serve, the historian James Epstein has argued, as an alternative to a costly British empire.

As these passages show, the idea of Anglo-America would change over the course of the century. For Harriet Martineau, in the 1830s, being an Anglo-American had been a matter of willed affiliation. It was an identity made possible by ties of politics, religion, intermarriage, and trade. By the end of the century, being an Anglo-American—or, rather, being an Anglo-Saxon—was a matter of race. In this shift, we can see the effects of the more general rise of racial science over the course of the century. But we also see an attempt to resolve specifically transatlantic contests. The concept of the Anglo-Saxon race negotiated an end to the military rivalry between the United States and Great Britain. It also served to ease certain tensions within both the United States and Great Britain. Within the United States, it served as a way to imagine reconciling the southern states to the rest of the nation in the aftermath of the Civil War, a reconciliation that explicitly required the exclusion of the newly enfranchised African Americans. And in Great Britain as well as the United States, it served to distinguish national subjects of long standing from recent immigrants from southern and eastern Europe.

3. Quoted in Paul Giles, "Transnationalism and Classic American Literature," *PMLA* 118, no. 1 (January 2003): 69.

The rise of racialism and the rise of imperialism altered the terms of Anglo-American reformist collaboration. Of the novelists I have discussed, only Henry James supported imperialism—and he did so in largely aesthetic terms. He confesses, when speaking of the British expedition in Sudan, to finding "no spectacle more touching, more thrilling and even dramatic" than the battle of a "great precarious, artificial empire" at war with native forces.[4] The others were far more critical. As early as the 1850s, Charles Dickens had been skeptical of an empire that lost sight of England in its focus on Booriboola-Gha. George Eliot attacked imperialism in her last published essay, "The Modern Hep, Hep, Hep" (1878). And Thomas Hardy, entering into public life after setting his novel-writing career aside, spoke in favor of a Zionist state in Palestine but did not otherwise support imperial endeavors.

But it was Mark Twain whose engagement with imperialism was most rich and complex. It began in the early years of his career, when he returned to London after his triumphal first tour and was asked to give a public lecture. He decided to reprise his Hawaiian lectures, a telling choice at a moment when the United States had just begun considering whether or not to annex Hawaii. Twain was therefore speaking about a potential object of U.S. imperialism in the very metropolis of the British Empire.[5] In this way, his lecture looks forward to the shared imperial future that would come to pass before the end of Twain's own life, with the U.S. annexation of Cuba and the Philippines. At the same time, Twain's choice of title for the talk, "Our Fellow Savages of the Sandwich Islands," points in another direction. Ironically identifying Twain and his audience as "savages" themselves, the title challenges the ascription of savagery that makes imperialism possible and in this way functions as a broadly anti-imperialist strategy. But it also points to the structural similarity between the potentially colonial subjects of Hawaii and the postcolonial subjects of the United States. Twain's lecture thus recalls that transatlantic relations are undergirded by an imperial history as well as an imperial future.

Twain tried to reverse that history in *A Connecticut Yankee in King Arthur's Court* (1889), which describes the colonization of Arthurian Britain by a nineteenth-century citizen of the United States. Finding himself in a strange land and condemned to death by the natives, the Yankee borrows a trick from Cortez: recalling that an eclipse is soon to come, the

---

4. James, *Henry James Letters: 1895–1917*, 67.
5. Twain had initially supported such annexation, but by 1873 he had come to oppose it. In a letter he published in the *New York Tribune*, he sarcastically concluded: "We must annex those people. We can afflict them with our wise and beneficent government" ("The Sandwich Islands," *New York Tribune*, 9 January 1873).

Yankee announces that he will make the sun disappear. The trick comes from Cortez by way of contemporary British romance, and in playing it the Yankee uses Britain's own imperial discourse to position the British as a backward people and himself as the civilizing colonizer. This inversion is made most explicit right before the novel's end, after the Yankee has succeeded in establishing schools, navies, newspapers, and telephone lines. So far has the country advanced under his guidance, he announces, that he is "getting ready to send out an expedition to discover America" (365). The Yankee neatly rewrites the history of U.S. colonization so that it is a U.S. citizen who discovers the United States. In doing so, Twain suggests that the United States is bridling at its status as former colony and covertly eager to colonize in turn.

In the 1890s, personal bankruptcy forced Twain to make good his debts by going on a worldwide reading tour. The tour took him through what Dilke had called "Greater Britain." Twain began in Canada, then traveled through New Zealand and Australia, through Sri Lanka, India, and Pakistan, and then to South Africa before ending up in London. Twain traveled less as an American than as an Anglo-American. In *Following the Equator* (1897), Twain describes his fellow passengers, a companionable group of Australians and New Zealanders as well as Scotsmen, Englishmen, Irishmen, and South Africans. There are some small differences between them: the Australians, Twain notes, call London "home," and the passengers spend considerable time debating the proper pronunciation of various words.[6] But these differences aside, they speak the same language, observe the same customs, and find commonalities among their various settler outposts: they are the Anglo-Saxon race that so many of Twain's contemporaries were claiming would soon conquer the world. In this context, it is hardly surprising that Twain shares the imperial views of his fellow passengers through much of the trip. He admires the efficiency of British rule in India, for instance, and congratulates the Indians on being ruled by the British rather than the French. It is only when Twain sees a Briton strike his Indian servant in the face and recalls that his own father used to strike their slaves in precisely the same way that Twain pauses in his celebration of British imperialism. Twain, as a citizen of a nation that has outlawed slavery, views the British treatment of their servants in much the same way as the British once viewed the slave-owning United States after having abolished slavery in their own colonies. The striking of the Indian servant and the recollecting of the U.S. slave recall a history of transatlantic reformist collaboration, and Twain was

6. Mark Twain, *Following the Equator: A Journey around the World* (1897; New York: Harper Collins, 1996), 49.

soon drawn into a similar kind of collaboration in his own campaign against imperialism.[7]

Along with a number of other U.S. authors, Twain protested the Spanish-American War (1899), the Boer War (1899–1902), and the Boxer Rebellion (1900), as well as King Leopold's rule in the Congo. In the process, he wrote what is now his most famous statement against imperialism, an essay entitled "To the Person Sitting in Darkness" (1901), as well as the text that I will focus on most extensively here, *King Leopold's Soliloquy* (1905). In "To the Person Sitting in Darkness," Twain denies the imperial longings he expressed in *Connecticut Yankee* and his Hawaii lectures and instead calls for a return to what he takes to be U.S. innocence. Twain condemns the recent U.S. occupation of the Philippines following U.S. victory in the Spanish-American War. In making this condemnation, Twain draws a distinction between what he calls "the European game," which is subjecting vulnerable nations to imperial rule, and "the American game," which is—or, at least, has been—defending those vulnerable nations against the Europeans.[8] In this way, Twain condemns the United States for becoming like other nations, but in doing so he is implicitly affirming the idea that the United States should be—and has been—unique.

In *King Leopold's Soliloquy*, by contrast, Twain acknowledges U.S. complicity in the imperialism of other nations. But he also finds in Anglo-American reformist collaborations a way of campaigning against what was happening in the Congo. This campaign began in 1904, when a group of British and U.S. missionaries protested King Leopold's treatment of the Congolese. These missionaries formed the Congo Reform Association, which then divided into two wings, one British, one American. In typically transatlantic fashion, Twain was persuaded to join the U.S. association by a petition from a British acquaintance, the earl of Norbury, who was on the board of the British association. Twain was horrified by what he learned of conditions in the Congo. In 1884, King Leopold of Belgium had asserted a personal claim to all of Congo, and the United States was the first to recognize his sovereignty. In order to adjudicate this and other African land claims, the German chancellor Otto von Bismarck then convened the Congress of Berlin, which was attended by the United States and fourteen European nations. The congress agreed, among other things, that Leopold could retain sovereignty

7. The history of this campaign is most fully described in Hung Hawkins, "Mark Twain's Involvement with the Congo Reform Movement: 'A Fury of Generous Indignation,'" *New England Literary Quarterly* 51, no. 2 (June 1978): 147–75. I will be drawing on this account in my own summary.

8. Mark Twain, "To the Person Sitting in Darkness," in *Mark Twain* (1901; New York: Library of America, 2000), 746, 745. All further references will be to this edition.

in Congo so long as he preserved the moral well-being of the Congolese and continued to allow free trade. In Twain's account, the congress made these concessions to Leopold because he went "parading under the guise of philanthropy," claiming to ensure that the Congolese would no longer be sold into slavery.[9] This is a rather idiosyncratic account of the political motivations behind the Treaty of Berlin, but it makes Leopold the last—and by far the most dangerous—of Twain's con artist reformers. Leopold assented to these terms, but in the 1890s he began instituting the murderous policies that would make the colonization of Congo the most catastrophic of all imperial conquests.

When Twain was approached by the Congo reformers, he was informed that the United States had signed the Congress of Berlin. He therefore presumed that the United States was not only permitted, but indeed required, to intervene in Congo. Twain, that is to say, understood the situation in Congo as a problem of international law, and he therefore directed his energies to petitioning the U.S. government. And Twain was, of course, celebrity enough to do so. He commanded a private audience with Theodore Roosevelt, who was then president, as well as two long meetings with the secretary of state. Indeed, Twain even tried to pass diplomatic messages between the secretary of state and his aristocratic friends in Britain, assuring them, and asking them to assure the British prime minister in turn, that the United States would support Britain should Britain act first. This message prompted considerable diplomatic embarrassment and some discreet backpedaling because the United States had no intention of doing any such thing. At some point after this, Twain was finally informed of what he should have known all along, namely, that the United States was not at all obligated to act. For while the United States had signed the Treaty of Berlin, the treaty had never been sent to the Senate for ratification. Upon learning this, Twain resigned in disgust from the U.S. Congo Reform Association and refused to have anything more to do with Congo—or with reform.

What we can see in this episode is a shift in the nature of reform, the emergence of a humanitarianism grounded in international law and attentive to human rights. That this emergence is only partial with respect to Congo, that it is quickly stifled by U.S. self-interest, should not distract us from the fact that it ultimately became the predominant mode of international action through much of the latter part of the twentieth century. But what is most interesting about this episode is the persistence of an earlier mode of international—or transnational—action, namely, Anglo-American reform. Twain's discovery that the Senate had not ratified the Treaty of Berlin was

9. Mark Twain, *King Leopold's Soliloquy* (1905; New York: Seven Seas Books, 1961), 41.

not the end of the story in Congo, although he thought that it was. In his first flush of outrage upon hearing about the abuses in Congo, Twain wrote a long essay that his usual publishers refused to print. And so he published it himself as a freestanding pamphlet entitled *King Leopold's Soliloquy*. The text is a collage of various reformist modes, with Twain trying on all of these modes in turn, in search of one that might work—and even developing some new techniques of his own. Rather than making a sentimental appeal based on the inner sufferings of the Congolese, he instead adduces their maimed bodies as sign enough of suffering. The text is filled with references to, and even illustrations of, the amputated limbs of Congolese who were unable to meet Leopold's quotas. The interiority that interests Twain is not the victim's but rather the victimizer's, and so he writes, as the title reveals, Leopold's own soliloquy. Written from Leopold's perspective, the text is bitterly comic; the sufferings it depicts are mediated and so do not prompt in us the tears of an *Uncle Tom's Cabin* or even of the early sections of *Huckleberry Finn*. Tears, in this text, are what were shed by the European nations taken in by Leopold's false claims of antislavery concern, and so tears are what Twain refuses to produce, so that we may more clearly see.

In all of these ways, familiar and innovative, Twain's pamphlet seeks to rouse public opinion against Leopold's rule in Congo. At the same time, Twain remained quite hopeless about the capacity of public opinion to make a difference in this case. He believed that Leopold, as an absolute monarch, was entirely insulated from the opinions of his subjects and his own people, and he therefore believed that only the pressure of other governments could force Leopold to relinquish his power. When he learned that other governments were unwilling to act, he was unable to imagine any other recourse. And yet his own pamphlet had already become such a recourse. It roused such outrage in his readers that they continued to petition the British and American governments to intervene—and ultimately these governments did so. In January of 1906, Twain resigned from the U.S. Congo Reform Association and refused to hear another word about Congo. By December of that same year, Roosevelt bowed to public opinion and invented a legal pretext for intervening in Congo after all. Leopold was forced to step aside, and the colony came under the control of the Belgian government. And in this way Twain achieved, without ever knowing that he had done so, one of the last victories of Anglo-American reform.

Works Cited

"$10 Premiums." *The Lily,* 1 May 1854, 1.

Abzug, Robert H. *Cosmos Crumbling: American Reform and the Religious Imagination.* Oxford: Oxford University Press, 1994.

Ackroyd, Peter. *Dickens.* New York: HarperCollins, 1990.

Alcott, Louisa May. *Silver Pitchers: and Independence, a Centennial Love Story.* Boston: Roberts Brothers, 1876.

Alfano, Christine. "Under the Influence: Drink, Discourse, and Narrative in Victorian Britain." Ph.D. diss., Stanford University, 1996.

"American Slavery, and Emancipation by the Free States." *Westminster Review* 59, no. 1 (January 1853): 125–67.

Anderson, Benedict. *Imagined Communities.* 1983. London: Verso, 1991.

Anderson, Frederick, and Kenneth M. Sanderson, eds. *Mark Twain: The Critical Heritage.* New York: Barnes and Noble, 1971.

Arac, Jonathan. *Commissioned Spirits: The Shaping of Social Motion in Dickens, Carlyle, Melville, and Hawthorne.* 1979. New York: Columbia University Press, 1989.

——. *Huckleberry Finn as Idol and Target: The Functions of Criticism in Our Time* Madison: University of Wisconsin Press, 1997.

Arata, Stephen. "1897." In *A Companion to Victorian Literature and Culture,* ed. Herbert F. Tucker. London: Blackwell, 1999.

Armitage, David. "Three Concepts of Atlantic History." In *The British Atlantic World, 1500–1800,* ed. Armitage and Michael J. Braddick. London: Palgrave, 2002.

Armstrong, Nancy. *Desire and Domestic Fiction: A Political History of the Novel.* Oxford: Oxford University Press, 1987.

Arnold, Matthew. "Civilization in the United States." *Nineteenth Century* 23, no. 134 (April 1888): 481–96.

Ashton, Rosemary. *George Eliot: A Life.* London: Penguin, 1996.

Auerbach, Erich. *Mimesis: The Representation of Reality in Western Literature.* Trans. Willard R. Trask. 1946. Princeton: Princeton University Press, 1974.

Austen, Zelda. "Why Feminist Critics Are Angry with George Eliot." *College English* 37 (1976): 549–61.

Baetzhold, Howard G. *Mark Twain and John Bull: The British Connection.* Bloomington: Indiana University Press, 1970.

Bailyn, Bernard. Preface. In *The British Atlantic World, 1500–1800,* ed. David Armitage and Michael J. Braddick. London: Palgrave, 2002.

Barker, Juliet. *The Brontës.* London: Weidenfeld and Nicolson, 1994.

Baym, Nina. *Novels, Readers, and Reviewers: Responses to Fiction in Antebellum America.* Ithaca: Cornell University Press, 1984.

Becker, George J., ed. *Documents of Modern Literary Realism.* Princeton: Princeton University Press, 1963.

Beer, Gillian. *George Eliot.* Bloomington: Indiana University Press, 1986.

Bell, Michael Davitt. *The Problem of American Realism: Studies in the Cultural History of a Literary Idea.* Chicago: University of Chicago Press, 1993.

Bellesiles, Michael. "Creating Empires." *Journal of British Studies* 40, no. 4 (October 2001): 586.

Besant, Walter. *All Sorts and Conditions of Men: An Impossible Story.* 1882. London: Chatto and Windus, 1924.

——. *The Art of Fiction: A Lecture Delivered at the Royal Institution, April 25, 1884.* Boston: Cupples, Upham, 1884.

Blake, Kathleen. "Middlemarch and the Woman Question." *Nineteenth-Century Fiction* 31 (1976): 285–312.

Boston, Ray. *British Chartists in America, 1839–1900.* Manchester: Manchester University Press, 1971.

Boumelha, Penny. "Sexual Ideology and Narrative Form." In *New Casebooks: "Jude the Obscure,"* ed. Boumelha. 1991. London: St. Martin's, 2000.

Bourdieu, Pierre. *The Rules of Art: Genesis and Structure of the Literary Field.* Trans. Susan Emanuel. 1992. Palo Alto: Stanford University Press, 1996.

Boyeson, H. H. "Why We Have No Great Novelists." *Forum* 2 (1887): 615–22.

Bradbrook, Muriel C. "Barbara Bodichon, George Eliot and the Limits of Feminism." In *Women and Literature, 1779–1982: The Collected Papers of Muriel Bradbrook.* New York: Barnes and Noble, 1982.

Brantlinger, Patrick. *The Spirit of Reform: British Literature and Politics, 1832–1867.* Cambridge: Harvard University Press, 1977.

Brodhead, Richard. *The School of Hawthorne.* Oxford: Oxford University Press, 1984.

Brontë, Anne. *The Tenant of Wildfell Hall.* 1848. Oxford: Oxford University Press, 1993.

Brown, Christopher Leslie. *Moral Capital: Foundations of British Abolitionism.* Chapel Hill: University of North Carolina Press, 2006.

Budd, Louis J. "Mark Twain as an American Icon." In *The Cambridge Companion to Mark Twain,* ed. Forrest G. Robinson. Cambridge: Cambridge University Press, 1995.

——. *Mark Twain: Social Philosopher.* Bloomington: Indiana University Press, 1962.

——, ed. *Mark Twain: The Contemporary Reviews.* Cambridge: Cambridge University Press, 1999.

Buell, Lawrence. "American Literary Emergence as a Postcolonial Phenomenon." *American Literary History* 4, no. 3 (Autumn 1992): 411–42.

———. "Rethinking Anglo-American Literary History." *Clio* 33, no. 1 (Fall 2003): 65–72.

Bulwer, Edward. *England and the English.* Ed. Standish Meacham. 1833. Chicago: University of Chicago Press, 1970.

Cable, George Washington. "The Freedman's Case in Equity." *Century Magazine* 29, no. 3 (January 1885): 409–19.

Cady, Edwin. *The Road to Realism: The Early Years of William Dean Howells, 1837–1885.* Syracuse: Syracuse University Press, 1956.

Camfield, Gregg. "Sentimental Liberalism and the Problem of Race in Huckleberry Finn." *Nineteenth-Century Literature* 46, no. 1 (June 1991): 96–113.

Cardwell, Guy A. *Twins of Genius.* Lansing: Michigan State College Press, 1953.

Carlyle, Thomas. "Shooting Niagara—And After?" *Macmillan's Magazine* 16 (April 1867): 64–87.

Carton, Evan. "Speech Acts and Social Action: Mark Twain and the Politics of Literary Performance." In *The Cambridge Companion to Mark Twain,* ed. Forrest G. Robinson. Cambridge: Cambridge University Press, 1995.

Cash, W. J. *The Mind of the South.* New York: Knopf, 1941.

Chai, Leon. *The Romantic Foundations of the American Renaissance.* Ithaca: Cornell University Press, 1987.

Chapman, Maria Weston, ed. *Harriet Martineau's Autobiography, with Memorials.* Boston: J. R. Osgood, 1877.

Charvat, William. *Literary Publishing in America, 1790–1850.* Amherst: University of Massachusetts Press, 1959.

Chaudhuri, Brahma. "Dickens and the Question of Slavery." *Dickens Quarterly* 6, no. 1 (March 1989): 3–9.

Cognard-Black, Jennifer. *Narrative in the Professional Age: Trans-Atlantic Readings of Harriet Beecher Stowe, George Eliot and Elizabeth Stuart Phelps.* London: Routledge, 2004.

Cohen, Hennig, and William B. Dillingham. *Humor of the Old Southwest.* Athens: University of Georgia Press, 1975.

Cohen, William B. "Epilogue: The European Comparison." In *Charity, Philanthropy, and Civility in American History,* ed. Lawrence J. Friedman and Mark D. McGarvie. Cambridge: Cambridge University Press, 2003.

Colley, Linda. *Britons: Forging the Nation, 1701–1837.* New Haven: Yale University Press, 1992.

Collins, Philip. *Dickens and Education.* London: Macmillan, 1963.

———, ed. *Dickens: The Critical Heritage.* London: Routledge, 1971.

Cooke, Rose Terry. "The Ring Fetter." *Atlantic Monthly,* August 1859.

Coward, Rosalind, and John Ellis. *Language and Materialism: Developments in Semiology and the Theory of the Subject.* London: Routledge, 1977.

Cox, R. G. *Thomas Hardy: The Critical Heritage.* London: Routledge, 1970.

Crowley, John W. *Drunkard's Progress: Narratives of Addiction, Despair, and Recovery.* Baltimore: Johns Hopkins University Press, 1999.

Cunningham, Gail. *The New Woman and the Victorian Novel.* London: Macmillan, 1978.

Davidoff, Leonore, and Catherine Hall. *Family Fortunes: Men and Women of the English Middle Class, 1780–1850.* Chicago: University of Chicago Press, 1987.

Davis, David Brion. *The Problem of Slavery in the Age of Revolution, 1770–1823.* Ithaca: Cornell University Press, 1975.

Dellamora, Richard. "Male Relations in Thomas Hardy's *Jude the Obscure.*" In *New Casebooks: "Jude the Obscure,"* ed. Penny Boumelha. 1991. New York: St. Martin's Press, 2000.

Demetz, Peter. "Zur Definition des Realismus," *Literatur und Kritik* 2 (1967): 333–45.

De Voto, Bernard. *Mark Twain at Work.* Cambridge: Harvard University Press, 1942.

Dickens, Charles. *American Notes for General Circulation.* 1842. London: Penguin, 1972.

———. *Bleak House.* 1851–53. London: Penguin, 1996.

———. *Martin Chuzzlewit.* 1884–85. Oxford: Oxford University Press, 1998.

———. *Nicholas Nickleby.* 1839. London: Penguin, 1978.

———. *Oliver Twist.* 1839. Oxford: Oxford University Press, 1966.

———. *The Posthumous Papers of the Pickwick Club.* 1837. London: Penguin, 1986.

———. *Sketches by Boz.* 1836. New York: Penguin, 1995.

Dickens, Charles, and Henry Morley. "North American Slavery." *Household Words,* 18 September 1852.

Dickinson, Emily. *Poems by Emily Dickinson.* Ed. Martha Dickinson Bianchi and Alfred Leete Hampson. 1890. Boston: Little Brown, 1957.

Dimock, Wai Chee, *Empire for Liberty: Melville and the Poetics of Individualism.* Princeton: Princeton University Press, 1989.

———. *Residues of Justice: Literature, Law, Philosophy.* Berkeley: University of California Press, 1997.

Dixon, Chris. *Perfecting the Family: Antislavery Marriages in Nineteenth-Century America.* Amherst: University of Massachusetts Press, 1997.

Douglas, Ann. *The Feminization of American Culture.* New York: Knopf, 1977.

Dowling, Andrew. "'The Other Side of Silence': Matrimonial Conflict and the Divorce Court in George Eliot's Fiction." *Nineteenth-Century Literature* 50, no. 3 (December 1995): 322–36.

DuBois, Ellen Carol. *Feminism and Suffrage: The Emergence of an Independent Women's Movement in America, 1848–1869.* 1978. Ithaca: Cornell University Press, 1999.

Edel, Leon. *The Life of Henry James: The Conquest of London, 1870–1881.* Philadelphia: J. B. Lippincott, 1962.

Edwards, Brent Hayes. *The Practice of Diaspora: Literature, Translation, and the Rise of Black Internationalism.* Cambridge: Harvard University Press, 2003.

Eigner, Edwin M., and George J. Worth. *Victorian Criticism of the Novel.* Cambridge: Cambridge University Press, 1985.

Eliot, George. *Adam Bede.* 1859. New York: Signet, 1981.

———. *Armgart.* In *Complete Poems.* 1870. New York: Doubleday, 1901.

———. "Art and Belles Lettres." *Westminster Review* 65, no. 2 (April 1856): 625–50.

———. "Belles Lettres." *Westminster Review* 66 (October 1856): 571–78.

———. *Daniel Deronda.* 1876. London: Penguin, 1986.

——. *Essays of George Eliot*. Ed. Thomas Pinney. New York: Columbia University Press, 1963.

——. *Felix Holt*. 1866. London: Everyman, 1997.

——. *The George Eliot Letters*. Ed. Gordon S. Haight. 8 vols. New Haven: Yale University Press, 1954–1978.

——. "Margaret Fuller and Mary Wollstonecraft." *Leader* 6 (13 October 1855): 988–89.

——. *Middlemarch*. 1871–72. London: Penguin, 1994.

——. "The Morality of Wilhelm Meister." *Leader* 6 (21 July 1855): 703.

——. *Romola*. 1862–64. London: Everyman, 1999.

——. *Scenes of Clerical Life*. 1857. Oxford: Oxford University Press, 1985.

[Eliot, George]. "Prospectus of the Westminster and Foreign Quarterly Review." *Westminster Review* 57, no. 1 (January 1852): 1.

Eliot, T. S. Introduction. In *The Adventures of Huckleberry Finn*. New York: Chanticleer Press, 1950.

Ellis, Sarah Stickney. *Family Secrets; or, Hints to Those Who Would Keep Home Happy*. Vol. 1. Philadelphia, 1842.

——. *The Wives of England: Their Relative Duties, Domestic Influence, and Social Obligations*. In *The Prose Works of Mrs. Ellis*. Vol. 1. New York: Langley, 1844.

Emerson, Ralph Waldo. "The American Scholar." In *Ralph Waldo Emerson: Essays and Lectures*, ed. Joel Porte. New York: Library of America, 1983.

——. *English Traits*. Cambridge: Harvard University Press, 1929.

——. "Man the Reformer." *Nature: Addresses and Lectures*. Boston: James Monroe, 1849.

Englander, David. *Poverty and Poor Law Reform in Britain: From Chadwick to Booth, 1834–1914*. London: Longman, 1998.

Ermarth, Elizabeth Deeds. *Realism and Consensus in the English Novel*. Princeton: Princeton University Press, 1983.

Fisher, Philip. *Hard Facts: Setting and Form in the American Novel*. Oxford: Oxford University Press, 1987.

Fishkin, Shelley Fisher. *Lighting Out for the Territories: Reflections on Mark Twain and American Culture*. Oxford: Oxford University Press, 1996.

Flint, Kate. "George Eliot and Gender." In *The Cambridge Companion to George Eliot*, ed. George Levine. Cambridge: Cambridge University Press, 2001.

——. *The Woman Reader, 1837–1914*. Oxford: Oxford University Press, 1993.

Foner, Philip S. *Mark Twain: Social Critic*. New York: International Publishers, 1958.

Ford, Anne-Marie. "Gothic Legacies: Jane Eyre in Elizabeth Stoddard's New England." In *Special Relationships: Anglo-American Affinities and Antagonisms, 1854–1936*, ed. Janet Beer and Bridget Bennett. New York: Palgrave, 2002.

Forster, John. *The Life of Charles Dickens*. 1872–74. London: Chapman and Hall, 1879.

Frankel, Oz. "Blue Books and the Victorian Reader." *Victorian Studies* 46, no. 2 (Winter 2004): 308–18.

Franklin, Benjamin Fisher. "King Arthur Plays from the 1890s." *Victorian Poetry* 28, nos. 3–4 (Autumn 1986): 153–76.

Frierson, William C. "The English Controversy over Realism in Fiction, 1885–1895." *PMLA* 49, no. 4 (December 1934): 533–50.

Fulton, Valerie. "Rewriting the Necessary Woman: Marriage and Professionalism in James, Jewett, and Phelps." *Henry James Review* 15, no. 3 (Fall 1994): 242–56.

Gage, Frances Dana. "Tales of Truth, Number One." *The Lily*, 1 January 1852, 2–3.

Gagnier, Reginia. *Subjectivities: A History of Self-Representation in Britain, 1832–1920.* Oxford: Oxford University Press, 1991.

Gainor, Ellen. "G.B.S. and the New Woman." *New England Theatre Journal* 1, no. 1 (1990): 1–17.

Gallagher, Catherine. "George Eliot: Immanent Victorian." *Proceedings of the British Academy* 94 (1997): 157–72

——. *The Industrial Reformation of English Fiction: Social Discourse and Narrative Form, 1832–1867.* Chicago: University of Chicago Press, 1980.

Gatrell, Simon. "England, Europe, and Empire: Hardy, Meredith, and Gissing." In *The Ends of the Earth: 1876–1918*, ed. Gatrell. London: Ashfield Press, 1992.

——. "Wessex." In *The Cambridge Companion to Thomas Hardy*, ed. Dale Kramer. Cambridge: Cambridge University Press, 1999.

Gilbert, Sandra M., and Susan Gubar. *The Madwoman in the Attic: The Woman Writer and the Nineteenth-Century Literary Imagination.* 1977. New Haven: Yale University Press, 1989.

Giles, Paul. "Transnationalism and Classic American Literature." *PMLA* 118, no. 1 (January 2003): 69.

——. *Virtual Americas: Transnational Fictions and the Transatlantic Imaginary.* Durham, NC: Duke University Press, 2002.

Gilroy, Paul. *The Black Atlantic: Modernity and Double Consciousness.* Cambridge: Harvard University Press, 1993.

Gissing, George. *The Immortal Dickens.* London: Cecil Palmer, 1925.

Glazener, Nancy. *Reading for Realism: The History of a U.S. Literary Institution.* Durham, NC: Duke University Press, 1997.

Goodlad, Lauren M. E. *Victorian Literature and the Victorian State: Character and Governance in a Liberal Society.* Baltimore: Johns Hopkins University Press, 2003.

Goodman, Susan, and Carl Dawson. *William Dean Howells: A Writer's Life.* Berkeley: University of California Press, 2005.

Grady, Henry W. "In Plain Black and White." *Century Magazine* 29, no. 6 (April 1885): 909–17.

Grand, Sarah. "The New Aspect of the Woman Question." *North American Review* 158 (1894): 270–76.

Grattan, Thomas Colley. *Civilized America.* London: Bradbury and Evans, 1859.

Gravil, Richard. *Romantic Dialogues: Anglo-American Continuities, 1776–1862.* London: Macmillan, 2000.

Green, Laura. *Educating Women: Cultural Conflict and Victorian Literature.* Athens: Ohio University Press, 2001.

Griest, Guinevere. *Mudie's Circulating Library and the Victorian Novel.* Bloomington: Indiana University Press, 1970.

Griffith, George V. "Elizabeth Stuart Phelps and George Eliot—An Epistolary Friendship." *Legacy* 18, no. 1 (2001): 94–100.

Gruesz, Kirsten Silva. *Ambassadors of Culture: The Transamerican Origins of Latino Writing.* Princeton: Princeton University Press, 2002.

Guy, Josephine. *The Victorian Social-Problem Novel: The Market, the Individual, and Communal Life*. London: Macmillan, 1996.

Habegger, Alfred. *Henry James and the "Woman Business."* Cambridge: Cambridge University Press, 1989.

Habermas, Jürgen. *The Structural Transformation of the Public Sphere: An Inquiry into a Category of Bourgeois Society*. Trans. Thomas Berger. 1965. Cambridge: MIT Press, 1989.

Haight, Gordon S. *George Eliot: A Biography*. Oxford: Oxford University Press, 1968.

Hardy, Thomas. "Candour in English Fiction." *New Review* 2 (January–June 1890): 15–21.

——. *The Collected Letters of Thomas Hardy: 1840–1892*. Ed. Richard Little Purdy and Michael Millgate. Oxford: Oxford University Press, 1978.

——. *The Collected Letters of Thomas Hardy: 1893–1901*. Ed. Richard Little Purdy and Michael Millgate. Oxford: Oxford University Press, 1980.

——. "How Shall We Solve the Divorce Problem?" *Nash's Magazine*, March 1912.

——. *Jude the Obscure*. 1895. London: Penguin, 1998.

——. *The Mayor of Casterbridge*. 1886. Oxford: Oxford University Press, 1987.

——. *Tess of the d'Urbervilles*. 1891. London: Penguin, 1985.

——. *The Woodlanders*. 1887. Oxford: Oxford University Press, 1996.

[Hardy, Thomas]. *The Early Life of Thomas Hardy, 1840–1891*. 1928. London: Studio Editions, 1994.

Harrison, Brian. *Drink and the Victorians: The Temperance Question in England, 1815–1872*. Pittsburgh: University of Pittsburgh Press, 1971.

——. *The Peaceable Kingdom: Stability and Change in Modern Britain*. Oxford: Oxford University Press, 1982.

Hawkins, Hung. "Mark Twain's Involvement with the Congo Reform Movement: 'A Fury of Generous Indignation.'" *New England Literary Quarterly* 51, no. 2 (June 1978): 147–75.

Hawthorne, Nathaniel. *The Blithedale Romance*. 1852. London: Penguin Books, 1986.

——. "The Custom House." In *The Scarlet Letter*. 1851. London: Penguin, 1983.

Hayes, Kevin J., ed. *Henry James: The Contemporary Reviews*. Cambridge: Cambridge University Press, 1996.

Hedrick, Joan D. *Harriet Beecher Stowe: A Life*. Oxford: Oxford University Press, 1994.

Heilmann, Ann. *New Woman Fiction: Women Writing First-Wave Feminism*. New York: St. Martin's Press, 2000.

Hobart, Anne. "Harriet Martineau's Political Economy of Everyday Life." *Victorian Studies* 37, no. 2 (Winter 1994): 223–52.

Hoffman, Andrew. *Inventing Mark Twain: The Lives of Samuel Langhorne Clemens*. New York: William Morrow, 1997.

Howe, Maud, and Florence Howe Hall. *Laura Bridgman: Dr. Howe's Famous Pupil and What He Taught Her*. Boston: Little, Brown, 1903.

Howells, William Dean. *Criticism and Fiction*. 1891. New York: New York University Press, 1959.

——. "Henry James, Jr." *Century Magazine* 25, no. 1 (November 1882): 24–29.

——. "Mark Twain." *Century Magazine* 24, no. 5 (September 1882): 780–84.

——. *A Modern Instance.* 1882. New York: Penguin, 1984.

Hutchinson, Stuart, ed. *George Eliot: Critical Assessments.* 4 vols. The Banks, Mountfield: Helm Information, 1996.

Ingham, Patricia. "The Evolution of *Jude the Obscure.*" *Review of English Studies* 27 (1976): 27–37.

Jackson, Shannon. *Lines of Activity: Performance, Historiography, Hull-House Domesticity.* Ann Arbor: University of Michigan Press, 2000.

Jaffe, Audrey. *Scenes of Sympathy: Identity and Representation in Victorian Fiction.* Ithaca: Cornell University Press, 2000.

James, Henry. "The Art of Fiction." *Longman's Magazine,* September 1884. Reprinted in *Henry James: The Critical Muse: Selected Literary Criticism,* ed. Roger Gard. New York: Penguin, 1987.

——. *The Bostonians.* 1884–85. London: Penguin, 2000.

——. "Charles de Bernard and Gustave Flaubert: The Minor French Novelists." *Galaxy,* February 1876, 219–34.

——. *The Complete Notebooks of Henry James: The Authoritative and Definitive Edition.* Ed. Leon Edel and Lyall H. Powers. Oxford: Oxford University Press, 1987.

——. *French Poets and Novelists.* 1878. London: Macmillan, 1893.

——. *Henry James Letters,* vol. 2: *1875–1883.* Ed. Leon Edel. Cambridge: Harvard University Press, 1975.

——. *Henry James Letters,* vol. 3: *1883–1895.* Ed. Leon Edel. Cambridge: Harvard University Press, 1980.

——. *Henry James: Literary Criticism, Continental Writers.* Ed. Leon Edel. New York: Library of America, 1984.

——. *Henry James: The Critical Muse: Selected Literary Criticism.* Ed. Roger Gard. New York: Penguin, 1987.

——. "Ivan Turgenieff." *Atlantic Monthly,* January 1884, 42–55.

——. *The Letters of Henry James.* Ed. Percy Lubbock. London: Macmillan, 1920.

——. *The Middle Years.* New York: Scribner's, 1917.

——. *Nathaniel Hawthorne.* 1879. Ithaca: Cornell University Press, 1997.

——. *The Princess Casamassima.* 1885–86. London: Penguin, 1987.

Johnson, Edgar. *Charles Dickens: His Tragedy and Triumph.* 2 vols. New York: Simon and Schuster, 1952.

Jordan, W. K. *Philanthropy in England, 1480–1660.* London: G. Allen and Unwin, 1959.

Kaplan, Amy. *The Social Construction of American Realism.* Chicago: University of Chicago Press, 1988.

Kaplan, Fred. *Dickens: A Biography.* 1988. Baltimore: Johns Hopkins University Press, 1998.

——. *Henry James: The Imagination of Genius.* New York: William Morrow, 1992.

Keating, P. J. *The Working Classes in Victorian Fiction.* New York: Barnes and Noble, 1971.

Kelly, Katherine E. "Imprinting the Stage: Shaw and the Publishing Trade, 1883–1903." In *The Cambridge Companion to George Bernard Shaw,* ed. Christopher Innes. Cambridge: Cambridge University Press, 1998.

Kemble, Frances Anne. *Journal of a Residence on a Georgian Plantation in 1838–1839.* Ed. John A. Scott. 1863. New York: Knopf, 1961.

Kerr, Andrea Moore. *Lucy Stone: Speaking Out for Equality*. New Brunswick: Rutgers University Press, 1992.

Kestner, Joseph. *Protest and Reform: The British Social Narrative by Women, 1827–1867*. Madison: University of Wisconsin Press, 1985.

Kramer, Dale. "Hardy and Readers: *Jude the Obscure*." In *The Cambridge Companion to Thomas Hardy*, ed. Dale Kramer. Cambridge: Cambridge University Press, 1999.

Krauth, Leland. "Mark Twain: The Victorian of Southwestern Humor." *American Literature* 54, no. 3 (October 1982): 368–84.

Landow, George P. *Elegant Jeremiahs: The Sage from Carlyle to Mailer*. Ithaca: Cornell University Press, 1986.

Leavis, F. R. *The Great Tradition: George Eliot, Henry James, Joseph Conrad*. New York: George W. Stewart, 1950.

Ledger, Sally. *The New Woman: Fiction and Feminism at the Fin de Siècle*. New York: St. Martin's Press, 1997.

Levin, Harry. *The Gates of Horn: A Study of Five French Realists*. Oxford: Oxford University Press, 1963.

Levine, Caroline. *The Serious Pleasures of Suspense: Victorian Realism and Narrative Doubt*. Charlottesville: University of Virginia Press, 2003.

Levine, George. *The Realistic Imagination: English Fiction from "Frankenstein" to "Lady Chatterley."* Chicago: University of Chicago Press, 1981.

Lillibridge, George Donald. *Beacon of Freedom: The Impact of American Democracy upon Great Britain, 1830–1870*. Philadelphia: University of Pennsylvania Press, 1955.

Loeffelholz, Mary. *From School to Salon: Reading Nineteenth-Century American Women's Poetry*. Princeton: Princeton University Press, 2004.

Logan, Deborah. "Harriet Martineau and the Martyr Age of the United States." *Symbiosis* 5, no. 1 (April 2001): 33–49.

———. *The Hour and the Woman: Harriet Martineau's "Somewhat Remarkable" Life*. DeKalb: Northern Illinois University Press, 2002.

Lowry, Richard S. *"Littery Man": Mark Twain and Modern Authorship*. Oxford: Oxford University Press, 1996.

Lukács, Georg. *Studies in European Realism: A Sociological Survey of the Writings of Balzac, Stendhal, Zola, Gorky, and Others*. Trans. Edith Bone. 1948. London: Merlin Press, 1984.

Makela, Klaus, et al. *Alcoholics Anonymous as a Mutual-Help Movement*. Madison: University of Wisconsin Press, 1996.

Manning, Susan. "Did Mark Twain Bring Down the Temple on Scott's Shoulders?" In *Special Relationships: Anglo-American Affinities and Antagonisms, 1854–1936*, ed. Janet Beer and Bridget Bennett. New York: Palgrave, 2002.

———. *Fragments of Union: Making Connections in Scottish and American Writing*. London: Palgrave, 2002.

Marcus, Sharon. "Comparative Sapphism." In *The Literary Channel: The International Invention of the Novel*, ed. Carolyn Dever and Margaret Cohen. Princeton: Princeton University Press, 2002.

Martineau, Harriet. *Deerbrook*. 1839. London: Penguin Books, 2004.

———. *Society in America*. 3 vols. London: Saunders and Otley, 1837.

Marx, Leo. "Mr. Eliot, Mr. Trilling, and Huckleberry Finn." *American Scholar* 22 (Autumn 1953): 423–40.

Masson, David. *British Novelists and Their Styles, Being a Critical Sketch of the History of British Prose Fiction*. 1859. Philadelphia: Folson Press, 1969.

Matthiessen, F. O. *The American Renaissance: Art and Expression in the Age of Emerson and Whitman*. Oxford: Oxford University Press, 1941.

Mattingly, Carol, ed. *Water Drops from Women Writers: A Temperance Reader*. Carbondale: Southern Illinois University Press, 2001.

McCabe, Colin. *James Joyce and the Revolution of the Word*. London: Macmillan, 1978.

McGill, Meredith. *American Literature and the Culture of Reprinting, 1834–1853*. Philadelphia: University of Pennsylvania Press, 2003.

Michelson, Bruce. "Realism, Romance, and Dynamite: The Quarrel of *A Connecticut Yankee in King Arthur's Court*." *New England Quarterly* 64, no. 4 (December 1991): 609–32.

Miller, D. A. *The Novel and the Police*. Berkeley: University of California Press, 1988.

Miller, J. Hillis. *The Ethics of Reading: Kant, de Man, Eliot, Trollope, James, and Benjamin*. New York: Columbia University Press, 1987.

Millet, Kate. *Sexual Politics*. Garden City: Doubleday, 1970.

Millgate, Michael. *Thomas Hardy: A Biography*. New York: Random House, 1982.

Mintz, Steven. *Moralists and Modernizers: America's Pre–Civil War Reformers*. Baltimore: Johns Hopkins University Press, 1995.

Mitchell, Sally. "New Women, Old and New." *Victorian Literature and Culture* 27, no. 2 (1999): 579–88.

Moers, Ellen. *Literary Women*. Garden City: Doubleday, 1976.

Morris, Pam. *Realism*. London: Routledge, 2003.

Mulvey, Christopher. *Transatlantic Manners: Social Patterns in Nineteenth-Century Anglo-American Travel Literature*. Cambridge: Cambridge University Press, 1990.

Murray, Donald M. "Henry James and the English Reviewers, 1882–1890." *American Literature* 24, no. 1 (1952): 1–20.

Nestor, Pauline. *George Eliot*. London: Palgrave, 2002.

Olmstead, John Charles, ed. *A Victorian Art of Fiction: Essays on the Novel in British Periodicals, 1851–1869*. 2 vols. New York: Garland, 1979.

Ouida. "The New Woman." *North American Review* 158 (1894): 610–19.

Owen, David. *English Philanthropy, 1660–1960*. Cambridge: Harvard University Press, 1964.

Pasterson, John. "The Genesis of *Jude the Obscure*." *Studies in Philology* 57 (1960): 87–98.

Patten, Robert L. "*Pickwick Papers* and the Development of Serial Fiction." *Rice University Studies: Studies in English* 61, no. 1 (Winter 1975): 51–74.

Pell, Nancy. "George Eliot and Barbara Leigh Smith Bodichon." In *Nineteenth-Century Women Writers of the English-Speaking World*, ed. Rhoda B. Nathan. Westport, CT: Greenwood Press, 1985.

Pizer, Donald, ed. *Documents of American Realism and Naturalism*. Carbondale: Southern Illinois University Press, 1998.

Poovey, Mary. *Making a Social Body: British Cultural Formation, 1830–1864*. Chicago: University of Chicago Press, 1995.

Pykett, Lyn. Foreword. In *The New Woman in Fiction and in Fact: Fin-de-Siècle Feminisms*, ed. Angelique Richardson and Chris Willis. London: Palgrave, 2001.

"Representative Reform." *Westminster Review* 57, no. 1 (January 1852): 1–41.

Review of *Society in America*, by Harriet Martineau. *Edinburgh Review*, April 1838, 181.

Review of *The Chimes*, by Charles Dickens. *Economist*, 18 January 1845, 53–54.

Review of *The Tenant of Wildfell Hall*, by Anne Brontë. *Spectator*, 18 December 1847, 1217.

Reynolds, David S. *Beneath the American Renaissance: The Subversive Imagination in the Age of Emerson and Melville*. Cambridge: Harvard University Press, 1988.

Riis, Jacob. *How the Other Half Lives: Studies among the Tenements of New York*. 1890. New York: Penguin Books, 1997.

Roach, Joseph. *Cities of the Dead: Circum-Atlantic Performance*. New York: Columbia University Press, 1996.

Robbins, Bruce. "Telescopic Philanthropy: Professionalism and Responsibility in *Bleak House*." In *Nation and Narration*, ed. Homi K. Bhabha. London: Routledge, 1990.

Roberts, Caroline. *The Woman and the Hour: Harriet Martineau and Victorian Ideologies*. Toronto: University of Toronto Press, 2002.

Rorabaugh, W. J. *The Alcoholic Republic: An American Tradition*. London: Oxford University Press, 1979.

Rowe, John Carlos. "Nineteenth-Century United States Literary Culture and Transnationality." *PMLA* 118, no. 1 (January 2003): 78–89.

Rush, Benjamin. *An Inquiry into the Effects of Spirituous Liquors on the Human Body, to Which Is Added a Moral and Physical Thermometer*. Boston, 1790.

Saint-Amour, Paul K. *The Copywrights: Intellectual Property and the Literary Imagination*. Ithaca: Cornell University Press, 2003.

Sánchez-Eppler, Karen. "Bodily Bonds: The Intersecting Rhetorics of Feminism and Abolition." *Representations* 24 (Autumn 1988): 28–59.

Scanlan, Margaret. "Terrorism and the Realistic Novel: Henry James and *The Princess Casamassima*." *Texas Studies in Literature and Language* 34, no. 3 (Fall 1992): 380–402.

Schaffer, Talia. "'Nothing but Foolscap and Ink': Inventing the New Woman." In *The New Woman in Fiction and in Fact: Fin-de-Siècle Feminisms*, ed. Angelique Richardson and Chris Willis. London: Palgrave, 2001.

Schor, Hilary. "Fiction." In *A Companion to Victorian Literature and Culture*, ed. Herbert F. Tucker. London: Blackwell, 1999.

Seltzer, Mark. *Henry James and the Art of Power*. Ithaca: Cornell University Press, 1984.

Shaw, George Bernard. "Author's Apology." In *Plays by George Bernard Shaw*. 1902. New York: Signet, 1960.

Shaw, Harry E. *Narrating Reality: Austen, Scott, Eliot*. Ithaca: Cornell University Press, 1999.

Showalter, Elaine. "Family Secrets and Domestic Subversion: Rebellion in the Novels of the 1860s." In *The Victorian Family: Structure and Stresses*, ed. Anthony S. Wohl. New York: St. Martin's Press, 1978.

——. "The Greening of Sister George." *Nineteenth-Century Fiction* 35 (1980): 292–311.

——. *A Literature of Their Own: British Women Novelists from Brontë to Lessing.* 1977. Princeton: Princeton University Press, 1999.

Silber, Nina. *The Romance of Reunion: Northerners and the South, 1865–1900.* Chapel Hill: University of North Carolina Press, 1993.

Skilton, David. *The Early and Mid-Victorian Novel.* London: Routledge, 1993.

Smith, Sydney. Review of *Statistical Annals of the United States of America,* by Adam Seybert (Philadelphia, 1818). *Edinburgh Review* 33, no. 65 (January 1820): 69–80.

Sommer, Doris. *Foundational Fictions: The National Romances of Latin America.* Berkeley: University of California Press, 1991.

Spector, Stephen J. "Masters of Metonymy: *Hard Times* and Knowing the Working Class." *ELH* 51, no. 2 (Summer 1984): 365–84.

Staines, David. "King Arthur in Victorian Fiction." In *The Worlds of Victorian Fiction,* ed. Jerome H. Buckley. Cambridge: Harvard University Press, 1975.

Stang, Richard. *The Theory of the Novel in England, 1850–1870.* New York: Columbia University Press, 1959.

Stanton, Elizabeth Cady, Susan B. Anthony, and Matilda Joslyn Gage. *The History of Woman Suffrage.* Vol 1. New York, 1881.

Stevens, Laura M. "Transatlanticism Now." *American Literary History* 16, no. 1 (Spring 2004): 93–102.

Stoddard, Elizabeth. *The Morgesons and Other Writings, Published and Unpublished.* Ed. Lawrence Buell and Sandra Zagarell. Philadelphia: University of Pennsylvania Press, 1984.

Stone, Harry. "Charles Dickens and Harriet Beecher Stowe." *Nineteenth-Century Fiction* 12, no. 3 (December 1959): 188–202.

Stone, Lawrence. *The Road to Divorce: England, 1530–1987.* Oxford: Oxford University Press, 1990.

Stowe, Harriet Beecher. *Uncle Tom's Cabin; or, Life among the Lowly.* 1851. New York: Norton, 1994.

Sutherland, J. A. *Victorian Novelists and Publishers.* Chicago: University of Chicago Press, 1976.

Tamarkin, Elisa. "Black Anglophilia; or, The Sociability of Antislavery." *American Literary History* 14, no. 3 (2002): 444–77.

Taylor, Andrew. *Henry James and the Father Question.* Cambridge: Cambridge University Press, 2002.

Techi, Cecelia. "Women Writers and the New Woman." In *The Columbia Literary History of the United States,* ed. Emory Elliot. New York: Columbia University Press, 1988.

"Tendencies of England, The." *Westminster Review* 58, no. 1 (July 1852): 1–41.

Thistlethwaite, Frank. *The Anglo-American Connection in the Early Nineteenth Century.* Philadelphia: University of Pennsylvania Press, 1959.

Thompson, E. P. *Customs in Common.* London: Penguin Books, 1991.

Tocqueville, Alexis de. *Democracy in America.* 1835. New York: Modern Library, 1981.

Tomashevsky, Boris. "Thematics." In *Russian Formalist Criticism: Four Essays.* Trans. Lee T. Lemon and Marion J. Rees. 1925. Lincoln: University of Nebraska Press, 1965.

Tompkins, Jane. *Sensational Designs: The Cultural Work of American Fiction, 1790–1860.* Oxford: Oxford University Press, 1985.

Traub, Valerie. "Beyond the Americana: Henry James Reads George Eliot." In *Special Relationships: Anglo-American Affinities and Antagonisms, 1854–1936,* ed. Janet Beer and Bridget Bennett. New York: Palgrave, 2002.

Trilling, Lionel. *The Liberal Imagination.* New York: Charles Scribner's Sons, 1950.

Trollope, Anthony. *The Warden.* 1855. London: Penguin, 1984.

Turley, David. *Culture of English Antislavery, 1780–1860.* London: Routledge, 1991.

Tusan, Michelle Elizabeth. "Inventing the New Woman: Print Culture and Identity Politics during the Fin-de-Siècle." *Victorian Periodicals Review* 31, no. 2 (Summer 1998): 169–82.

Twain, Mark. *The Adventures of Huckleberry Finn.* 1885. In *Mark Twain.* New York: Library of America, 2000.

——. *A Connecticut Yankee in King Arthur's Court.* 1889. London: Penguin, 1986.

——. *Following the Equator: A Journey around the World.* 1897. New York: Harper Collins, 1996.

——. *King Leopold's Soliloquy.* 1905. New York: Seven Seas Books, 1961.

——. *Mark Twain's Letters,* vol. 5: *1872–1873.* Ed. Lin Salamo and Harriet Elinor Smith. Berkeley: University of California Press, 1997.

——. *Mark Twain's Letters to His Publishers, 1867–1894.* Ed. Hamlin Hill. Berkeley: University of California Press, 1967.

——. *Mark Twain's Own Autobiography: The Chapters from the North American Review.* Ed. Michael J. Kiskis. Madison: University of Wisconsin Press, 1999.

——. "Only a Nigger." *Buffalo Express,* 26 August 1869.

——. *The Prince and the Pauper.* 1882. New York: Modern Library, 2003.

——. "The Sandwich Islands." *New York Tribune,* 9 January 1873.

——. "To the Person Sitting in Darkness." In *Mark Twain.* 1901. New York: Library of America, 2000.

——. "A True Story, Repeated Word for Word As I Heard It." *Atlantic Monthly* 34, no. 205 (November 1874): 591–94.

——. "The United States of Lyncherdom." In *Europe and Elsewhere.* New York: Harpers, 1923.

Unwin, Stanley. *The Truth about Publishing.* 1926. Boston: Houghton, Mifflin, 1927.

"Useful Advice to Temperance Societies." *Preston Temperance Advocate,* May 1836, 34.

Vaidhyanathan, Siva. *Copyrights and Copywrongs: The Rise of Intellectual Property and How It Threatens Creativity.* New York: New York University Press, 2001.

Vicinus, Martha. *Independent Women: Work and Community for Single Women, 1850–1920.* Chicago: University of Chicago Press, 1985.

Walters, Ronald. *American Reformers, 1815–1860.* New York: Hill and Wang, 1978.

Warner, Michael. *The Letters of the Republic: Publication and the Public Sphere in Eighteenth-Century America.* Cambridge: Harvard University Press, 1990.

Watt, Ian. *The Rise of the Novel.* Berkeley: University of California Press, 1957.

Webb, Igor. *From Custom to Capital: The English Novel and the Industrial Revolution.* Ithaca: Cornell University Press, 1981.

Weber, Carl J. *Hardy in America: A Study of Thomas Hardy and His American Readers.* Waterville: Colby College Press, 1946.

Weisbuch, Robert. *Atlantic Double-Cross: American Literature and British Influence in the Age of Emerson*. Chicago: University of Chicago Press, 1986.

Weld, Theodore. *American Slavery As It Is*. New York: American Anti-Slavery Society, 1839.

Welsh, Alexander. *The City of Dickens*. 1971. Cambridge: Harvard University Press, 1986.

West, James L. W. "The Chace Act and Anglo-American Literary Relations." *Studies in Bibliography* 45 (1992): 303–11.

Whipple, E. P. "Novels of the Season." *North American Review*, October 1848, 354–69.

Widdowsdown, Peter. *Hardy in History: A Study in Literary Sociology*. London: Routledge, 1989.

Williams, Raymond. *The Country and the City*. 1973. Oxford: Oxford University Press, 1975.

——. *Culture and Society, 1780–1850*. 1958. New York: Columbia University Press, 1983.

"Woman's Rights and Woman's Wrongs." *Milwaukee Daily Free Democrat*, 22 October 1853, 3.

Wright, T. R. Hardy and His Readers. London: Palgrave, 2003.

Zboray, Ronald. *A Fictive People: Antebellum Economic Development and the American Reading Public*. Oxford: Oxford University Press, 1993.

Zola, Émile. "Topics of the Day by Heroes of the Hour—My New Novel." *Pall Mall Gazette*, 3 May 1884.

Zwerdling, Alex. *Improvised Europeans: American Literary Expatriates and the Siege of London*. New York: Basic Books, 1998.

Index